About Island Press

Since 1984, the nonprofit organization Island Press has been stimulating, shaping, and communicating ideas that are essential for solving environmental problems worldwide. With more than 1,000 titles in print and some 30 new releases each year, we are the nation's leading publisher on environmental issues. We identify innovative thinkers and emerging trends in the environmental field. We work with world-renowned experts and authors to develop cross-disciplinary solutions to environmental challenges.

Island Press designs and executes educational campaigns, in conjunction with our authors, to communicate their critical messages in print, in person, and online using the latest technologies, innovative programs, and the media. Our goal is to reach targeted audiences—scientists, policy makers, environmental advocates, urban planners, the media, and concerned citizens—with information that can be used to create the framework for long-term ecological health and human well-being.

Island Press gratefully acknowledges major support from The Bobolink Foundation, Caldera Foundation, The Curtis and Edith Munson Foundation, The Forrest C. and Frances H. Lattner Foundation, The JPB Foundation, The Kresge Foundation, The Summit Charitable Foundation, Inc., and many other generous organizations and individuals.

The opinions expressed in this book are those of the author(s) and do not necessarily reflect the views of our supporters.

Pathways to Success

Pathways to Success

Taking Conservation to Scale
in Complex Systems

*Nick Salafsky and Richard Margoluis
in collaboration with Foundations of Success*

Illustrations by Anna Balla

● **ISLAND**PRESS | Washington | Covelo

Library of Congress Control Number: 2021934508

All Island Press books are printed on environmentally responsible materials.

Manufactured in the United States of America
10 9 8 7 6 5 4 3 2 1

Keywords: Island Press, adaptive management, biodiversity conservation, collaborative learning, *Conservation Standards*, decision support systems, evidence-based practice, evidence-informed conservation, impact assessment, information management, monitoring and evaluation, *Open Standards for the Practice of Conservation*, outcome assessment, performance measures, program effectiveness, program management, scaling up, strategic philanthropy, strategic planning, systems thinking, theory of change

To our families

The wayfarer,
Perceiving the pathway to truth,
Was struck with astonishment.
It was thickly grown with weeds.
"Ha," he said,
"I see that none has passed here
In a long time."
Later he saw that each weed
Was a singular knife.
"Well," he mumbled at last,
"Doubtless there are other roads."

—Stephen Crane, 1905

Contents

Foreword

The most common critique that I sometimes hear about works such as *Pathways to Success* and its precursor, *Measures of Success*, is that they endeavor to take the richness and nuance of skilled work done by deeply experienced conservation practitioners and reduce it to a set of systematically structured, and by necessity simplified, principles, roadmaps, and tools. It's as if the critics take offense at the notion of attempting to reconceive the masterworks of artisans as building blocks for journeymen. But I've always been a bit puzzled by this line of reasoning. For while it is no doubt hard to fully capture the subtleties of intuition and judgment that animate the craft of seasoned practitioners driving conservation to scale in complex systems, that simply cannot be the reason that we let ourselves off the hook from learning from the accumulated knowledge before us. We're in a moment when the conservation field is facing an all-hands-on-deck emergency of global proportions, and time is not on our side, but wisdom can be if we commit to unlocking it.

The reality of the challenges facing us in conservation calls on all of us, masters and journeymen alike, to look more systematically at how we can improve our program design, strategy selection, execution, and adaptive management to amplify the pace and scale of our impact. We simply cannot afford to be purely experiential learners, muddling through on instinct alone. Indeed, one of the most important contributions of *Pathways to Success* is that it equips us to be both better learners and more deliberate teachers, distilling hard-won lessons about taking conservation to scale in complex systems that allow us to examine our own challenges with heightened insight but also providing us with a roadmap for structuring our work in a manner that will allow us to add to the collective knowledge of our field.

Pathways to Success deftly navigates the challenge of respecting the artful, messy, and context-specific realities of conservation on the ground while illuminating principled, structured, and generalizable themes and approaches that can help us better manage conservation programs designed to achieve change at large scales. It doesn't fall into the trap of prescribing a formulaic, step-by-step recipe, but it also avoids overwhelming the reader with an exhaustive laundry list of options. Instead, it arms the reader with a roadmap and frameworks to inform a clear and focused personal learning journey, enabling them to tap more deeply and deliberately into their own knowledge about the problem and solution space. For example, by introducing a conceptual framework for considering different scaling approaches, *Pathways* pushes the reader to carefully consider the assumptions behind their choices of strategic interventions and whether they add up coherently to the change envisioned. And importantly, *Pathways* explores these important concepts without detouring too long into the abstract or theoretical; it brings the guidance to life with practical, real-world examples.

In focusing on the question of how to take conservation to scale in complex systems, *Pathways* brings a disciplined approach to one of the most important challenges bedeviling the conservation field today. It pushes us to take a hard look at the silver-bullet, leap-of-faith thinking that often stands in for the hard work of testing our theories of change about how interventions link to outcomes and how that plays out as you move across different scales in the systems we are trying to navigate. *Pathways* reminds us that driving systems change isn't about finding the magical start button in an elaborate Rube Goldberg machine. Rather, it's about taking the time to lay out our assumptions about how the system works and how it should respond and then being methodical about learning and adapting based on the evidence of what actually transpires. Only in this way can we deliver conservation solutions at the scale needed to shift complex systems.

Aileen Lee
Chief Program Officer, Environmental Conservation
Gordon and Betty Moore Foundation

Preface

More than twenty years ago, we published *Measures of Success*, a practitioner's guide to designing, managing, and monitoring conservation and development projects. *Measures* was focused on helping field-based conservation teams plan, implement, and adapt their projects over time. It helped operationalize the then emerging concept of adaptive management, which entails taking action in the face of uncertainty by treating these actions as hypotheses that could be tested and improved over time. Although most people understood the word *measures* in the book's title to refer to the indicators and methods used to monitor conservation work (the measures you make), in our minds it always had an equally important second meaning referring to the deliberate actions a project team implements to accomplish their goals (the measures you take).

Measures was one part of a broader initial wave of related work (per Thomas Kuhn) seeking to transform conservation practice by improving the analytical thinking behind the design, management, monitoring, and learning from conservation actions and projects. Perhaps the most important initiative in this wave is:

- ***The Open Standards for the Practice of Conservation* (i.e., *Conservation Standards*).** An open-source set of principles and practices that bring together common concepts, approaches, and terminology for conservation project design, management, monitoring, and learning.

This wave also involves a number of organizations from around the world supporting the *Conservation Standards* and related frameworks, guidance, and tools including:

- **Conservation Measures Partnership (CMP).** A global community of conservation-oriented nongovernment organizations, government agencies, funders, and businesses that work collectively to guide conservation around the world. CMP is responsible for developing and stewarding the *Conservation Standards* and related guidance and tools.

- **Conservation Coaches Network (CCNet).** A global community of trained professional coaches who use the *Conservation Standards* to strengthen conservation action and results.
- **Teaching Adaptive Management (TAM) Network.** A network of university teachers leading courses to train the next generation in the *Conservation Standards*.
- **Organizational adaptive management teams.** In-house departments in many organizations and agencies, such as WWF, The Nature Conservancy, and the U.S. Agency for International Development, developing and supporting their own versions of the *Conservation Standards*.
- **Foundations of Success (FOS).** A mission-driven global collective dedicated to accelerating and amplifying the impact of the conservation community, including providing support and training to programs and organizations using the *Conservation Standards*.
- **Consulting businesses.** Firms around the world, ranging from sole proprietorships to large consulting firms that are supporting the *Conservation Standards*.

Finally, this wave includes many data systems that build on the *Conservation Standards* including:

- **Miradi.** A software system designed to support learning and use of the *Conservation Standards*.
- **International Union for Conservation of Nature (IUCN)/CMP Conservation Threat and Actions Standard Classifications.** A standard taxonomy codifying both the problems conservation teams face and the solutions available to them.
- **Conservation Actions and Measures Library (CAML).** A library of generic theories of change for key conservation actions.
- **Evidence-based conservation.** A set of initiatives and websites, such as Conservation Evidence.com and the Collaboration for Environmental Evidence, focused on developing and sharing the global evidence base behind key conservation interventions.

As you can see from the lengthy list above, this initial wave has turned into a substantial global movement, seeking to transform the practice of conservation. But this transformation is not yet complete. We need to start thinking about the next wave.

Taking Conservation to Scale in Complex Systems

When we first discussed writing a second edition of *Measures of Success*, we quickly realized the world does not need yet another step-by-step project-level adaptive management guide given the vast array of materials from the many sources listed above. That said, in recent years there has been a growing interest and need to take conservation to scale. The magnitude of the issues we collectively are facing—continental, oceanwide, or even global biodiversity loss, land use change, invasive species, and climate change—means that we can no longer just focus on individual projects. Instead, we need to more effectively take action across the much larger range of program scales needed to combat these increasingly global issues.

Even at local sites, conservation has always taken place in complex systems. But as we increase the scale of our issues and ambitions, the levels of complexity increase exponentially. Scaling up conservation efforts entails dealing with global markets for commodities that stretch from the forest frontier or remote coral reefs to consumer dinner tables on the other side of the world. It entails navigating sociopolitical landscapes in which armed insurrectionists trafficking in wildlife products are also involved in smuggling drugs, arms, and people. And it involves taking action in the face of climate change, global pandemics, social inequities, systemic racism, skepticism about science and expertise, massive social change, and competition for scarce resources needed for other urgent civil society problems. To address this increasingly complex mix of challenges, conservation teams have become increasingly multidisciplinary.

Concurrent with the growing scale and complexity of the problems conservation teams are facing, there has also been massive growth in the approach to and complexity of solutions available to these teams. This complexity starts with who is involved in conservation. The conservation community has embraced more inclusive and participatory approaches, understanding the imperative for transparency and honesty in terms of who is sitting at the table, who controls the agenda, who prioritizes actions, and who carries out these actions at the end of the day. The conservation community is also beginning to understand that enduring justice for the environment is based on justice for people, especially those most affected by environmental action or inaction. Conservation has moved far beyond just setting up protected areas, to an entire toolbox of different actions that can be taken under different conditions, from restoring wetlands to setting up sustainable seafood market value chains. There are also an increasing number of tools for surveying and monitoring conservation systems (e.g., remote sensing, camera traps, audio recordings, and environmental DNA). There is a continuing need to reach out to, partner with, and learn from complementary disciplines such as social science, public health, economics, and business that are dealing with shared challenges. And there are greatly expanded possibilities for generating and sharing data, information, and knowledge; when we first wrote *Measures of Success*, the internet was only barely coming into existence! But despite all this enhanced technology and flood of data, the question still remains of how to use it well.

Effective conservation on a large scale is hard. The pathway to success, like the pathway to truth in our epigraph, is overgrown with many singular knives. It's usually much easier to put your head down and keep working at a local scale, comfortably doing what you have always done and what you are good at doing. But if we individually and collectively are going to achieve our desired conservation outcomes, we are going to have to brave those knives and do the thinking and analysis necessary to take our actions to scale.

About This Book

This book is intended as a guide to analytical frameworks and tools for conservation program managers and funders who want to increase the scale and the effectiveness of their work. By *conservation* we mean biodiversity protection, species and ecosystem restoration, climate change mitigation and adaptation, market and policy-based approaches to changing human behaviors, natural resource management, integrated conservation and development work, and similar nature-based solutions. Furthermore, although this book focuses on conservation, many of the principles and practices covered here readily translate to economic development, public health, human rights, social equity, and other civil society building efforts that are working to achieve defined goals at scale under uncertain conditions in complex systems.

Many other guidance books of this type present a broad survey of the analytical techniques that can be used to complete a given step of the program cycle and then leave it to the reader to decide which ones best fit their specific situation. We are a lot more selective in what we cover and present: a focused set of analytical approaches that in our years of frontline experience have been the most effective in helping program teams do the critical thinking needed to go through the program cycle.

Furthermore, although many experts advocate for "gold-standard" analytical approaches to systems thinking, strategy prioritization, work planning, monitoring and evaluation, and evidence synthesis, we believe that in most cases their return on investment does not warrant the necessary resource expenditures. Instead, we emphasize "aluminum-standard" analytical approaches that are lightweight, inexpensive, flexible, and, above all, useful for practitioners.

No book by itself will automatically turn you and your team into expert conservation practitioners; good conservation is as much an art as it is a science. And like any art, it requires years of hands-on practice to achieve mastery and to know when to follow the rules and when to bend, break, and reinvent the rules. But it is our hope that this book can help you realize what knowledge and skills you need, what you currently lack, where you can go to find additional training and support, and most importantly, give you confidence in traveling along your pathways to success.

Acknowledgments

We recognize the specific people and sources we have drawn on in the "Sources and Further Information" sections at the end of each chapter. That said, there are many people we need to thank for their contributions to both this book and the broader body of work it is based on.

The staff members of Foundations of Success (FOS) are collectively credited as coauthors of this book, which is woefully insufficient to capture the dedication, creativity, and passion that they have each individually brought to this work. These coauthors include (in rough order of their service time with FOS) Caroline Stem, Marcia Brown, Janice Davis, Guillermo Placci, Vinaya Swaminathan, Ilke Tilders, Arlyne Johnson, Judy Boshoven, Armando Valdés, Nico Boenisch, Valeria Martinez, Amanda Jorgenson, Ashleigh Baker, Adrienne Marvin, Vladimir Milushev, Daniela Aschenbrenner, Annette Olsson, Paola Mejía Cortez, Katya Milusheva, Kari Stiles, Varsha Suresh, Jaclyn Lucas, Sara Estlander, and Xavier Escuté. Additional inputs have also come from the Miradi Software Team, including Dan Salzer, Brian Knowles, Andy Phenix, Warren Lockwood, Felix Cybulla, Ari Bakoss, and Nuno Freire, plus Kevin Smith and Nima Ansari. We and FOS have also been ably guided by our Board of Directors, many of whom have been with us since the beginning (again in rough order of service time): Bernd Cordes, Tom Lovejoy, John Robinson, Jeff Langholz, Brett Jenks, Bonnie Cockman, and Anne Savage.

We also thank our colleagues at the Gordon and Betty Moore Foundation, who provided insightful input on earlier drafts of the book, including Paulina Arroyo, Genny Biggs, Harvey V. Fineberg, Aileen Lee, Ken Moore, and Mari Wright. We are grateful to Dwayne Marsh, president and CEO of the Northern California Grantmakers, for providing extremely valuable advice and guidance on the sections related to diversity, inclusion, and equity.

We thank the hundreds of colleagues and friends in the Conservation Measures Partnership, Conservation Coaches Network, and the wider conservation community who have collaborated with us to develop these ideas, concepts, and materials over the past two decades. It's impossible to acknowledge them all by name, but those who contributed directly to this book include Will Beale, Giselle Block, Sara Carlson, Hank Cauley, Erica Cochrane, Emily Corwin, Stuart Cowell, Amielle DeWan, Carlos Drews, Natalie Dubois, Cynthia Gill, Shelly Hicks, Megan Hill, Mike Honey, Robyn Irvine, Dane Klinger, Liz Lauck, John Morrison, Matt Muir, Catherine Payne, Shawn Peabody, Lilian Pintea, Stephen Pratt, Kent Prior, Andrew Pullin, Kent Redford, Mark Schwartz, Annette Stewart, and Bill Sutherland.

Of course, the usual caveats apply here that the views and opinions expressed in this book do not necessarily reflect the position of these organizations and individuals.

Finally, we thank Anna Balla for sharing her unique perspective of the world through her amazing illustrations and Erin Johnson, Sharis Simonian, and the rest of the production team at Island Press for their help in bringing this book to life.

Introduction

Pathways to Success is centered around a fictional coastal management scenario that shows the many challenges of managing terrestrial, marine, and freshwater conservation strategies at different spatial and institutional scales. In particular, we take the perspectives of program managers from four different organizations involved in this work. Each organization has its own program, but they also interact and interrelate with one another. Although this scenario is hypothetical, it is based on real-world issues and approaches. We hope you will find elements of this scenario that apply or are at least analogous to your own work.

Community program manager. Suppose you are the formally educated daughter of a traditional leader who has been selected by your coastal community to help develop a plan to sustainably manage the natural resources on which much of the local economy is based. Your community is located at the mouth of a river flowing from upland forests to a large bay. Community members have depended for generations on harvesting several salmon species that migrate up the river to spawn, as well as clams that live in the mudflats of the bay. In recent years, residents have taken jobs in local timber and mining operations and have been working on commercial fishing boats and whale watching ecotourism boats. Community elders have been warning for years that current practices will lead to severe declines in available stocks, and over the past decade there have been steadily declining fish harvests due to a number of factors including competition with outside fishing fleets, dams that restrict fish from accessing their spawning habitat, and increased pollution and sediment in the water from mining and timber harvesting operations in your watershed. There are also growing signs of sea-level rise and changes to climate patterns that seem as if they will affect your livelihoods and lives.

NGO regional program manager. Suppose you work for a Capital City–based nongovernment organization (NGO) whose mission is to promote conservation in your region. In particular, you are the manager of a program composed of multiple community-managed watershed projects. This program seeks to bring together all the coastal communities in your region to help them better manage and conserve their natural resources in the face of growing demand and looming effects of climate change. The board and managers of your NGO have challenged you and your colleagues to raise the funds needed to develop projects and programs that will allow you to take your impact to scale.

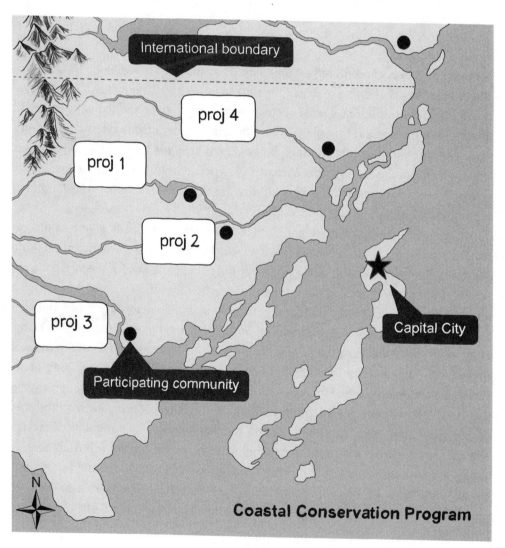

Government agency monitoring expert. Suppose you are a monitoring specialist in the government agency that is responsible for managing the fisheries and associated aquatic habitats in this region of your country. You are also the leader of an interagency task force that is responsible for setting fishery quotas that weigh the competing needs of humans, seals, and endangered cetaceans that depend on the fish as their main food source.

Foundation program officer. Or finally, suppose you are a program officer in a private foundation responsible for designing a sustainable fisheries initiative in this part of the world. Your foundation has a mandate from its founder to find durable solutions to intractable problems. You are thus expected to help convene a working group of key stakeholders who will co-design and manage this initiative.

Focus of This Book

Two decades ago, when we wrote our original book *Measures of Success*, our focus was on designing, managing, and monitoring individual conservation efforts, which we defined as:

▸ **Project.** A set of actions being taken by a defined team of people to achieve agreed-upon outcomes, often at a specific geographic site or within a thematic scope. For example, the Community Lands Management Project shown in Figure 0.1 might involve taking a range of actions to benefit salmon, restore wetlands, and promote traditional cultural practices within one site on the community lands. Other examples of projects might include managing a park or wildlife refuge or promoting sustainable seafood production within a city.

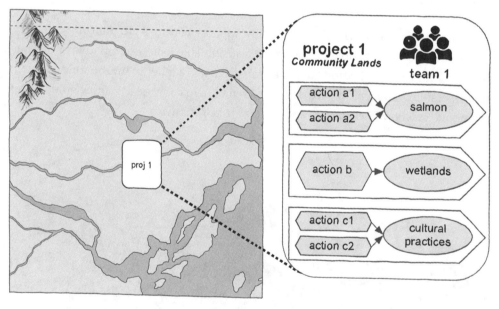

Figure 0.1. A project is a set of actions to achieve agreed-upon outcomes.

Conservation projects make sense as a management unit when we view the world from the perspective of the specific project team that has to decide on how to allocate their limited time and treasure across multiple actions and multiple desired outcomes. For example, how much effort should the team devote to removing dams to enable salmon to access spawning areas rather than restoring wetland habitat?

Although technically projects can be at any scale, in practice they tend to be smaller site-based endeavors. In addition, they are also often developed and managed as groups of related projects. When working in increasingly larger and more complex situations such as those in the above scenario, we thus found that we needed to adopt a higher-order management unit as our focus to think about and implement conservation work:

▶ **Program (or initiative).** A set of related projects or actions designed to achieve a set of higher-level outcomes. For example, the foundation's Sustainable Fisheries Program shown in Figure 0.2 might be focused on restoring salmon populations across all watersheds in the region. In this case, ACTION A might involve making a grant to project 1 along with many similar projects in other watersheds. But the program might also fund ACTION X, which involves policy work or other program-level actions. Other programs might include establishing and managing a network of protected areas, restoring wetlands to capture carbon on a large scale, or promoting sustainable seafood production across an industry supply chain.

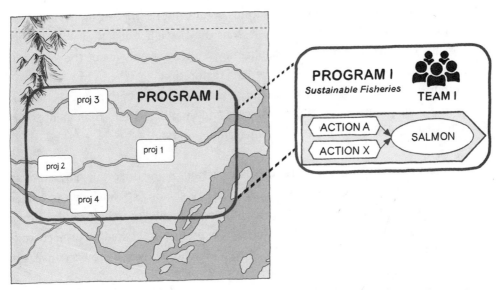

Figure 0.2. A program is both a set of related projects and a larger-scale project of its own.

A program can be thought of as both a larger-scale project in its own right ("a collection of actions being taken by a defined team of people leading to agreed-upon outcomes") and a functional unit to think about managing, funding, or learning from a group of related component projects. *Programs* and *projects* are relative rather than absolute terms. The "parent" program is at a higher scale than its lower-order "child" projects and thus contains work at multiple scales, a roll-up of project-level actions plus other actions being taken at the program-level scale.

Combining and linking projects and programs is the key to taking conservation to scale, enabling the conservation community to:

- Efficiently replicate actions so that we can increase the scale of our work,
- Provide funds to projects and track how they are contributing to higher-order results, and
- Compare experiences from individual projects to learn how to make our actions more effective.

But unfortunately, when it is necessary to directly aggregate or link projects to programs, we run into both practical and conceptual disconnects. For example, although the foundation implementing Program I may be interested in funding the salmon conservation work that project 1 is doing, they probably have no official interest in that project's wetland work. And likewise, if various organizations working on wetland restoration want to pool their data or share lessons they have learned, they want to find other teams working on similar issues, but they really care only about the subset of each project or program that relates to wetland restoration.

To address these disconnects, it is useful to first break down both projects and programs into their component strategy pathways and then link these components (Figure 0.3). We thus define two additional management units:

▸ **Project strategy pathway.** A set of related actions being undertaken by a project team to achieve specific results (e.g., ACTION a1, shading stream banks to reduce water temperatures, and ACTION a2, building fish ladders to help adult salmon get over dams—all in service of restoring salmon to a watershed). A project strategy pathway is a building block of a project; put another way, a project consists of one or more project strategy pathways.

▸ **Program strategy pathway.** A set of related actions being undertaken by a program team to achieve specific program-level results. A program strategy pathway can include both rolled-up project-level strategy pathways and its own independent actions (e.g., ACTION A, providing funding to a suite of watershed-scale

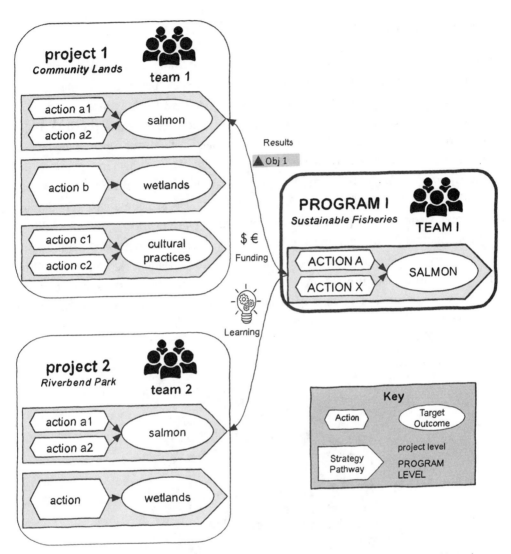

Figure 0.3. Using strategy pathways to link project and program results, funding, and learning.

projects that are improving salmon habitat, and ACTION X, convening key stakeholders to develop sustainable fishing policies in the region).

As you will see throughout this book, we believe this subtle shift in focus to designing, managing, funding, and learning from conservation efforts based on strategy pathways at different scales is key to improving conservation practice in complex systems.

How This Book Is Organized

Although there are many planning and management frameworks used by different organizations, most of them follow a typical project cycle pattern that goes back to W. Edwards Deming's concept of Plan–Do–Check–Adjust. In the conservation community, many leading organizations in the Conservation Measures Partnership (CMP) have agreed on a version of this continuous feedback cycle in the *Open Standards for the Practice of Conservation* (hereafter *Conservation Standards*) shown in Figure 0.4. The *Conservation Standards* offer consensus "good analytical practices" for managing conservation projects and, along with Miradi Software, also provide a carefully defined common lexicon and symbology for describing conservation work.

This book is about applying the *Conservation Standards* framework to plan and manage large-scale programs in complex systems. In particular, we focus on modifying and adapting basic project-level analytical approaches to meet the distinct needs of larger programs. But instead of strictly following the steps in the *Conservation*

1. ASSESS
- Purpose & team
- Scope, vision, & targets
- Critical threats
- Conservation situation

2. PLAN
- Goals, strategies, assumptions, & objectives
- Monitoring plan
- Operational plan

5. SHARE
- Document learning
- Share learning
- Foster learning

3. IMPLEMENT
- Work plan & timetable
- Budget
- Implement plan

4. ANALYZE & ADAPT
- Prepare data
- Analyze results
- Adapt plans

Figure 0.4. *The Open Standards for the Practice of Conservation.*

Standards, this book is divided into two main parts (Figure 0.5). Part I of this book is about assessing your program's situation (Chapter 1) and then developing your strategies (Chapter 2) and operations (Chapter 3). But your program does not exist in a vacuum. Instead, it is surrounded by your program's evidence base, which contains the relevant data, information, and knowledge that collectively can help you and your partners to better design and manage your work. In Part II, we turn to using and expanding this evidence base to better design and manage your work through evidence synthesis (Chapter 4), monitoring, evaluation, and research (Chapter 5), and cross-program learning (Chapter 6).

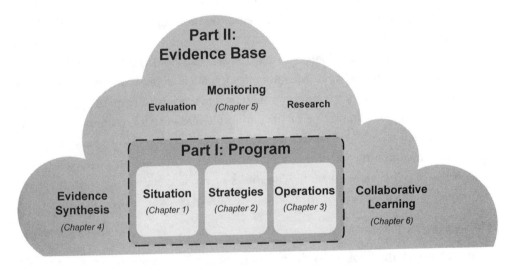

Figure 0.5. How this book is organized.

Throughout this book, we have adopted the following conventions:

- ▶ **Chapter structure.** Each chapter of this book describes the key analyses that conservation programs are likely to need to undertake in relation to the subject of the chapter. For each of these analyses, we first share some basic principles and then provide guidance on how to apply these principles to your work.
- ▶ **Use of the example scenario.** Throughout this book, we rely on our fictional conservation scenario, encompassing several programs as described above, to provide examples and illustrations. Although this scenario focuses on coastal conservation, the principles and guidance readily transfer to other conservation situations—and indeed to other complex social problems such as combating disease outbreaks or promoting economic development.

▶ **Illustrations and references.** In the print version of this book, we are necessarily restricted to small gray-scale illustrations. However, we also provide links to more detailed full-color examples that are available in online supplemental materials. At the end of each chapter, we list references for additional reading and guidance.

▶ **Learning questions.** At the end of each chapter, we raise key learning questions that outline areas of inquiry that we and the broader community need to continue exploring. For example, in Chapter 1 we introduce our current thinking about diversity, equity, inclusion, and social justice movements in the context of large conservation programs. This material is only one starting point for additional research and thinking about better integrating these topics throughout the *Conservation Standards* cycle.

▶ **Terms and symbols.** Finally, we have mostly adopted the terms and symbols of the *Conservation Standards*. However, we have introduced some new conventions where necessary to represent new concepts or provide greater clarity where existing terms are imprecise or have multiple and conflicting meanings. These changes, which are described in the Glossary, are intended to improve the conservation community's collective ability to understand and use these concepts. As Ludwig Wittgenstein said, "The limits of my language are the limits of my world.... What we cannot speak about we must pass over in silence."

Overarching Themes

As you go through this book, you will notice a number of key themes that weave through each of the sections. These themes are summed up in the following quotes:

"I would not give a fig for the simplicity on this side of complexity. I would give my right arm for the simplicity on the far side of complexity."
—Attributed to Oliver Wendell Holmes, Sr., ~1860

"An approximate answer to the right question is worth a great deal more than a precise answer to the wrong question."
—John Tukey, 1962

"All models are wrong but some are useful.... Just as the ability to devise simple but evocative models is the signature of the great scientist so overelaboration and overparameterization is often the mark of mediocrity."
—George Box, 1978

"Remember, always, that everything you know, and everything everyone knows, is only a model. Get your model out there where it can be viewed. Invite others to challenge your assumptions and add their own."
—Donella Meadows, 2008

"Become less and less and less wrong."
—Nate Silver, 2012

Complex Systems

A complex system consists of many different components (detail complexity) that can interact with one another in many different ways (dynamic complexity). Conservation work undoubtedly takes place in complex systems. As a thought experiment, consider the complex web of biophysical and ecological relationships between the living and nonliving components of a coral reef or a forest. Then, intersect these ecosystems with the human political, economic, social, institutional, and cultural systems that can potentially lead to their degradation or conservation. It's not too much of a stretch to argue that conservationists are probably working in some of the most complex systems in the world, if not the galaxy! A key theme in this book is how we can better understand and take action in these extremely complex systems.

Making Choices with Limited Time and Treasure

Given the complexity of the systems we are dealing with and inevitably limited resources, program teams cannot hope to do every needed action or get the data to meet every evidence need. Instead, teams need to figure out how to most strategically allocate their scarce time and treasure. A key tenet of good strategic planning is that it involves specifying not just what you will do, but also what you will not do. It is about understanding your options for a given decision, making a decision about how to proceed, and then moving forward along your pathway. It also requires documenting your assumptions and noting uncertainties that may require additional evidence. And it demands that you adapt your work as circumstances change and your understanding of the situation and strategies change.

Pathways and Models

Given the complexity of the systems we are dealing with, project and program teams trying to take action in these systems need to develop a shared understanding of what they know—and just as importantly what they do not know—about how these systems currently function and how they will respond to these actions.

At its most basic, a pathway is a set of factors in a system that have an assumed causal relationship to one another. A pathway can be described in text, a table, an economic cash flow analysis, mathematical notation, or even a three-dimensional sculpture. In this book, however, we will usually represent pathways in flow diagrams as shown in Figure 0.6.

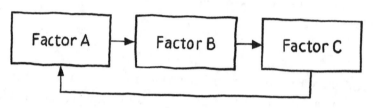

Figure 0.6. A basic pathway diagram.

A pathway represents a series of assumptions (or claims or hypotheses) about the system. These assumptions include whether a given factor is present in the system (e.g., Factor A is a key factor) and presumed causal relationships between factors (e.g., Factor A affects Factor B and, through Factor B, affects Factor C; there is a feedback loop from Factor C to Factor A). More sophisticated versions of pathway diagrams can show additional information about key assumptions such as the status of a given factor, the direction, strength, and nature of the relationship between factors, and the degree of certainty about a given assumption. As we will see, these diagrams can include both situation pathways that are components of your situation assessment and strategy pathways that help you develop and implement your theories of change and take them to scale.

It is important to remember that a pathway is only a model of the underlying system; each assumption depicted in the pathway may or may not actually be a true property of the system in question. Furthermore, each pathway is only a narrow linear slice of the underlying system that is inevitably not showing many factors and relationships. Although in conservation we hear that some pathways are too simple and linear, we believe simplicity can be a feature rather than a bug. Indeed, as George Box reminds us, the only thing we know for certain is that our pathway models are wrong, but the critical question is whether they are useful to help us understand the workings of our system of interest. To this end, we do not want our pathway models to be the most detailed representations of the system. Instead, we intentionally recommend making models as streamlined as possible while still capturing the necessary detail to make good management decisions, striving for the "simplicity on the far side of complexity" for which Oliver Wendell Holmes purportedly would have given his arm.

Sources of Evidence

Much of the work of designing and managing a conservation program involves acquiring and analyzing the evidence needed to improve decision making. Your program's evidence base consists of the relevant data, information, knowledge, and wisdom (collectively called evidence) that helps you and your partners develop your understanding of the situation and design, manage, and adapt your strategies. Per Figure 0.7, there are a number of sources of evidence:

▸ **Existing evidence.** Available data and information used to support claims you make as you develop your program's situation assessment and design your strategies. It can include both scientific and traditional knowledge. It is synthesized from two sources:

  • **Specific evidence base.** What your program team, partners, and stakeholders already know about your program's particular situation and strategies
  • **Generic evidence base.** What the rest of the world knows about similar situations and strategies

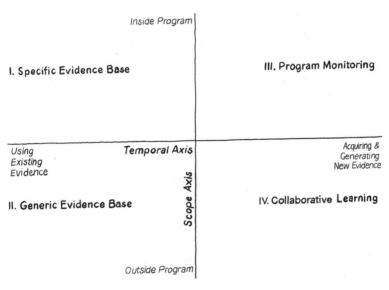

Figure 0.7. Overview of sources of evidence for your program's evidence base.

▶ **Future evidence.** The data and information you need to collect going forward to answer the questions needed to adapt and learn from your program. It is generated from two sources:

- **Program monitoring.** How you plan to answer questions about your program's situation and strategies through monitoring, evaluation, and research
- **Collaborative learning.** How you plan to answer questions about your program's situation and strategies through collaboration with similar programs

Appropriate Investments in Evidence Acquisition and Analysis

Acquiring and analyzing evidence needed to improve decision making occur throughout the program planning and implementation cycle. There is a tendency when working with complex systems and strategies to assume that investing in more sophisticated approaches for gathering and analyzing evidence will necessarily lead to better understanding of both the underlying system and your proposed interventions. This better understanding will in turn lead to better decision making and ultimately better outcomes.

In our experience, however, the relationship between investment in evidence and better decision making is itself nonlinear, as shown in Figure 0.8. The graph plots increasing investment of time and treasure in evidence acquisition and analysis against the increasing probability of a program team making a correct decision. The y-intercept here (Point A) is greater than zero because there is some chance that the team would get the right answer just by gut instinct or luck. Next, there is the steep part of the curve between points A and B where a minimal investment in evidence will greatly improve the probability of a correct decision. In particular, this investment lies in framing the conceptual underpinnings of the decision being made, or defining the exact problem and then using available evidence to compare options. Then there is a flatter part of the curve between Points B and C where there are still positive but diminishing returns to expending additional effort on evidence acquisition and analysis. This phase of investment generally involves trying to more precisely and quantitatively compare trade-offs between different decision options. It often involves handing the problem over to specialized researchers who then report back to the primary decision makers. The curve then starts to dip south between Points C and D when additional analysis may just start to confuse the situation. Finally, the curve plummets to the x-axis at Point E, representing the cases when planning paralysis sets in and no decision is ever reached.

The choice of how much to invest in evidence acquisition and analysis is governed by both the return to effort and the costs of making the wrong decision. In a few situations where there is a high cost of being wrong (i.e., where there is a high burden of proof, as discussed in more detail in Chapter 4), it may be necessary to invest in the most sophisticated gold-standard analyses that remove as much uncertainty as possible from the decision. For example, if you are working on the last population of an endangered species, or if your program will severely disrupt the lives of human stakeholders, or if your action is likely to involve expensive legal challenges, you may have to invest in sophisticated analyses so as to ensure that you get to the maximum confidence level (Point C in Figure 0.8).

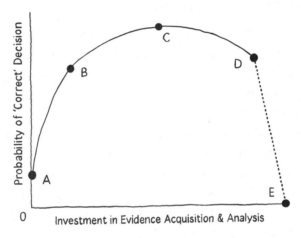

Figure 0.8. Return on investment in evidence.

In most conservation situations, however, it's probably sufficient to try to maximize the return on your analytical investments (Point B). To this end, rather than investing in gold-standard approaches, practitioners will be better served by quick and low-cost aluminum-standard approaches. If you can get your program team to clearly define the decision being made and collect and analyze readily available evidence about your options, then you will probably have "approximate answers to the right question." And if you do this analysis in a format that all your partners and stakeholders can internalize, understand, and own, you can then "invite others to challenge your assumptions and add their own" and bring in the wisdom of the crowd. By contrast, if you insist on using gold-standard decision support tools for every analytical need, it is highly likely that the necessary investment will bankrupt your program, it will take so long to get answers that the decision moment will be long past, and the critical underlying assumptions (and your confidence levels in these assumptions) will be invisible to your partners and team members who need to understand them, unless you make extensive investments in translating the results.

The reality of conservation today is that often the choice is not between the gold and the aluminum standards but rather between *no* analysis and *any* analysis. To this end, we recommend you use the simplest analysis you can, given the system you are working in, the capacity of your team and stakeholders, and the consequences of the decision you are making. Subsequent sections provide more explicit guidance on how to make these trade-offs.

Taking Action in the Face of Uncertainty

Analysis of evidence in a program context is ultimately about helping your team choose the right actions to take. Your level of investment in analysis is thus governed by your level of certainty about the situation and your strategies and the cost of either taking the wrong action or choosing not to act when action is warranted.

In some cases in which you have a great deal of certainty about your theory and evidence about your situation and strategies *and* there is a low burden of proof (Chapter 4), you can take action with confidence and invest minimal resources in confirming the results of your actions. In other cases, if you have high certainty but also a higher burden of proof, you may have to invest a bit more in validating the results of your actions.

In many cases, however, practitioners are often in a position of having to take action in the face of a great deal of uncertainty in key assumptions about their program. Adaptive management is the incorporation of deliberate learning into professional practice to reduce uncertainty in decision making. Specifically, it enables practitioners to systematically and efficiently test key assumptions, evaluate the results, adjust management decisions, and learn while taking action. Adaptive management is closely related to the concept of agile design in software development and other fields. Both of these approaches are particularly useful when you need to take action but don't have sufficient evidence to be certain about key assumptions in your system, as is typically the case when you are working in complex systems. Instead of being paralyzed by uncertainty, you take action but then make sure you monitor the results of this action so that you can learn from both successes and failures and adapt as needed.

In any case, there is no substitute for good thinking. The complex nature of the systems we are working in and the relative lack of good information about these systems mean that in most cases, we cannot just build and parameterize a decision model and then run it to have the right answer to a given management question magically pop out the other end. Instead, you and your team will have to work with your model to frame the situation, discuss and debate various pathways, and then agree on how to move forward and what additional evidence you will need to track to reduce uncertainty or, as Nate Silver puts it, "become less and less and less wrong" over time.

Scale

Finally, throughout this book we will be talking a great deal about scale and working across scales. There are a number of overlapping dimensions in which we can think about scale in relation to conservation work. Each dimension plays out across the factors in a given strategy pathway from actions to ultimate outcomes:

- **Spatial and ecological scale.** Is the strategy pathway aimed at conserving a small run of salmon in a specific stream? Or the entire population of salmon in the ocean?
- **Temporal scale.** Are the actions in the strategy pathway being implemented over a week? Over several months? Over many years? And are the results of the strategy pathway expected to last for a season or for decades?
- **Social, Political, and Institutional Scale.** Is the strategy pathway part of a specific project being implemented by a community or a local NGO in a municipality? Or part of a much larger program being implemented by a consortium of government agencies and private foundations across international boundaries? Is the program or strategy pathway funded sufficiently to actually achieve the intended goals at whatever scale is desired?

As we will see, there are often hierarchical relationships between factors in pathways at different scales. For example, the salmon in a small stream are part of the overall salmon population in the ocean. And a small community NGO project may be funded as part of a program being run by a consortium. One of the biggest challenges in thinking about scale is that similar patterns repeat at different levels of the hierarchy, which can lead to confusion among people trying to work together across these levels.

As an analogy, consider how the concepts of strategy and tactics change in a business setting depending on one's frame of reference. A local grocery store franchise might have a strategy to increase sales by bringing new customers into the store from surrounding neighborhoods. The store's managers can decide on different tactics to accomplish this strategy, such as holding sales on new products that might appeal to these customers or by targeted advertising. By contrast, the regional headquarters for the chain of grocery stores might have a strategy to sell more new franchise licenses. For the regional managers, having the local store increase sales is now merely a tactic en route to their higher-level strategy. The same action could thus either be a tactic or strategy depending on one's perspective.

In a similar fashion, a local conservation project might have as its main strategy to work with the local community to set up a sustainable fishing operation. But this entire project might itself only be a small activity within a larger program's strategy to develop a national or global market for sustainable seafood. As a result, the exact same work can simultaneously be both a project-level strategy and a program-level activity; again, it all depends on your perspective. The key is to understand your frame of reference at any given point as you develop and implement your work.

Sources and Further Information

(See FOSonline.org/pathways for links and updated guidance material.)

There are a number of places to go to learn more about basic project and program planning in the conservation sector. A good starting point is the *Open Standards for the Practice of Conservation* (i.e., *Conservation Standards*), which provide high-level principles and good practices for conservation project management. The *Conservation Standards* were developed by the CMP, a consortium of leading conservation organizations, agencies, and funders. CMP regularly updates these standards, in collaboration with and drawing on the experience of the broader *Conservation Standards* community. The Conservation Standards Website provides a trove of materials related to various aspects of the *Conservation Standards* and contacts for becoming more actively involved in this community of practice.

There are also many training guides and approaches to help implement the *Conservation Standards*. Although we are undoubtedly a bit biased, some of our favorites include:

Foundations of Success (FOS) Training Guides. These are a series of training guides and presentations designed to provide a solid introduction to each of the steps in the *Conservation Standards*.

Healthy Country Planning. A powerful adaptation of the *Conservation Standards* for use with indigenous and local community project teams.

CMP/FOS/University of Wisconsin–Madison Online Conservation Standards Course. An online training course that walks through the basic steps in the *Conservation Standards*.

As our colleague Annette Stewart has pointed out, although most conservation organizations make substantial investments in the centralized information technology (IT) systems needed to support their financial and administrative business processes, they don't make comparable investments in the IT systems to support their programmatic work. Instead, they rely on a patchwork of word processing forms, spreadsheets, and document sharing websites. To address this problem, there is a growing movement to design a set of integrated IT systems to help collect and analyze the data needed to implement the *Conservation Standards*. These systems are centered around:

Miradi Software. A software system that supports step-by-step implementation of the *Conservation Standards*. Miradi started out as a desktop software package and has become a powerful online data sharing platform. It also has a set of application programming interfaces (APIs) that allow Miradi users to easily import and export data with other elements of their IT ecosystem.

If you are interested in coaching and training teams or students who are using the *Conservation Standards*, we recommend:

Conservation Coaches Network (CCNet). CMP's sibling consortium provides training materials, information about courses, and even certification for people who want to provide training and coaching in using the *Conservation Standards*.

Teaching Adaptive Management (TAM) Network. A community of practice made up of university professors who offer courses and training in the *Conservation Standards* and related methods and tools. Their website offers a range of course syllabi and teaching materials.

In writing this book, we have tried to provide analytical approaches for implementing the *Conservation Standards* with large-scale programs in complex systems. A memorable article by Giovani Gavetti and Jan Rivkin published years ago in the *Harvard Business Review* described the power and limitations of developing a new business strategy by adapting a strategy borrowed from an analogous industry. The article emphasized that although using a template analogy can help you quickly make 90 percent of your decisions, it can also steer you disastrously wrong if you fail to adapt the template for the 10 percent that are different in the new situation. The challenge, of course, is to know which 10 percent of the decisions are the ones that need adaptation. Thus, in this book we especially focus on the elements of the *Conservation Standards* that need to be adapted when moving from a single project to a program scale.

Finally, throughout this book we focus on what we have come to call aluminum-standard analytical approaches for acquiring and analyzing evidence to support your conservation work. We are inspired by Robert Pirsig, who wrote in his classic 1974 book *Zen and the Art of Motorcycle Maintenance*,

> A man conducting a gee-whiz science show with fifty thousand dollars' worth of Frankenstein equipment is not doing anything scientific if he knows before-hand what the results of his efforts are going to be. A motorcycle mechanic, on the other hand, who honks the horn to see if the battery works is informally conducting a true scientific experiment. He is testing a hypothesis by putting a question to nature.

Our aim is to provide practitioners with the analytical tools they need to honk the horns of their conservation programs.

PART I

Designing and Implementing Your Program

The first half of this book is about designing and implementing your program. As shown in Figure Ia, we focus in particular on three components of your program:

- **Situation (Chapter 1).** Defining your program's focus and developing a shared situation assessment of the system you are working in.
- **Strategies (Chapter 2).** Finding key intervention points in the system and developing strategy pathways that will enable your program to achieve desired outcomes at scale.
- **Operations (Chapter 3).** Operationalizing and implementing your program, including developing a work plan and an overall program investment portfolio.

In the second part of this book, we focus on using and expanding the evidence base needed to support and improve these components of your program.

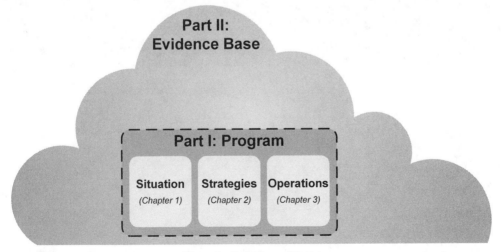

Figure Ia. Overview of Part I.

1

Framing and Assessing the Situation

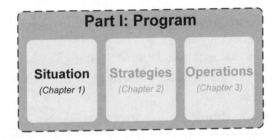

To get started when you are considering a new program (or initiative), you need to both define what you want to focus on and understand the complexities of the system you are working in. Framing your situation includes defining your program's focus, which includes three interrelated components:

- Clarifying your purpose
- Selecting target factors and bounding the scope of your program
- Assembling the right team and program partners

Once you have defined your program's focus, key analyses include:

- Understanding the system in which you are working
- Developing a shared situation model

Clarifying Your Purpose

The first component of defining your program's focus involves answering the question, "What are we ultimately trying to accomplish?" Answering this question about what you ultimately value will affect everything you do.

The purpose (or ultimate outcome) of a program is a high-level statement of what you would like to accomplish with your time and treasure. It is closely related to the concept of a mission statement, which applies to an organization or agency rather than a program. A good purpose statement concisely and ideally eloquently describes either or both:

- ▶ **The challenges you are facing.** This outlines the existing or coming set of problems you are looking to take on. The clearer and more specific you can be, the better. Are you interested in saving endangered whales? Reversing the decline in regional salmon populations? Helping key ecosystems and human communities adapt to inevitable climate change? Empowering marginalized indigenous communities?
- ▶ **Your vision for the future.** This defines what success looks like in the future when you have solved the current problems. Healthy whale populations. Sufficient salmon to sustain the animals and humans that depend on them. Resilient ecosystems and communities that can adapt to climate change. Vibrant indigenous communities managing their lands and resources.

As you can see from these examples, a vision for the future is often the inverse of a challenge. To this end, good purpose statements often do not address these two points separately but instead find an effective way to bring them together. Our example programs might have these purposes:

Purpose: Protect whales against all threats so that we have healthy whale populations.
Purpose: Manage salmon sustainably in a way that sustains both the marine mammals and human communities that depend on them.
Purpose: Address looming climate change by mitigating atmospheric CO_2 levels and creating resilient natural ecosystems and human communities that can adapt to their effects.

Perhaps the most important point to keep in mind as you develop your program's purpose is that there is often little or no strategy associated with choosing what to focus on. Instead, choosing a purpose is primarily a values question. Conservation organizations choose to work on conservation issues because they and their members believe it is imperative to protect species and ecosystems. Government agencies work on issues mandated by policies driven by decision makers and ultimately constituent preferences. Philanthropists choose to work on topics that they feel are important or are particularly interesting to them. The common thread is that all these entities choose to spend their time and treasure to take action in an area in which they believe it is important to achieve certain outcomes. It's all about preference and choice. At the same time, it's important to have a common purpose across all program partners—what Peter Senge (1990) calls a shared vision. If you and other members of your program can't agree on a common purpose, you probably should think about splitting into separate programs.

Guidance for Clarifying Your Purpose

Often, especially if you work for an existing program or are starting a new program in the context of an organization or agency that has established priorities or mandates, you will be given the ultimate purpose of your program and instructed to go make it happen. If your community has decided to take on a specific concern, the leaders and members of your nongovernment organization (NGO) have agreed on a course of work, your agency has received an appropriation from society to tackle a certain issue, or the decision makers in your foundation have selected a topic to work on, then you can skim the rest of this section and get on with the work.

But other times, it will be up to you and your colleagues to go through a more systematic process to select—or at least refine—the purpose of your work. If you find yourself in the latter circumstance, some key points to keep in mind include:

- **Pick a purpose that reflects your values.** Selecting a purpose can be daunting and can expose you to a great deal of external criticism and self-questioning about whether you are working on the right thing. As psychologists have discovered, having unlimited and unconstrained options for a given decision can be stressful and even paralyzing. For example, there is an argument that it is immoral to work on environmental issues when there are so many urgent human needs. "How can we worry about saving the whales or the bears or the trees when there are so many oppressed humans who don't have health care or enough to eat?" In effect, these people are saying, "How can you justify a conservation purpose?" There is no one right answer to this question. Instead:

  - Some people might advance the argument that there is a strong link between the environment and human well-being through the various ecosystem services such as food, livelihoods, and culture that the natural world provides to people. As a result, conservation of the environment is in the human interest.

- Some people might also argue that regardless of the benefits to humans, whales and bears and trees have an intrinsic moral right to exist. In particular, though at an individual level few of us would hesitate to cut down a tree to pay for medicine for our sick child, it is a lot harder to justify cutting down trees to pay for designer clothing or a ski vacation. As Gandhi said, "The earth has enough for everyone's need but not for everyone's greed."

- Finally, some people might observe that framing the question as a trade-off between human needs and environmental conservation is asking the wrong question. Given that our collective spending on either of these issues pales next to the vast resources humans devote to pursuits such as arts, sports, fashion, and pets, to name just a few, why should these two causes fight one another for the limited resources we get from society? Instead, why not try to grow the pie so that we all have what we need to achieve social and environmental justice?

At the end of the day, the choice of purpose is almost exclusively a values decision—and it's your values decision! If you want to spend your time and treasure on providing food and healthcare for humans, that's your choice. And if you want to spend it on saving the whales, bears, and trees, that's also your choice. Whatever your purpose, the approach presented in this book can help you more effectively plan how to get there and raise the resources needed to reach it.

- **Develop a coherent focus.** As a rule, you want to have a program purpose that is not too broad and all-encompassing but is constrained in some way. It's fine to have a purpose that encompasses multiple closely related ultimate outcomes such as healthy salmon populations and a vibrant rural economy or healthy coastal ecosystems and mitigation of global warming. But if you are trying to mash together a range of unrelated outcomes, you might need to consider focusing on a subset or at least setting up separate programs to deal with each. For example, it probably does not make sense to set up a program to work simultaneously on salmon conservation and getting people to quit tobacco use. Both of these could be topics worthy of attention, but they are too unrelated to allow for a coherent program.
- **Dream big but be realistic.** To achieve great things, you need to dream big dreams—to have what the business writer Jim Collins (2005) calls "Big Hairy

Audacious Goals." However, big dreams alone will not get you to your destination. You also need to be able to develop a strategic plan that will get you to your goals given the resources you have and can raise. There is a real art to choosing a purpose that is important and big enough to make a difference at the scale of a program but also small enough that it is manageable and feasible given the amount of resources you have. At this point, although you should think more about what you want to accomplish rather than how you will do it, you need to have some sense of whether what you are proposing is doable by your program and your potential partners.

- **Don't get too hung up on ends versus means at this point.** There is often a complex relationship between different potential purposes in an overall system. For example, as shown in Figure 1.1, conserving salmon populations depends on having healthy river and estuary ecosystems. And establishing a vibrant economy and culture depends on having a healthy salmon population and thus, by extension, on having a healthy river ecosystem. And finally, healthy rivers and estuaries depend on having a vibrant economy and culture so that local people are present to steward the watershed. The regional NGO's program might establish as its ultimate purpose to <*Conserve rivers and estuaries*>. The government agency program could state that its purpose is to <*Sustainably manage salmon*>. And the indigenous people's program might decide that its purpose is to <*Maintain and grow a vibrant local economy and culture*>. Because of the interlinked nature of these factors, one program's end purpose is only a means for the others to achieve their respective purposes. But that doesn't make one program right and the other wrong. Instead, because choice of purpose is a values decision, you define your program by the purpose you choose to focus on in a big complex system. As we will see later on, the key is to understand how these factors fit together and how your different programs can work together so that each can achieve their desired ends.

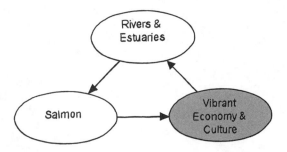

Figure 1.1. Three interrelated purposes.

- **Compare your options.** If you have several options for a purpose (which is effectively the same as having several candidate programs that you could initiate), you can have your organization's decision makers evaluate each of them against criteria including:

  - Does it fit with our organizational mission and priorities or those of our members, constituents, or financial backers?
  - Can we take this work to a meaningful scale to make a substantial and lasting difference?
  - Do we have the skills and capacity to do this work, or can we raise the sufficient resources (people, partners, and money) to be successful, especially at scale?
  - Is there a gap in other people's work on this topic that we can help fill?

  Although in some cases it may help to do a more quantitative comparison, in most cases a relative or absolute criteria rating exercise (per Chapter 3) should be sufficient to distinguish between the higher- and lower-ranked candidate programs. If after this initial analysis you still have no clear favorite among several plausible candidates, you may need to develop a strategic plan for each of the candidates as a way to get more information before you make a final selection.
- **Remember there is no one right purpose.** Always keep in mind that the choice of a purpose is much more of a values decision than a strategic decision. At the end of the day, you will have to pick a purpose and get on with the work.

Selecting Target Factors and Bounding the Scope of Your Program

Few programs have the resources to work at a global scale, so you need to think about how you can both focus and bound your work. To this end, the second component of defining your focus involves delineating the target factors and the spatial, thematic, and temporal scope of your work:

▸ **Target factors.** At the core of any given program purpose, you can almost always identify some specific entities that represent the ultimate values you care about. These entities typically include both ecological targets, such as species, ecosystems, and ecological processes, and human well-being targets, which include aspects of human communities such as food security, livelihoods, protection from flooding, and culture (although some groups do not divide ecological and human well-being targets into separate categories). As programs expand into other disciplines, it may also be useful to consider target factors that represent other purposes such as human health, education, water and sanitation, environmental justice, social and racial equity, and human rights.

Examples of purposes converted into target factors include:

Purpose: Protect whales against all threats so that we have healthy whale populations.
Target factors:
   Resident whale populations
   Migratory whale populations

Purpose: Reverse the decline in salmon populations and create a sustainable salmon fishery that sustains the marine mammals and human communities that depend on them.
Target factors:
   Salmon populations
   Marine mammal populations
   Salmon fishery
   Human community livelihoods

Purpose: Address looming climate change by mitigating atmospheric CO_2 levels and creating resilient natural ecosystems and human communities that can adapt to its effects.

Target factors:
  Atmospheric CO$_2$ levels
  Wetland, river and estuary, and nearshore ocean ecosystems
  Human community well-being

One key distinguishing technical feature of the *Conservation Standards* when compared with most other planning approaches is that rather than jumping straight to stating your desired outcomes, each of these target factors is a neutral tangible entity expressible as a noun. Later on, we will talk about how to assess the current status of each of these target factors and define a goal that describes their desired future status. But for now, it's better to identify these target factors in our system as literally the things that we ultimately care about to fulfill our purpose, thus allowing us to focus our systems analysis.

▶ **Spatial scope.** The target factors mentioned above are unbounded; it's not clear which specific salmon populations or human communities we are talking about (the exception being truly global targets such as atmospheric CO$_2$ levels). A program's scope thus involves setting boundaries or otherwise demarcating which specific targets you care about, which is closely related to the scale at which you are working. These boundaries can be set across a number of dimensions, which often intertwine and conflict:

  • *Ecological boundaries.* Ecological targets often have natural ecosystem or geophysical boundaries such as the watershed of a large river system, the historical range of a kelp forest ecosystem, a population of salmon that return to a given river, or the home range of a resident pod of whales. You might thus use the boundaries of these ecosystems and species to define the boundaries of your program. Or for migratory species, you might focus only on the target factor during part of its lifecycle. For example, you might choose to focus on salmon while they are in inland waters or migratory birds in their summer breeding grounds. In these cases, you are deliberately saying that you will not invest your time and treasure in the salmon when they are out in the ocean or the birds when they fly to the tropics for the winter. You are thus accepting the risk that your target salmon or bird populations may be affected by threats that you are choosing not to address.
  • *Political–cultural boundaries.* Ecological targets inevitably intersect with human divisions of the land and water. So your program scope might be legally

or practically bounded by a political unit such as a district, state or province, or even a country. Or it might be defined by the traditional lands and waters of an indigenous community.

- *Institutional boundaries.* A given program is typically part of a larger organization or has funding from one or more donors. So your program scope might be bounded by the region administered by your branch of a government agency. Or by the lands or species and ecosystems that are legally under your jurisdiction, such as a network of wildlife refuges or a population of endangered whales. Or the geography of interest established by the founder of a philanthropy. Or the lands directly owned and managed by the large timber company you are working for.

- *Threatshed boundaries.* Finally, if your program is focused on mitigating or eliminating the effects of a human activity that directly affects your target factors, you might bound your scope by the footprint of that direct threat, such as sites vulnerable to mine development, watersheds with large dams, or salmon populations being harvested by small-scale fisheries.

As discussed in more detail below, the art of program design involves selecting the right mix of these different boundary types to define a cohesive spatial scope. And of course, this scope is not necessarily static but can change over time. For example, you may start a pilot project with one coastal watershed but then expand to all the watersheds in your district over time, and then maybe even expand across the international boundary to additional watersheds.

- ▶ **Thematic scope.** In many threat- or problem-focused programs, it can be hard to develop a specific spatial scope. Instead, it may make more sense to start with a thematic scope. For example, if you are working on a program that is trying to establish a wild-caught sustainable seafood certification or rating system, then you are effectively saying that your targets are the fisheries and the fish stocks they depend on, wherever they may occur in the world. Your scope thus delimits which specific fisheries and which fish stocks you ultimately hope to influence. For instance, is your scope the Western Pacific Ocean or the Atlantic Ocean? In inland, nearshore ocean, or pelagic waters? With small-scale or industrial fisheries? Even here, however, you can almost always trace the ultimate impact of the thematic focus to specific conservation or human well-being target factors that have some spatial footprint.

- ▶ **Temporal scope.** People often think about scope in the three dimensions of space. But it is also important to think about the temporal scope of your work.

Time is a particularly challenging concept to consider in conservation programs because of the long time frames, high degree of uncertainty, and fundamental asymmetry between the duration of failure and that of success. If you are trying to protect the last individuals of an endangered species or a patch of old-growth forest or even just a local wetland, then if you fail even just once, the consequences extend far into the future; extinction is forever, and ecosystems can take many decades or even many centuries, if ever, to recover. On the other hand, success is only one year or even one day at a time; if you protect the species or the ecosystem today from the threats that it is facing, you will probably have to do it all over again tomorrow, and the day after, and the year after, and the decade after.

As a result, in defining your program scope, and indeed throughout the strategic planning process, you need to constantly think about the temporal nature of the threats you are facing and the timeshed of the actions you are taking. You also need to think about the durability of your actions. Each action you take is going to buy your team not an infinite amount of conservation but rather some defined period. For example, trucking salmon around a dam might work for one migration season but will have to be redone every year. By contrast, a fish ladder might last for a decade before it needs to be repaired or replaced. And removing the dam might last for a much longer period but still requires some vigilance to ensure that a new barrier is not put in place in the future. Because no action lasts forever—and any major failure could be permanent—you have to plan accordingly. Yes, this is a depressing thought. But it's a fundamental reality of this work.

Guidance for Selecting Target Factors and Bounding the Scope of Your Program

Defining the target factors and scope of your program is a highly iterative process:

- **Select a limited number of coarser target factors.** A good starting point for thinking about target factors is to take your program's purpose and use it to establish one or two, or at most a handful of target factors that represent the ultimate values of your program's purpose. As discussed above, your target factors should be tangible entities such as an ecosystem, a species, or a human community.

    For those who are familiar with the *Conservation Standards* process as applied to conservation projects, you may notice that at a program scale we are proposing some subtle yet important changes in the target selection process. In a typical conservation project planning process, you would start by defining your project scope, such as a small watershed or a large bay. You would then work with your ecologists to select up to eight focal ecological targets (ecosystems and species) that would represent and encompass the full range of biodiversity across your scope. For example, as shown in the "Local Project" column in Table 1.1, this project team has focused primarily on ecosystem types but also lists as nested targets key species that live in or use the ecosystems as part of their lifecycle.

    Jumping up to the regional level, this higher-scale program might again select a set of focal ecological target factors, but in this case the ecosystem factors are more lumped. Furthermore, the regional team also uses key migratory species as target factors in their own right, using them to then develop apex indicators of overall ecosystem health and interconnectedness. The regional team also has

Table 1.1. Target factors become coarser as program scale increases

Examples of Factors	Programmatic Scale		
	Local Project (e.g., small watershed)	Regional Program (e.g., large bay)	National Program[a]
Conservation target factors Nested targets	Floodplains Feeding cranes Marshes Striped newt Migrating ducks Tributary streams Spawning salmon River mainstem Migrating salmon River delta Juvenile salmon Shoreline habitats Beaches Dune systems Feeding shorebirds Breeding seals Nearshore marine Mud clams Seagrass beds	Riparian wetlands Floodplains Marshes Rivers Tributary streams River mainstems Estuaries River deltas Tidal marshes Marine systems Shoreline habitats Islands Nearshore marine Open ocean Migratory shorebirds Migratory waterfowl Salmon Killer whales Seals	River systems Riparian wetlands Rivers Estuaries Migratory birds Shorebirds Waterfowl Raptors Songbirds Anadromous fish Marine mammals Whales and dolphins Seals and sea lions Manatees

[a] A national program typically would select only one target factor.

additional targets that are not relevant at the site level (e.g., <tidal marshes> or <killer whales>).

At a program level, however, we have found (somewhat paradoxically) that it's more effective to have fewer coarser-scale target factors as your focus and then use your scope to bound or delimit them. This is in part because programs, even though they are often larger in scale, tend to be narrower in conceptual scope than a typical project. For example, as you move from the local scale to the regional scale in Table 1.1, the local project targets actually become nested targets for the regional project. Indeed, as shown in the "National Program" column, a truly large program might only have one high-level target factor such as <river systems> or <marine mammals>. Likewise, a global sustainable fisheries program might have as its sole target factor <key fisheries>. Of course, only some of the nested targets at the national level might be relevant to a given regional program.

The choice of target factors stems from your purpose and thus is largely a values decision, even when it seems to have scientific grounding. As one example, say you are part of the planning team for a large lake that historically had a native population of landlocked salmon that became genetically distinct. Seventy-five years ago, these salmon became overfished and suffered disease. Managers thus decided to introduce nonnative salmonids, which soon flourished, providing a healthy salmon population as the basis for both top ecological predators and a robust sports fishery. In your planning workshop for conservation of this lake, the question comes up whether the team should maintain the nonnative salmon population as a target factor or try to replace them (at great expense) with the nearest living "local" salmon population (i.e., treating the nonnative salmon as a threat). The key here is to realize that there is no right answer to this question. Nonetheless, for your project to move forward, you need to have an answer to this question.

- **Consider the relationship between target factors.** As discussed in the preceding section, there is a complex relationship between different purposes that carries over into the relationship between different target factors. There is a strong desire in conservation to find win–win solutions that simultaneously improve both conservation and development target factors. As illustrated in Figure 1.2, if you are sailing your program boat toward the islands of conservation and development, a given strategy pathway can take you toward both destinations if they are conceptually next to each other (Panel A) or are at least aligned with each

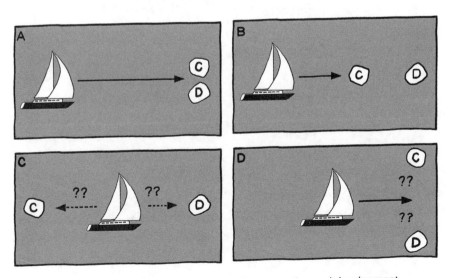

Figure 1.2. Navigating to the islands of conservation and development.

other relative to your current position (Panel B). But if your two destinations are in different directions (Panel C) or at opposite ends of the map relative to your current position (Panel D), then at some point you have to make some difficult trade-off decisions.

The key is not just to hope your target factors are adjacent but to explicitly sketch out how they relate to one another. As an example of a win–win solution in Panel A or B in Figure 1.2, Figure 1.3 shows conserving or restoring <wetlands> for their conservation benefits may also lead to <protection from flooding> and <wetland natural filtration>, which directly benefit both local and global human populations. This filtration may in turn benefit <nearshore ocean> shellfish beds, which then provide <livelihoods, food and culture>. By contrast, an example of a trade-off situation in Panel C or D of Figure 1.2 might occur when a drastic decline in fish stocks means that managers have to choose between allocating fish to either seals and killer whales or recreational, commercial, and subsistence fisheries.

Understanding these relationships helps you and your partners figure out where there are synergies and where trade-offs or decisions must be made. There is now an extensive body of practice in the *Conservation Standards* community

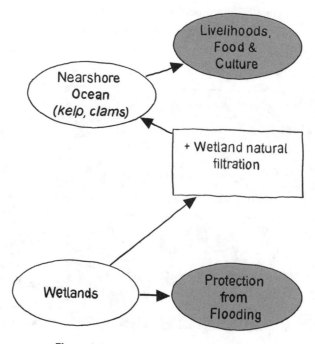

Figure 1.3. A potential win–win situation.

related to understanding and modeling the links between ecological and human well-being factors, in particular looking at ecosystem services.

• **Set a program scope to bound these target factors.** Once you have your candidate target factors, you should think about how you can bound them both in the near term and over time. As discussed above, a program scope is typically defined by a combination of relevant ecological, political–cultural, institutional, and threatshed boundaries.

As a rule, you probably want to start with the boundaries of your ecological targets and the political–cultural boundaries of your human well-being targets. For example, a salmon-focused program in Figure 1.4 might start with the river areas that salmon depend on for spawning in the parts of watersheds managed by your indigenous partners.

Boundary A in the map in Figure 1.4 shows one such spawning area in a pilot watershed. As you think about expanding the pilot to additional river systems,

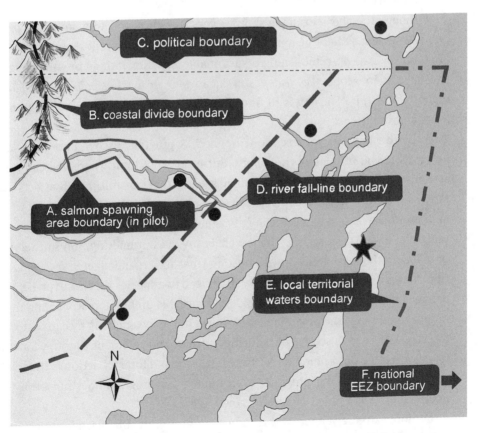

Figure 1.4. Using ecological and sociopolitical boundaries to determine program scope.

you might bound your program scope in the west by Boundary B, which is the mountain ridgeline that divides the coastal river systems from the inland river systems. Going to the north, however, you might (at least for now) limit your program scope with Boundary C, which is the international political border. Finally, in the east you have three options. You could restrict yourself to the freshwater portions of the river systems as represented with Boundary D, which is the fall line demarcating the transition from flowing freshwater to tidal saltwater. Or you could expand your program to include salmon in the nearshore ocean environment as defined by Boundary E, which shows the zone of local government territorial control over ocean waters. Or finally, you could choose to cover salmon over their entire lifecycle going out to Boundary F, which is the national exclusive economic zone (EEZ) boundary or even into the international waters of the high seas. Here again, there is obviously no right answer as to how to set your program's scope. But to have a successful program, you need to come up with an answer, however you choose to define it.

Although the above example shows a very specific scope, in many other programs your scope might be a much more general thematic scope. For example, a program focused on establishing a sustainable fisheries ratings program might just have as its scope *<key fisheries in our region>* or even *<small-scale fisheries around the world>*. The key is to find a scope that best matches your program's focus and ambitions.

• **Take action beyond your scope if needed.** A program's scope puts boundaries on what you ultimately care about. But it does not limit where you can take action; you can work outside your defined scope if that work ultimately affects the target factors within your scope. As one example, consider two different pathways built around an action of getting logging companies to adopt better management practices (BMPs) (Figure 1.5). The top chain involves promoting BMPs in service of reducing the loss of old-growth nesting trees for an endangered owl population. In this case, because the forestry BMPs lead to a species that is not one of the defined target factors for our example program, this upland forestry action does not make sense for the program to undertake. In the lower chain, by contrast, the forestry BMPs are in service of reducing nutrient and sediment runoff, which in turn is affecting our salmon target factor. This upland forestry action is thus well within the scope of our program, even though our program does not have the upland forests as a target factor in its own right.

A more extreme version of this concept of actions taking place far away from the scope of the program involves policy actions that may be taken in a national

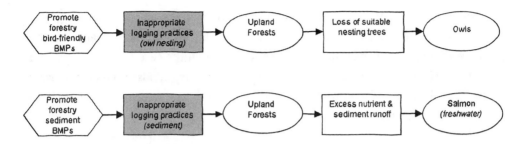

Figure 1.5. Determining whether an action is in scope depends on linkages to the target factor.

capital on the other side of the country or market demand actions that might affect commodity production on the other side of the world.

- **Match your program's strategies to the appropriate scopes.** For place-based programs, the strategic planning challenge starts with selecting a specific purpose and scope and then figuring out the right set of strategies and tools to address the problems found in that place. However, some programs specialize in deploying a specific strategy and its associated tools to help other place-based projects and programs address specific challenges. For example, a program may focus on working with indigenous communities to help them do land and water planning. Or a program may specialize in promoting desired human behavior change. Or a program may specialize in setting up sustainable seafood production. These thematic-based programs thus have the inverse challenge of starting with their strategy and tools and figuring out the right set of places (i.e., spatial scopes) where their approach can make a meaningful difference.

Assembling the Right Team and Program Partners

The third component of your program's focus involves determining who should be involved in this work. This choice of "who" really matters. As business writer Jim Collins (2005) states, success is largely about "getting the right people on the bus. . . . The number-one resource for a great social sector organization is having enough of the right people. . . . Time and talent can often compensate for lack of money, but money cannot ever compensate for lack of the right people." At the same time, if you don't have the right people on the bus, then you probably will not find a truly sustainable and durable solution to the problem you are trying to address.

It is often helpful to think about the individuals and the organizations involved in a given program across different functional roles (note that in this book we are using the word *organization* to mean all types of entities including nonprofits and NGOs, consortia, government agencies, communities, tribes and other indigenous groups, foundations, and firms). These roles are not completely discrete categories but rather, as shown in Figure 1.6, overlapping circles; a person on the core team can also be an implementing partner and even a stakeholder. There also tends to be an increasing level of involvement in the program as you move from the outer to the inner circles. Common roles include:

- ▶ **Core team.** Individuals and organizations who are directly involved in designing and managing your program. The core team also typically includes one or more coaches or facilitators who can provide process support and advice.
- ▶ **Implementing partners.** Individuals and organizations who are involved in helping to implement your program's pathways. Generally people who can be assigned activities and tasks used to implement program strategies. Specific types of implementing partners include:

  - *Staff.* Work for the core organizations involved in the program
  - *Funders.* Provide financial and other support through grants and contracts
  - *Grantees or contractors.* Use financial and other support to implement activities
  - *Cooperating partners.* Participate in program implementation without direct compensation

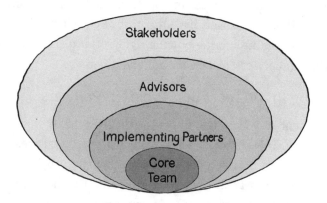

Figure 1.6. Overlapping program roles.

- ▶ **Advisors.** Individuals and organizations who provide advice and oversight for your work. These advisors can include your organizational leaders and board members as well as similar individuals from your program partners. They can also include key stakeholders such as community elders, citizen groups, watchdog organizations, or researchers.

▶ **Stakeholders.** Individuals and organizations who are potentially affected by your work and whose inclusion you want to ensure. These can include people who need to be engaged or informed through either two-way or one-way communication about your work. But as we discuss in more detail below, the level of engagement among different stakeholders may vary.

Conservation is at least as much a human behavior issue as an ecological issue. As a result, even small conservation projects need an interdisciplinary project team. So it should be no surprise that at a program scale, it is even more important that you have a dynamic and diverse set of individuals and organizations involved in your program. The key is to make sure that you involve all these people not just in doing the work but also in the full cycle of planning, managing, monitoring, and learning from this work. One key concept to consider is:

▶ **The wisdom of the crowd.** There is an established concept in the social science and business worlds that large groups of people are inherently smarter than any of the individuals in the group, assuming that their knowledge can be properly harnessed and tapped. The classic example is that if you give a group of people a very large jar full of jellybeans and you ask everyone in the group to guess how many jellybeans are in the jar, the individual guesses will vary greatly, but the average of all the guesses is almost always within 5 percent of the actual total number if you have a large enough group of people guessing. The key is to record the individual guesses without allowing them to bias each other. This wisdom of the crowd is the basis for both the stock market and market-based predictive systems.

At their best, the pathway diagrams and other participatory techniques described in this book provide a powerful tool to harness the collective wisdom of the crowd. You can share your models with different people and obtain their perspectives and input into the situation. The challenge is to get input from a wide enough range of people so that you have more confidence in arriving at the right answer. To this end, a simpler but more accessible model that can be understood and commented on by many people may be more robust than a more complex and "sophisticated" model that can only really be understood by and receive input from its creators.

An important corollary to the wisdom of the crowd is that your models, decisions, and work will almost always be better if there is a greater range of perspectives in your team and among your partners. To get these diverse perspectives, we need to consider diversity, equity, inclusion, and justice and moral obligations. Although we are still learning how to best address these topics in the context of conservation programs, some initial principles, as framed by Dafina-Lazarus Stewart (2017), include:

- ▶ **Diversity.** Diversity answers the question, "Who is sitting at the program planning and management table?" Diversity comes in many forms, including organization types, cultures and religions, age, gender, race and ethnicity, and socioeconomic classes. It is also important to recognize that there is diversity within each sub-group. For example, one person from a given ethnic or racial group does not represent the perspectives of the entire group. Each of these different facets of your partnership will bring their own values, experiences, and ideas to your work and probably contribute to more successful outcomes. Diversity also helps build a stronger coalition that can give you more heft in political situations.

- ▶ **Inclusion.** Building on diversity, inclusion addresses the question, "Is each person or group at the table heard and valued?" Inclusion starts with creating an environment in which participants are respected and encouraged to participate. This is an area in which many program leaders can fool themselves. Just because a group's representative is invited to the table does not mean the person or their group is genuinely heard or valued. In other words, diversity does not ensure inclusion. If you are the leader bringing together a diverse team or partnership, don't assume you know whether people feel included; the only ones who can truly answer the question are your partners answering it for themselves.

- ▶ **Equity.** Diversity and inclusion in and of themselves will not pay dividends unless you ensure equitable outcomes. Equity answers the question, "Does everyone sitting at the table—and even those who may not be at the table—share risks and rewards equally?" Equity is crucial to ensure that both positive and negative outcomes do not disproportionately affect different racial, socioeconomic, cultural, political, or otherwise traditionally marginalized groups. This is an issue that has not traditionally been managed well in conservation programs. Power dynamics, structural social dynamics, money, educational levels, and history often work against achieving equity. In particular, implicit structural biases often work against participation in ways that most people in the program don't even realize, severely undermining progress on seemingly clear shared goals.

- ▶ **Justice and moral obligations.** Finally, it is important to remember that, as

discussed above, conservation does not take place in a vacuum. It takes place in the context of environmental justice, which intersects with many other social justice issues including public health, economic development, climate justice, and human rights that each create moral obligations. To some extent, modern environmentalism can trace its roots all the way back to practices that were fundamentally unjust and inequitable in that disempowered poor were excluded or expelled from lands they historically occupied to serve the extractive desires of royalty and affluent classes. Ironically, many of today's most important conservation areas exist because they belong to or have been stewarded for generations by their current inhabitants and users, such as indigenous groups and fishing or ranching communities.

As a result, conservation programs clearly have a moral responsibility to acknowledge and respect these original landowners and their contributions and to ensure that their rights, needs, and desires are integrated into the program's work. At the same time, many conservationists also feel they have a moral obligation to give voice and standing to the species and ecosystems that are otherwise unrepresented in human affairs that determine their fate. Although these two moral imperatives are most often aligned with one another, in some instances they may conflict. But even in these latter cases, being aware of implicit biases and developing clear understandings of your program strategy will go a long way toward finding equitable shared solutions and mitigating potential conflicts.

Guidance for Assembling the Right Team and Program Partners

Building your core team and program partners is at least as much an art as a science. To this end, you will ultimately have to decide which partners should play which role based on your situation, experience, intuition, and focus on appropriate inclusion and equity. That said, some pointers to keep in mind include the following:

• **Iteratively consider your program's purpose, target factors and scope, and partners.** There is a fair amount of overlap involved in defining the three components of your program's focus. Because the choice of a purpose is largely a values decision, it matters greatly whose values are considered in making this decision. The choice of target factors follows from the purpose, which in turn influences your program scope. And then these decisions in turn affect who you need to have as program partners, which then goes full circle and affects your program's purpose.

For example, if you select salmon during their spawning period in freshwater as a target factor, you will probably have to partner with the communities that live along the rivers as well as the government agencies responsible for managing these waters. If you decide to include the spawning watersheds across a political boundary (per Figure 1.4), you will have to expand your program partners to include the corresponding communities and government agencies in the relevant jurisdiction. If you decide to expand your target factors to include salmon in the nearshore marine environment, then you will have to further grow your roster of partners to include the people and companies involved in the fishing industry as well as the state or provincial government agencies involved in regulating them. And finally, if you expand your scope to include offshore national EEZ waters, you will have to bring in the federal agencies responsible for managing them as well as the companies involved in the salmon value chain.

• **Select partners who are complementary yet compatible.** As a rule, you will want a wide coalition of partners in your program so as to have a diverse and robust group of supporters, ensuring inclusion and equity. And you want to make sure you find partners who will bring complementary expertise and resources to your partnership and who will challenge your perspectives and thinking in a healthy way. Sometimes, it's also a good tactical move to include people or organizations who have the potential to cause problems for your work inside the partnership tent rather than having them throw rocks from the outside. But at the same time, each additional partner will also bring their own values and agenda to the partnership. This could put pressure on you to expand your program beyond where you want to go. And you probably want to avoid picking partners who will ultimately stall out or fragment your coalition or who may carry political baggage that will cause trouble for your work. At the end of the day, not all stakeholders need to be or should be partners.

As shown in the top row of Table 1.2, if you are pulling together a program focused on establishing a sustainable fishing industry, it may well make sense to include commercial boat operators or seafood companies in your program as advisors or even on the core team along with the other members of your coalition. But if you are working on a program aimed at stopping large-scale mining operations per the second row, even though they are clearly a stakeholder, it probably doesn't make much sense to include the mining companies or their political backers in your program—or even to inform them about your strategy and plans. However, if you think your program will focus on helping to make existing or planned mining more sustainable, then you might want to include the mining company. The bottom line is that although there is not necessarily a right answer, you need to have an answer.

Table 1.2. Examples of strategic selection of program partners and nonpartner stakeholders

Program	Program Partners	Nonpartner Stakeholders
Sustainable fishing industry	Indigenous communities Boat operators Environmental NGOs District government agencies Seafood companies	Foreign fishing fleets
Campaign against gold mines	Indigenous communities Environmental NGOs District government agencies Seafood companies	Mining companies Political backers

- **Start small and build up your partnership over time.** As in most human situations, it's usually easier to invite people to join the party along the way rather than start with a big group and then be forced to uninvite individuals and organizations who do not contribute constructively to the partnership. This speaks to your scaling strategy. As you consider each new partner, think about how their perspectives, values, skills, and resources fit into the existing partnership. What do they bring to the table? What baggage might come with them? What's their reputation within the broader community? Each candidate will probably have a mix of positive and negative factors. On balance, do the pluses outweigh the minuses? Are there any dealbreakers? This is definitely one set of decisions where you may have to trust your gut instincts as much as rational consideration of the problem.

- **Use your planning process to find common ground.** One of the advantages of going through an explicit planning process is that it gives you a set of tools to clearly articulate what your program is trying to achieve so that you can have frank discussions with potential partners about their involvement. As discussed above, you don't need to have 100 percent agreement with a partner to work together, but you do need to have sufficient common ground to justify joining forces. And if through your collective and inclusive planning process you can't get to a critical mass of partners and stakeholders who all find common cause and common ground, then that should be a clear signal to you that your efforts will probably fail.

  In particular, being open-minded and open-eyed about the relationship of your conservation purpose and target factors to other social issues is absolutely critical to your success. Given that most modern-day conservation efforts will not succeed over the short or long term without the fair distribution of risks and rewards among affected groups, you must pay attention to issues of diversity, inclusion, and equity. That does not necessarily mean that you must convert your conservation program into a human rights program, but it does require that you adequately incorporate relevant social issues into your planning and implementation processes. At the simplest level, this means you must explicitly negotiate the conservation goals that are important to you with the social goals that are most important to other groups in your partnership. Almost always, conservation work is about managing trade-offs, and you have to be willing to compromise to find common cause to make the gains you want to see. At the same time, you need to be vigilant not to compromise your conservation goals too much in the service of the goals of other organizations. To this end, having clear and shared models will go a long way toward developing a mutually acceptable common ground.

- **Enable equitable and inclusive participation.** As you start to build your partnership, it's important to ensure that your planning modalities and methods are designed to be inclusive to accommodate and encourage all key partners to participate in the work. To this end, the philosophy and approach in this book are based on using long-standing participatory community-based facilitation techniques and tools that focus on the achievement of equitable outcomes, which you need to adapt to your context. For example, you need to hold meetings in the appropriate language or languages and ensure that you have translation where necessary. You also need to schedule in-person meetings in locations and at times when key people can join and partner with local facilitators. And you might want to avoid online meetings if people don't have the tools or connectivity to join.

On the other hand, online approaches may actually enable wider and deeper participation. For example, introverts or people who feel shy about talking in the language being used in a workshop might be more willing to share their information and perspectives using a chat box. And obviously, with an online meeting you can reach people who are unable or can't afford to travel to an in-person workshop, assuming they have internet access. The key is to design your processes in such a way that all key participants are empowered to join.

- **Include all your partners and stakeholders in your process.** In our work over the years on systematic conservation planning, we have frequently heard criticism that it is not appropriate to impose a highly structured approach (what some refer to as "top down" or "scientific") on community planning processes. Although it is clearly important to use an approach that works for the stakeholders you are trying to reach, recognize your partners' abilities and aptitudes to do the type of systematic thinking and planning presented in this book. There is a long history of conservation planning and management work with groups such as the Locally Managed Marine Area Network across the Pacific Ocean and the Healthy Country Planning work with Aboriginal groups in Australia and First Nations groups in Canada. These efforts have shown that when appropriately shared and implemented, systematic conservation planning can be very effective for local and indigenous communities to regain control of and manage their resources. Furthermore, as discussed in more detail in Part II, these types of processes can easily incorporate and build on traditional knowledge where it augments and extends scientific evidence.

Certainly, in an era in which there is great skepticism about science and expertise in some communities, the kind of systematic approach presented in this book may not be the best fit in all situations. As an extreme example, if laws or dominant religious edicts mandate that resources be managed in a certain prescribed way, at some point you may not be able to implement anything different no matter what your logical plan says. That said, these processes can easily accommodate a wide range of worldviews. Both devout religious people who believe that humans have stewardship responsibility for the natural world and people who believe that all species have an inherent right to exist might be able to agree on a plan to maintain a healthy salmon population.

At the end of the day, although some people may argue that systematic planning reduces the creative process to boxes and arrows, we tend to side with Robert Pirsig (1974), who wrote "The Buddha . . . resides quite as comfortably in the circuits of a digital computer or the gears of a motorcycle transmission as he does at the top of a mountain or in the petals of a flower. To think otherwise is to demean the Buddha—which is to demean oneself."

Understanding the System in Which You Are Working

In traditional project planning, once you have defined your purpose, target factors and scope, and partners, the next step is to develop a situation assessment that models the various factors that affect your targets. As we noted in the Introduction, conservation programs typically work in some of the most complex systems in the world. Conservation program managers need to not only navigate around the shoals of this complexity but also to use the currents of the system to propel their work to scale. As a result, before diving into a situation assessment, it's helpful to have a basic understanding of systems analysis (or systems thinking) especially as applied to conservation work. A lot has been written about systems analysis over the past couple decades, but most of it boils down nicely to a basic definition articulated by Ross Arnold and Jon Wade (2015):

> Systems thinking is a set of synergistic analytic skills used to improve the capability of identifying and understanding systems, predicting their behaviors, and devising modifications to them in order to produce desired effects.

Systems analysis starts by defining three key characteristics of your system of interest:

▶ **System focus and boundaries.** Understanding a system starts with articulating its purpose, function, or goal and delimiting its boundaries. We are all familiar with systems that are named for their function, such as the human circulatory system, a home heating system, an urban school system, or a national transport system. This naming both defines the system and bounds it relative to other systems such as the human digestive system or an urban public safety system.

In conservation work on complex ecosystems, although it doesn't usually make sense to define these systems by their function, you can certainly define the focus and boundaries of your work by articulating your purpose, target factors and scope, and partners, as described in the preceding sections. These three components define the thing you want to influence and the boundaries of the system within which you will do your analysis.

▸ **System factors.** Understanding a system next requires describing component elements or factors. For example, the human circulatory system is made up of the heart, blood vessels, and blood, among other organs. Likewise, a national transport system is made up of the road network, rail network, and air travel system as well as many other components. As a rule, these components can be expressed as nouns, although they can be both tangible (e.g., roads, trains, airports) and intangible (e.g., policies, processes, perceptions, beliefs). Most if not all components of large-scale systems are themselves subsystems within the overall system of interest.

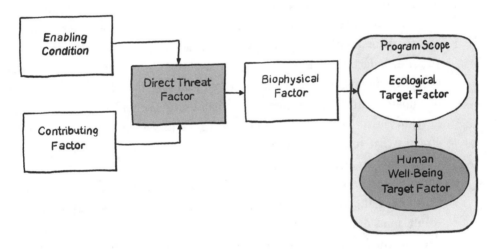

Figure 1.7. Types of factors in a situation model.

In any given discipline, it is helpful for communication and learning purposes to have a limited set of relevant factors that have commonly accepted names and definitions. For example, in medicine there are standard names for all the different parts of the human body, for different diseases, and for different treatments. Following the *Conservation Standards*, as shown in Figure 1.7, there are a number of basic factor types including:

- *Target factors.* As discussed above, target factors are no different from any other factors in the system, except that you have chosen them to represent the values you are ultimately interested in affecting. In analysis terms, they are your dependent variables. Conservation programs typically include ecological target factors (species, ecosystems, and/or natural processes) and human well-being target factors that represent aspects of human well-being that can be linked to the provision of ecosystem services. Species are typically named by the Linnaean classification system, whereas ecosystems are defined by an International Union for Conservation of Nature (IUCN) classification system. There have been some efforts to standardize human well-being and ecosystem services.

- *Biophysical factors.* Natural ecosystems are by themselves highly complex systems that have hundreds of interacting components from both the biotic and abiotic worlds. For example, the long-term health of a forest ecosystem might depend on soils, fire regimes, snowfall and melt patterns, the presence of migratory species that serve as pollinators or seed dispersers, and weather-related disturbance patterns, to name but just a few. It is particularly important to understand these interactive effects between biophysical factors when you are undertaking direct management actions in service of species and ecosystem restoration or in helping ecological systems adapt to the impacts of climate change. The conservation community has made some attempts to develop classifications of these biophysical factors, focused primarily on the stresses that represent altered ecological target attributes. However, these factors vary greatly between ecosystem types.

- *Direct threats (or pressures).* By definition, conservation involves taking action to stop or mitigate the effects of human activities on the natural world. As a result, some of the most critical factors to consider are the direct threats that describe the specific human activities that have adverse impacts on your ecological target factors. However, when working with potential program partners who use and manage natural resources, you need to be careful about how you select and refer to your threat factors. For example, fishing boat owners or loggers often take offense when their professions are labeled as threats; instead, you may want to label the threats as <unsustainable fishing> or <incompatible logging practices> and refer to them as pressures. Over the past two decades, the conservation community has developed a hierarchical and comprehensive standard classification of direct threats at all scales (see "Sources and Further Information" at the end of this chapter for relevant references).

- *Contributing factors (root causes or drivers).* Behind the direct threat factors, there are an unlimited number of different physical, social, political, economic, cultural, and other such factors that form the root causes or drivers of the human actions that constitute the direct threats. These contributing factors can include both positive opportunities or enabling conditions and negative indirect threats. However, it is often challenging to say a given factor is positive or negative; for example, a factor such as <ecotourism> can simultaneously be both a threat and an opportunity. Although there has been periodic interest in developing a standard classification of contributing factors, this has proven challenging because there are so many ways to divide up complex systems.
- *Exogenous factors.* Although they are technically a subset of contributing factors, it is often helpful in mapping conservation systems to think about the exogenous factors in the system that might affect your work but over which you have little or no control. For example, a program team might treat the global price of gold, or corruption, or an international treaty setting the boundaries of local ocean management as exogenous variables that need to be taken into account but cannot be changed by the program's actions.
- *Strategies and actions.* Finally, although they are not strictly part of a situation assessment, the last remaining factor type involves the strategies and actions that a program team uses to produce the desired effects in the system. It's also helpful to include strategies and actions being undertaken by other actors (outside your program team and partners) in your situation assessment so that you are aware of potential overlaps and gaps. The conservation community has developed a hierarchical and comprehensive standard classification of single conservation actions (see the Conservation Actions and Measures Library [CAML] website) but is only now starting to consider how to classify broader strategies that involve combinations of different actions.

In systems thinking, it is important not only to identify each of the relevant factors but also to assess both its current state (what systems thinkers refer to as the stock of the factor) and the changes in the factor over time (i.e., flows). We discuss how to make these assessments in Chapter 5.

▶ **System factor relationships.** Finally, understanding a system requires characterizing the connections between the factors in your system. When systems are described in diagram form, these connections involve the links between two specific factors. Each link can be used to convey several different aspects of the relationship:

- *Causality versus correlation.* As a rule, the presence of a link in a flow diagram depicts an assumed causal relationship between the two factors. Of course, if your assumption is wrong, it may only be a correlative relationship, or there may not be any relationship at all. It is also worth noting that the absence of a link in a diagram also means that you are assuming that no causal link exists, or at least that the link is not useful to show. It can be tempting in any systems analysis to connect every factor to every other factor because you can almost always come up with some claim about how the factors might be linked. The challenge is to show only the most important relationships.
- *Direction.* You can use arrowheads in your diagram links to show the direction of causality in the relationship. For example, in Figure 1.8, both Factor A and Factor B are assumed to cause Factor C. A double-headed arrow technically means that there is an iterative loop, as shown between Factor C and D, typically involving other implicit factors that are not shown in the diagram.

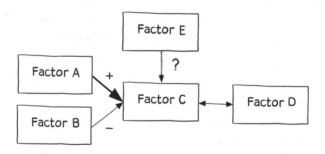

Figure 1.8. Different types of factor relationships.

- *Sign.* You can use your diagram links to show whether there is a positive relationship between two factors (if A increases, C also increases) or a negative (inverse) relationship between two factors (if B increases, C decreases).
- *Contribution.* You can use your diagram links to show the relative contribution of two or more independent factors to a dependent factor. For example, as shown in Figure 1.8, you might use the thickness of the link to show that Factor A is the main driver of Factor C, whereas Factor B plays a secondary role.

- *Variance and conditionality*. In addition to sign, you can use your diagram links to capture other aspects of the nature of the relationship between two factors. For example, you might describe the relationship as a mathematical function showing a linear, exponential, or other variable relationship between the two factors. In a conservation program, you might claim that there is an inverse nonlinear relationship between increases in water temperature and fish spawning success, meaning that as stream temperatures increase, spawning success decreases at a faster and faster rate. Alternatively, the nature of the relationship can be expressed as a set of conditional dependencies (e.g., for the statistically inclined, expressed as probabilities in a Bayesian network diagram). These variable and conditional relationships form the basis for a more dynamic systems analysis. One common example can be found in city-building video games in which parameters such as the number of road workers per thousand residents and number of firefighters per thousand residents are dynamically linked to outcomes such as the number of potholes and the response time to fires. If you reduce the number of road workers to pay for more firefighters, then your residents might be safer from house fires, but they will be more likely to get flat tires.
- *Certainty*. Finally, you can use your diagram links to express your level of certainty (or confidence) about the relationship. For example, you might use a solid line to indicate relative certainty versus a dotted line to show uncertainty. You can also annotate your links with evidence about the relationship, as discussed in more detail in Chapter 4.

In addition to these three primary characterizations of a given system (focus and boundaries, factors, and relationships), there are a number of ways to describe patterns and associations of factors that form subcomponents of the system. Although systems thinkers have developed dozens of named patterns, three of these subsystem types are particularly useful in conservation programs:

▶ **Nested factors.** Nested factors are wholly contained within a higher-order factor. The classic example of nested factors is species that are nested within an ecosystem target factor, such as those shown in Table 1.1. The same principle of nesting can also be used for other factor types. For example, as shown in Figure 1.9, there are three different types of fishing nested in the overall *<unsustainable fishing>* direct threat factor. Likewise, the value chain actors linking consumers

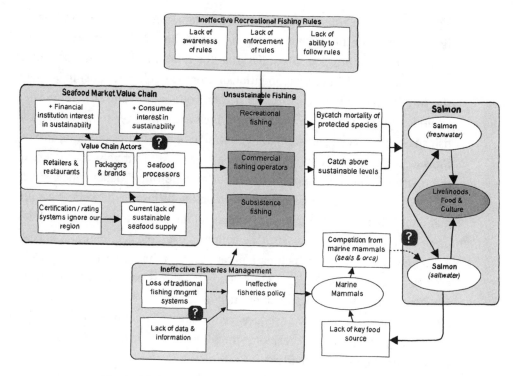

Figure 1.9. Situation model for an unsustainable fishing threat.

to producers <*retailers and restaurants, manufacturers and brands, seafood processors*> can also be considered nested factors in the overall <*seafood market value chain*> group box. As we will see later, nesting helps reduce detail complexity for working at scale.

▶ **Feedback loops.** Systems are inherently about the self-reinforcing circular cycles called feedback loops that influence both the stocks of any given resource in the system and the flows that govern changes in these resources. As Peter Senge (1990) points out using a simple example of filling a glass with water, humans tend to think in linear patterns, saying, "My hand on the faucet is controlling the rate of water flow into the glass." If you consider the problem with the circular system diagram Figure 1.10, you could as easily argue that the level of water in the glass is controlling your hand. The key insight here is to realize that the human actor is part of the system, not standing apart from it.

Systems thinkers have gone into great detail thinking about different types of feedback loops. For the purposes of conservation program design and management, it's most important to think about feedback loops that can quickly drive a

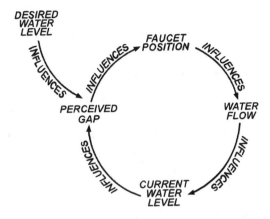

Figure 1.10. An example of a feedback loop. Source: Senge (1990).

system to an undesired state (i.e., vicious cycles) as well as feedback loops that can help scale up desired impacts (i.e., virtuous cycles). A third important type is the balancing loops, which represent patterns in the system that can limit the effect of vicious and virtuous cycles. As we will see below, overcoming the limitations imposed by balancing loops is a key component of leveraging the system to achieve impact at scale.

The simplest feedback loops can be expressed as double-headed arrows between two factors, as shown by the link between salmon in freshwater and salmon in saltwater in Figure 1.9. More complex feedback loops are shown as cycles such as the relationship between <*competition between marine mammals, salmon, lack of key food sources, marine mammals*>. In most cases, an arrow going against the main flow of the arrows in a diagram is a good indicator that there is a feedback loop.

▸ **Situation pathways.** Any given complex system can be subdivided into subsystems. For example, a national transport system can be subdivided into the road system, the rail system, and the air transport system. And each of these subsystems can be further divided into its component systems. As we will see in more detail below, a large part of systems thinking involves knowing how to usefully divide your overall system into meaningful subcomponents.

In conservation programs, some of the most useful subdivisions of the overall system are situation pathways. In the flow diagram models we use, situation pathways are typically horizontal chains of linked factors that lead into a given target factor. These situation pathways are generally self-contained, although there usually are linkages between different situation pathways. For example, in

Figure 1.13, the entire diagram could be considered a situation pathway related to fishing. Or you could subdivide it into three situation pathways, one related to commercial fishing, one to recreational fishing, and the third to the interactions between fishing policies and marine mammals.

Guidance for Understanding the System in Which You Are Working

A great deal of guidance and advice has been written about systems thinking. If you want to go deeper into this subject, you can start with some of the suggested materials we provide at the end of this chapter. Some high-level points to keep in mind include:

- **Keep your systems analysis as simple as possible.** As discussed in the Introduction, there is a tendency when working with complex systems to assume that because the underlying system itself is complex, investing in a more complex analytical approach is necessarily going to lead to better understanding of the system. This better understanding will in theory lead to better decision making and ultimately better outcomes.

  Following this logic, there has been substantial criticism over the years that the basic flowchart and pathway diagrams promoted under the *Conservation Standards* are too simple to model complex systems. These critics have advocated developing more sophisticated systems analyses that quantitatively account for more dynamic relationships between factors. As discussed above, there are certainly situations in which the consequences of making the wrong decision warrant investing in this gold-standard approach. In those cases we would advise you to use the appropriate approach and tools to conduct the needed analysis.

  In our experience, however, the relationship between investment in systems analysis and better decision making is itself nonlinear, as shown in Figure 0.8 in the Introduction. As a result, in most conservation situations, practitioners will be better served using an aluminum-standard approach. If you can get your program team and key stakeholders to define their focus, articulate the major factors in the system, and show their hypothesized causal links, this is probably 80 percent of the systems thinking that is needed. If you do this analysis in a format that all of your partners and stakeholders can internalize, understand, and own, you also bring in the wisdom of the crowd. To this end, we recommend you use the simplest systems analysis you can, given the system you are working in, the capacity of your team and stakeholders, and the consequences of the decision you are making.

- **Focus on the most relevant part of the overall system.** As described above, perhaps the most defining characteristics of a system are its focus and boundaries. Yes, everything in the universe is part of one big interconnected system, and it is tempting to consider all of it. But your challenge is to define and ideally modify a more tractable and manageable part of the universe. This need to focus is why we start the program planning process by iteratively defining the purpose, target factors and scope, and program partners—the three components that define the focus of the systems analysis.

  If you are working at a local project scale, your focus may be narrow enough to enable you to fill in all the details. But if you are working at a typical program scale, even the system you are focusing on may be too complex to fully analyze. To this end, you may want to sketch out the overall system at a high level but then come back and pay more attention to filling in the details of the parts of the system that are likely to be relevant to your eventual strategies. For example, Figure 1.13 (at the end of this chapter) focuses on management actions to ameliorate the impacts of <dams> on <salmon>; removal of the dams is beyond the feasible scope of this program. As a result, the model contains mostly biophysical factors that show the interaction between dams and salmon and very few contributing factors that lead to the direct threat of dams. By contrast, Figure 1.14 is focused on the contributing factors that lead to <unsustainable fishing>. This model thus contains very few biophysical factors because they are not relevant to the focal point of the story being told. However, if in Figure 1.13 the program team thought they might work on eliminating dams outright rather than managing them, then the model should focus on the various contributing factors that drive dam construction and removal.

- **Bind your systems analysis to your manageable interest.** A second temptation in any systems analysis is to keep expanding your analysis to wider and wider circles of factors until you end up trying to model the universe. For example, the situation pathway in Figure 1.11 shows an analysis of the drivers of a potential gold mine that is being proposed for your program area. Although this is an extreme exaggeration for teaching purposes, as you can see, your system analysis can quickly expand to encompass the core of the solar system and popular culture on the internet. But it's unlikely that you are going to be able to intervene in these distant parts of the system. So you are probably better off treating the price of gold as an exogenous factor and bounding your analysis at this point beyond which it is unlikely that you are going to be able to intervene.

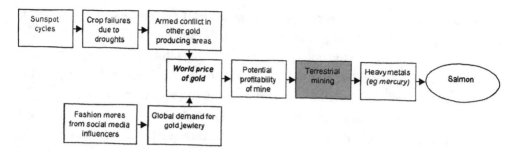

Figure 1.11. Taking a situation pathway way beyond your manageable interest.

- **Use situation pathways to subdivide your overall system into manageable components.** Although systems thinking is about a holistic approach to understanding a complex system, the limitations of the human brain mean that we need to break the system down into smaller, more manageable components to understand it. This does not mean that we are advocating for a completely reductionist approach, but we need to find the appropriate midscale units of analysis.

  For example, consider work over the past few decades on improving commercial aviation safety. The overall system focus here is to get the number of airline fatalities per passenger miles flown as close to zero as possible. Although it is clearly an integrated system, to tackle this problem engineers might subdivide the overall system into a number of component subsystems. For example, one group might focus on aircraft engineering and then subdivide into groups that focus on engine design versus the design and redundancies in the controls of flaps and rudders, among other components. Similarly, another group might focus on human error and then further subdivide into focusing on pilots versus mechanics versus air traffic controllers. At some point, it's still important to think about how these different subsystems interact with one another. But by breaking up the problem into actionable subsystems, engineers have been able to develop astounding gains in the overall goal of aviation safety. In a similar way, medical researchers have been able to look at different systems in the human body as a way to improve human health. There are clearly crossover effects that need to be considered, such as the impact of diet and mental stress on heart health. But overall, we need to find some way to reduce the complexity of the overall system to understand its components.

  There are many ways in which you can break down a typical conservation program system. As a rule, however, it's most helpful to think about your situation pathways. As defined above, a situation pathway typically incorporates a horizontal chain (in the orientation of our diagrams) that includes (from right to left) a target factor, one or more direct threats (and if needed, the biophysical factors that connect them to the target factor), and a set of contributing factors that drive the direct threats. When working at a program scale, some advantages of thinking about situation pathways as a midscale unit of analysis include that these pathways:

- *Form natural subsystems within your overall system.* If you divide up your system vertically by factor types (e.g., by columns in a typical model, such as all the target or direct threat factors), you are cutting across the system. By contrast, horizontal situation pathways form natural subsystems for analyzing problems and developing solutions.
- *Create a good framework for assessing evidence and learning.* As we will discuss in more detail in Chapter 4, the cause-and-effect linkages in situation pathways provide a useful framework for assembling and considering your evidence about how your system functions.
- *Serve as the basis for prioritizing problems.* In a typical site-based conservation project, practitioners are coached to prioritize the direct threats that are most in need of attention. In effect, each threat serves as a proxy for the situation pathway that lies behind that threat. In a larger-scale program in which there may be only one or two focal direct threats, although it may not make sense to prioritize direct threats per se, you can compare project pathways leading to the focal threat to identify potential intervention points, as discussed in more detail in Chapter 2.
- *Provide a template for developing strategy pathways.* Finally, situation pathways provide a good starting point for developing your strategy pathways that contain the actions you will take to achieve your goals.

- **Consider both the forest and the trees.** Although most people working at a program scale need to break down the system into more manageable subcomponents to deal with its detail complexity, it's also important from time to time to step back and consider the system as a whole to deal with its dynamic complexity. Peter Senge (1990) calls this "the art of seeing the forest and the trees." In particular, both within and between situation pathways, it's important to look at the emergent system properties that are driving the system. Senge sums this up very powerfully in a quote worth repeating:

In effect, the art of systems thinking lies in seeing *through* complexity to the underlying structures generating change. Systems thinking does not mean ignoring complexity. Rather, it means organizing complexity into a coherent story that illuminates the causes of problems and how they can be remedied in enduring ways. The increasing complexity of today's world leads many managers to assume that they lack information they need to act effectively. I would suggest that the fundamental "information problem" faced by managers is not too little information but too much information. What we most need are ways to know what is important and what is not important, what variables to focus on and which to pay less attention to—and we need ways to do this which can help groups or teams develop shared understanding.

In particular, it is important to look at the factors and relationships that have the potential to dramatically drive the system in either a positive or negative direction. For example, you might want to pay special attention to factors that have a multiplicative or even exponential relationship to one another. And you certainly need to look for and consider any potential feedback loops in your system.

- **Focus on problems but note opportunities.** A school of planning called appreciative inquiry states that rather than focus on problems to solve, planners should focus on opportunities and what their program team can do well. A related concept involves looking across the actors in your system to discover examples of things that are working, which is (somewhat oxymoronically) called positive deviance. It is certainly important to focus on opportunities, especially if you have a solution-focused organization that is looking for places to apply the skills and resources you have. But conservation is unfortunately a problem-oriented discipline. As an analogy, imagine that you hurt your knee while out running. You go to your doctor to get treatment, and your doctor promptly tells you that their expertise is in treating stomach ulcers, and therefore they are going to treat your stomach. It's highly unlikely that you would keep going to that doctor, unless maybe you subsequently develop a stomach condition from worrying about your knee. In a similar fashion, if you are trying to manage a declining salmon population, you first need to figure out what is going on with the salmon and then decide how to solve the problems.

Of course, as you try to understand the nature of the problems you are facing, you will also want to identify and take advantage of opportunities. You may also need to add new partners to your program to do so.

- **Acknowledge uncertainty but don't be paralyzed by it.** As we will discuss in more detail in Chapter 4, systems thinking is best when it incorporates evidence into your systems analysis. However, you will never have enough evidence to be fully certain about most assumptions in your analysis, and you obviously need to go forward with your work. The trick is to make sure that you acknowledge and track your known knowns and your known unknowns, and even try to be aware of your unknown unknowns. Over time, you can make your analysis, as Nate Silver puts it, "less and less wrong" as you frame and then answer key monitoring questions about your system under an adaptive management approach.

- **Integrate conceptual and spatial analyses.** When working at large scales, it is often helpful to combine your conceptual analyses with spatial maps of your program. Targets, threats, contributing factors, and strategies and actions can all be mapped as data layers that then correspond to your factors in your situation models.

- **Don't forget the thinking.** Finally, keep in mind that the most important part of systems thinking is not the approach you use or the specific tools used in your analysis. Systems thinking is fundamentally about thinking. The approach and tools presented in this book will not give your program the "right" answers. At the end of the day, they are at best aids to facilitate discussion, creativity, and sharing across your team and program partners. If you and your colleagues do not put the time and effort into thinking, you will probably fail no matter what analytical approach you are using. And if you do put the time and effort in, you will give your program the best chance to succeed.

Developing a Shared Situation Model

In the previous section, we covered the reasons for undertaking a systems analysis and some of the high-level principles and guidance for doing good systems thinking. In this section, we turn to a more practical discussion of how to use models to capture and share the results of all this good thinking.

As Peter Senge (1990) and many other thinkers have made it clear, all of us carry in our heads mental models of how the world works. These mental models are based on our life experiences, past observations, access to evidence, and personal beliefs and heuristics and are incredibly powerful because they govern both how we perceive the world and how we act. The challenge in any kind of management situation is to first make sure we surface and examine our individual mental models and then share and harmonize them with the other people we are working with. To this end, in developing a conservation program it is useful to work with your team and partners to create a shared situation model of your system in order to clearly define the problem you are trying to solve, synthesize your different perspectives, collect relevant evidence, compare alternative courses of action, and create a framework for ongoing learning.

Although developing models could easily be the subject of an entire book, some key bits of wisdom to consider as you develop your situation model (as well as your strategy pathway models later on in Chapter 2) include:

- **"All models are wrong, some are useful."** As expressed in George Box's famous quote, no model will ever perfectly capture all the nuances of the system you are working in. Instead, the key is whether or not the model helps you and your team and partners arrive at a better set of decisions about your program. So don't worry about making your model perfect. Yes, there are hundreds of factors in the system, and every factor could be linked to every other factor in theory. But showing all of them is not helpful in practice.

- **"The simplicity on the far side of complexity."** Models are essential tools for helping your team and partners to get a handle on the complexity of the system you are working in. That said, more complexity in your model is not necessarily more useful. Instead, following Oliver Wendell Holmes, you want your model to be as simple as possible to capture the necessary level of complexity. As one analogy, think about an illustrated birding field guide. Although one might think having realistic photos showing every detail of the bird's anatomy would be best, for most people, a hand-drawn illustration that shows only the most salient features of the bird necessary for identification is actually the most helpful type of guide. In a similar fashion, good models abstract out much of the clutter and detail, allowing the user to focus on the critical factors and interactions in the system that clearly outline the key assumptions you are making for everyone to see and understand.

- **"Approximate answers to an exact question."** A key aspect of the art of good model building involves estimation. As John Tukey says, it's better to have "approximate answers to the right question" than to have precise answers to questions that aren't relevant. But developing useful estimates of relevant parameters can be quite challenging. Following the classic analogy, it's more tempting to look under the lamplight for your keys rather than fumble around in the dark where you actually dropped them.

Somewhat ironically, good estimation is a learned skill that takes time and experience to master. If you ask a middle or high school student to calculate the exact answer to the following math problem using a pencil and paper, they can easily do it:

$$\begin{array}{r} 467 \\ \times\ 538 \\ \hline ??? \end{array}$$

But if you ask the students to estimate an approximate answer by eye, it's a lot harder to get many of them to realize that this is more or less 500 × 500, or about 250,000. This is a challenge, because good estimation can be the most profitable return on investment in many analyses. When working at large scales, if you can estimate the right parameter to a factor of 2 or even an order of magnitude, you will be looking at where your keys are rather than looking a block away under the lamplight.

If you are going to use estimates, however, it is important to clearly state the level of precision inherent in your model's assumptions. A mathematically based decision support table might display the benefit–cost ratio of different action scenarios down to last dollar or even to the last penny. But if you look under the hood of the model, you might find embedded assumptions that could swing the final totals by hundreds, if not thousands, of dollars. A more useful model ensures that users are aware of the error bars inherent in each assumption as well as the final results. At the end of the day, a rough approximation of the answer may be more than sufficient for the decision your team is looking to make.

▶ **"Invite others to challenge your assumptions and add their own."** As Donella Meadows wrote, one of the most important uses of a model is to help your team and your partners develop a shared understanding of the system in which you are working and the assumptions you are making about it. It is thus vital to develop your models in a format that at least enables your partners and stakeholders to review and understand the model and ideally enables them to easily develop and edit the model so that you can benefit from the wisdom of the crowd. To this end, it may be more useful to have a less precise model in a more accessible format rather than a more precise model in a less accessible format.

▶ **"Become less and less and less wrong."** Finally, although your model will never capture all the nuances of the system you are working in, it can become "less wrong" over time, as Nate Silver put it. The key is to document assumptions and uncertainties in your model and then develop monitoring and learning questions that you can ask and then answer over time. Of course, you also have to update your model over time as you get the answers to these questions and as the underlying system changes.

Guidance for Developing a Shared Situation Model

As discussed above, you will want to make sure your entire program team and all your partners are included in developing and providing input to your models. There are many facilitation techniques that you can use to get this input, depending on whether you are working in an in-person workshop or online via asynchronous sharing of information. Although these techniques are beyond the scope of this book, regardless of how you end up developing and updating your models, there are a number of key points to keep in mind when trying to develop models for large-scale programs:

- **Use a process and notation that is accessible by your team and partners.** If your program team is composed of economists and statisticians, then it may be entirely appropriate to build your model as a series of mathematical equations that encapsulate the key factors and relationships in the system you are working on. On the other hand, if you are working with a team of nonliterate people, it may be more appropriate to build your model as a series of pictographs or stories. In this book, we tend to use box-and-arrow flow diagrams because we find that they are generally understandable by many people but also allow a sufficient level of complexity. However, please be aware that although these types of models effectively communicate to many people, for some people they just don't work. If your boss or your donor or another key stakeholder is one of those people, then you need to find a way to share your thinking that resonates with them.
- **Start with templates.** Chances are good that you are not the first group of people to think about the system in which you are working. Wherever possible, see whether existing models can serve as a template for your work, either specifically for the system you are working in or from analogous systems elsewhere. Of course, make sure you don't blindly adopt these templates without ensuring that they are appropriate for your specific situation.
- **Sketch out the model first and then fill in the critical parts.** As a rule, you and your team should first try to sketch out your entire model and then go back and ink in the details in the parts that are most relevant.
- **Focus on factors as nouns.** In traditional logframe planning, you are asked to specify the goals and objectives for your strategy. However, we have found

that it is difficult for most program teams to articulate their goals and objectives when they haven't yet even defined the system they are working in. Thus, in the *Conservation Standards* you start by thinking about the key factors. These are generally concrete nouns. What species or ecosystems do you care about? What human activities are threatening these things? In Chapter 3 we will turn our attention to more detailed SMART formulations of the current and desired future state of these factors. But for now, it's easier to keep your factors more concrete.

- **Subdivide your situation models into situation pathways.** When dealing with complex systems, there is a natural tendency to create complex and detailed situation models. It is not uncommon to see spaghetti diagrams that have fifty or even a hundred different factors with dozens of links going every which way between them. Although these complex diagrams may be more accurate, they are almost inevitably much less useful. Most people have trouble absorbing information from or making sense of such complex diagrams, and they may even be turned off from the work you are doing. In our experience, if your diagram has more than 25 factors, it will not be as useful. One trick for managing this complexity is to present your situation as a series of related diagrams, each focused on a different situation pathway as shown in the full array of our models at the end of this chapter.

- **Develop high-level and detailed versions of your diagrams.** A second trick for managing complexity is to develop at least two versions of your situation diagrams. First, you can delve into more detail with your core team, showing more factors and more complex relationships between them. But you may also want to produce a higher-level, more simplified version of the model that nests much of the underlying detail. As shown below, the group boxes in the detailed situation model in Figure 1.14a (e.g., <*Unsustainable Fishing*>, <*Ineffective Recreational Fishing Rules*>, <*Ineffective Fishery Management*>, <*Seafood Market Value Chain*>) can become the factors in our higherlevel version in Figure 1.14b. In most cases, you would probably develop the detailed version first and then produce the higher-level diagram that shows "the simplicity on the far side of complexity."

- **Ensure that your model tells a story.** If you show someone an entire situation model with all the boxes and arrows in it, their eyes will probably glaze over and they will ignore the entire thing and perhaps even your entire program. However, if you reveal the model to them piece by piece, then you often can get them to understand the entire complex system in a few short minutes. The key in both building and presenting the model is to think about it as a storytelling aid that enables you to describe the key parts of the system that you want your audience to understand and think about. It also can be helpful to write text descriptions of your model to communicate to people who prefer written words to graphics. For example, Situation Pathway 1 (as shown below in Figure 1.13) might be described as follows:

> Salmon are a keystone species in our program area. In addition to playing a critical role in the ecosystem, they are the primary source of livelihood and food for the communities in the program area and an integral part of their culture. Salmon population health depends on the quality of rivers, estuaries, and nearshore coastal areas. One of the main threats to these aquatic systems is runoff of nutrients and sedimentation caused by inappropriate logging practices in upland forests. This runoff and sedimentation also have a direct influence on the amount and quality of water reservoirs. In our program area, salmon health is also affected by the direct alteration of spawning habitat from changes to the sediment regime, entrainment and impingement of juvenile fish, and barriers to spawning adults—all caused by large industrial and small local dams. Most of these dams have been built over the years as the demand for CO_2-free power and calls for enhanced flood control have increased.

- **Use your model to track what you know—and don't know.** A good model should serve as the guide to the key factors your team knows about the system of interest. To this end, you can use it to document the sources of evidence for key assumptions inherent in the model. But it can also serve as a guide to where you have information gaps or other uncertainties that need to be addressed, either through a review of available evidence or through ongoing adaptive management and learning. To this end, you can use dotted lines and question marks in your models to express uncertainties, as shown in the following situation model examples.

Situation Model Examples

The diagrams in Figures 1.12–1.16 present the overall high-level situation model and specific situation pathways for the conservation scenario used in this book. Note that each of the example programs might focus on only a subset of this overall model that is most relevant to their program's specific focus.

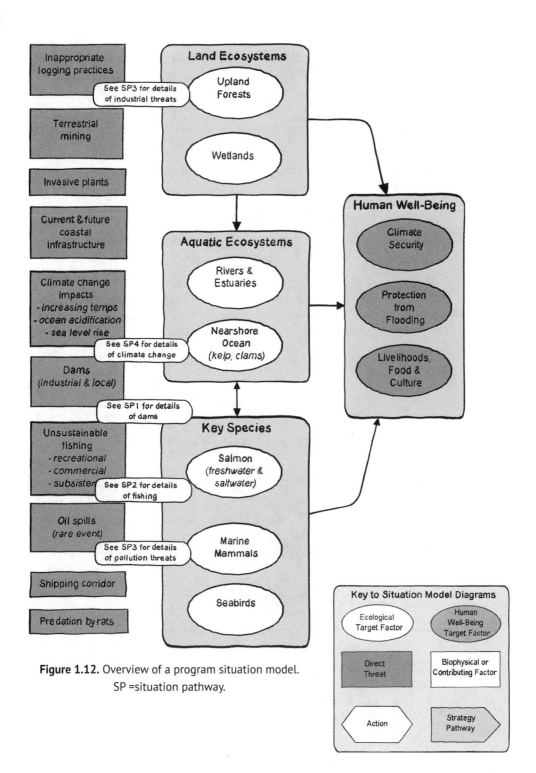

Figure 1.12. Overview of a program situation model.
SP = situation pathway.

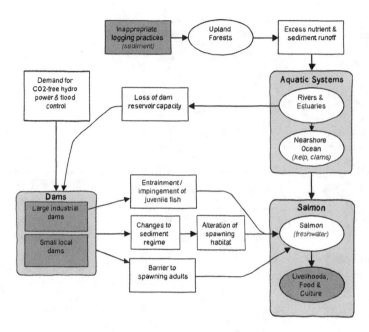

Figure 1.13. Situation Pathway 1: dams.

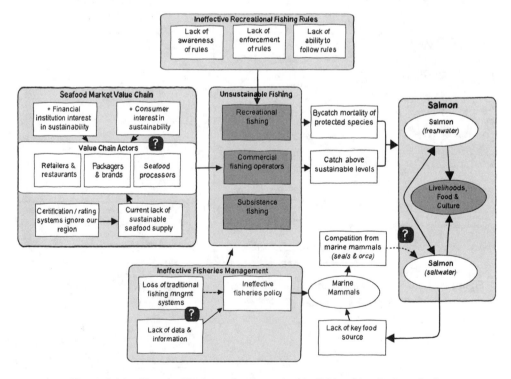

Figure 1.14a. Situation Pathway 2: unsustainable fishing (detailed version).

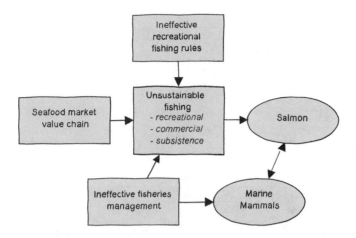

Figure 1.14b. Situation Pathway 2: unsustainable fishing (high-level version); group boxes from the detailed version become factors here.

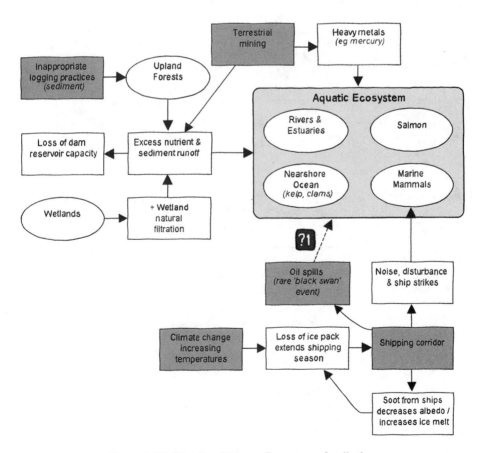

Figure 1.15. Situation Pathway 3: sources of pollution.

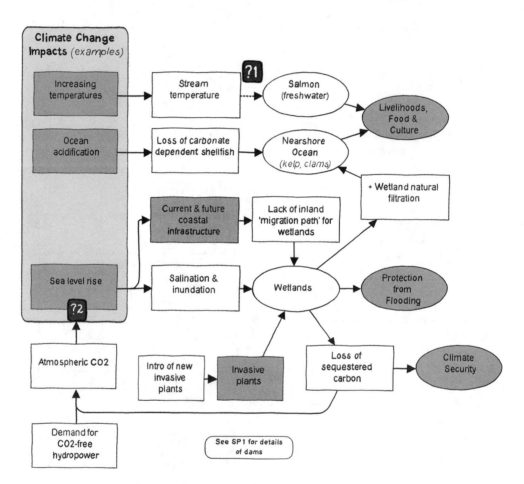

Figure 1.16. Situation Pathway 4: climate change.

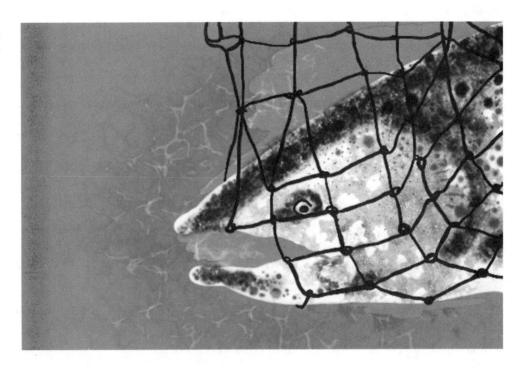

Sources and Further Information

(See FOSonline.org/pathways for links and updated guidance material.)

Clarifying Your Purpose

The business literature has many examples of authors advocating for what Peter Senge calls a "shared vision" and Jim Collins calls "big hairy audacious goals." That said, it's hard to provide much guidance on what is essentially a values decision. Four very different sources you might find useful:

Robert Pirsig (1974), *Zen and the Art of Motorcycle Maintenance.* A classic exploration of the relationship between classical Western science and romantic Eastern philosophy that argues that you don't define the right purpose, but rather you define yourself by what you choose as your purpose.

James Cone (2000), "Whose Earth Is It Anyway?" (*CrossCurrents* 50: 36–46). A powerful essay exploring the links between racism and environmentalism.

David Schlosberg (2007), *Defining Environmental Justice: Theories, Movements, and Nature.* A theoretical and political framework that draws together moral consideration for nonhuman nature with environmental justice concerns.

Foundations of Success (FOS) (2020), *Initiative Prioritization Tool.* A template for using both absolute rankings and time and treasure points to get feedback from a team to assess a number of candidate initiatives.

Selecting Target Factors and Bounding the Scope of Your Program

There is a long history of guidance for defining and selecting target factors:

The Nature Conservancy (2007), *Guidance for Step 2: Define Project Scope & Focal Conservation Targets in Conservation Action Planning Handbook.* The concept of target factors goes back to The Nature Conservancy's 5S/Conservation Action Planning method.

FOS (2021), *Planning for Conservation, Define Conservation and Human Wellbeing Targets: A How-To Guide.* A practical guide to selecting target factors.

There is also an extensive body of practice in the *Conservation Standards* community related to understanding and modeling the links between conservation and human well-being factors, in particular looking at ecosystem services:

Nick Salafsky (2011), "Integrating Development with Conservation: A Means to a Conservation End, or a Mean End to Conservation?" (*Biological Conservation* 144: 973–978). The source for the sailboat diagrams in this chapter.

Conservation Measures Partnership (CMP) (2015), *Integrating Human Wellbeing in the Open Standards.* A slide deck with guidance for thinking about the relationship between conservation and human well-being target factors.

CMP (2016), *Incorporating Social Aspects and Human Wellbeing in Biodiversity Conservation Projects.* A document version of this material.

Other potential conservation and human well-being targets are being developed by various international conventions:

Convention on Biological Diversity (2010), *Aichi Biodiversity Targets.* These are the global targets promoted by the convention. Note that the convention will soon release the post-2020 targets.

United Nations Development Programme (UNDP) (2015), *Sustainable Development Goals.* These are the broader sustainable development goals adopted by the United Nations.

Assembling the Right Team and Program Partners

Some good resources that discuss why building a broad coalition of partners matters:

Jim Collins (2005), ***Good to Great and the Social Sectors.*** A monograph applying business lessons to the social sector.

James Surowiecki (2004), ***The Wisdom of Crowds: Why the Many Are Smarter than the Few.*** A good exposition of why crowdsourcing is so powerful.

Michael Nielson (2013), ***Reinventing Discovery: The New Era of Networked Science.*** A discussion of how to harness the power of multiple perspectives when dealing with complex scientific problems.

Benjamin Chavis (1987), ***Toxic Waste and Race in the United States.*** One of the foundational publications of the environmental justice movement in the United States.

Dafina-Lazarus Stewart (2017), "Language of Appeasement." A blog post that we used to help define diversity, equity, and inclusion.

CIHR (2020), ***The Conservation Initiative on Human Rights.*** A website created by a number of conservation organizations focused on promoting the integration of human rights in conservation policy and practice.

Lacy Consulting Services (2020), ***Conservation Standards: Justice, Equity, Diversity, and Inclusion Approaches.*** A summary of guiding questions and considerations for incorporating DEIJ throughout the *Conservation Standards* cycle.

The following websites provide great resources and examples of working with indigenous communities to do effective conservation planning and management:

Locally Managed Marine Area Network. A learning network of communities around the Pacific and beyond seeking to help communities reinvigorate their traditional marine resource management systems.

Healthy Country Planning. An adaptation of the *Conservation Standards* for use with indigenous land management that has been successfully used with aboriginal groups in Australia, First Nations groups in Canada, and elsewhere.

Understanding the System in Which You Are Working

Systems thinking is a long-established and fast-growing discipline that easily could be the subject of an entire university course, or even a lifetime of study. Our goal in this book is thus merely to provide a brief introduction to some of the concepts we find most useful in conservation at scale. If you are interested in going deeper into systems thinking theory and practice, some of our favorite references include:

Peter Senge (1990), ***The Fifth Discipline: The Art and Practice of the Learning Organization.*** A classic of systems thinking as applied to business and management contexts.

Donella Meadows (2008), ***Thinking in Systems: A Primer.*** Another classic, full of ecological examples.

Ross Arnold and Jon Wade (2015), **"A Definition of Systems Thinking: A Systems Approach"** (*Procedia Computer Science* 44: 669–678). A short article that seeks to define systems thinking by using a systems thinking approach. Figure 3 from their article is also a useful summary of the skills needed to be a good systems thinker.

Developing a Shared Situation Model

Both the technical aspects of systems modeling and the practical aspects of facilitating inputs from a team could easily be the subject of an entire course. In addition to the sources listed above, you might want to consult:

Richard Margoluis et al. (2009), **"Using Conceptual Models as a Planning and Evaluation Tool in Conservation."** (*Evaluation and Program Planning* 32:138-147). A guide to situation models.

FOS (2021), ***Planning for Conservation, Assess the Conservation Situation: A How-To Guide.*** A practical guide to framing a project or program.

Miradi Software. A software system explicitly designed to support situation models.

Key Learning Questions

1. How can we collectively better incorporate justice, equity, diversity, and inclusion into the selection of conservation teams, the broader *Conservation Standards* cycle, and conservation? Specifically, how can the conservation community better:
   1a. Align and collaborate with the social justice movement?
   1b. Enable equitable and inclusive participation of all relevant stakeholders while maintaining a focus on conservation?
2. How can we develop better links between conservation and human well-being targets at larger scales?

3. How can we efficiently develop a library of generic situation assessments or models for different ecosystems around the world?

4. How can we develop standard ways of spatially mapping and sharing key information about targets, threats, and other factors?

5. How can we better incorporate systems thinking into the situation assessments and theory of change analyses used in the *Conservation Standards*? More specifically can we:

    5a. Develop common patterns of feedback loops?

    5b. Reconcile the concepts of stocks and flows as used by systems thinkers with the situation assessments in the *Conservation Standards*?

6. Can we develop a system for naming and tracking situation pathways within situation models?

2

Planning Your Strategies

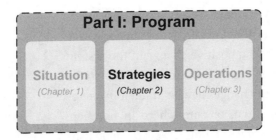

At this point, you have defined your program focus and completed your initial systems analysis and situation model. Your challenge now is to figure out your strategies to achieve your program's purpose. Key analyses in this process include:

- Understanding your overall impact trajectory
- Finding key intervention points in situation models
- Identifying candidate actions
- Creating strategy pathways to show theories of change
- Developing your approach for going to scale
- Determining your program's investment approach

Understanding Your Overall Impact Trajectory

The first analysis in planning your strategy pathways involves making sure you have a realistic understanding of what you are hoping to achieve. In Chapter 1, you first defined your overall program purpose and identified target factors that represent this purpose. At this point, having completed your situation assessment, it's a good time to take a brief step back to think about the overall impact you are hoping to have on your system of interest.

Liz Ruedy (2018) has developed a brilliant taxonomy of six potential impact trajectories for a program relative to the status quo. This analysis is worth sharing in its entirety, adapting her democracy promotion examples to our conservation situation:

▶ **Transformative impact.** This is *impact* the way it's most commonly thought of. With transformative impact, we expect a positive change in the system over time rather than the static rate of the status quo. The rate of change may be gradual or incremental, exponential, or somewhere in between. *Conservation examples*: building a sustainable fishery, restoring wetlands to protect a floodplain.

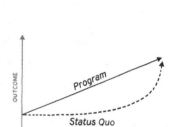

▶ **Proactive impact.** Some systems may already be moving in a positive direction, but an intervention can help accelerate that change. In this case, the ultimate change in outcomes is the same, but the accelerated pace and steeper rate of change are meaningful. We might facilitate these programs if the impact will allow us to pursue further opportunities that we are otherwise waiting to implement. *Conservation example:* developing a public awareness campaign to move opinion in support of an issue.

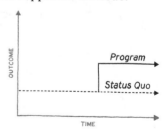

▶ **Opportunistic impact.** In the opportunistic model, the program lays the groundwork for change, but the outcomes will be entirely constrained by the context. There may be little perceivable difference in the system versus the status quo until there is a change in the context that creates an opportunity or removes an obstacle to change. If and when that happens, we expect to see a jump in the value of the outcome in the treatment scenarios compared with the status quo. The rate of change therefore looks like a stair step, with long periods of stasis interrupted by sudden increases. *Conservation example:* laying the groundwork for a policy so that you are prepared to implement it when conditions are favorable.

▶ **Stabilizing impact.** In some situations, we are working to prevent further decline in the system, to disrupt a vicious cycle, or to hold the system steady until the opportunity arises for positive change. In the stabilizing model, there is no measurable change to the outcome value throughout the program. The program thus appears to have 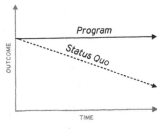 no impact unless you consider the negative trendline in the status quo. In this case, the benefit of the program lies in its ability to halt further decline. *Conservation examples:* stabilizing a declining whale population, keeping a fishery from crashing.

▶ **Preventive impact.** Perhaps the opposite of an opportunistic model, in this model the program lays the groundwork to strengthen the status quo and prevent certain events with the goal of having no change in the outcome. In this model, we recognize that there are vulnerabilities in the system that could lead a seemingly healthy system to 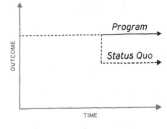 move suddenly in a negative direction. This model is similar to the stabilizing model, in which the impact is no change, but it differs in that the catalyzing event that spurs the decline may never actually happen. Proving impact in the preventive model is particularly challenging because the impact in this case is that a worse-case scenario did not occur. *Conservation example:* preventing rats from accessing islands with nesting seabirds.

▶ **Palliative impact.** One of the realities of working in a systems context is that, occasionally, systems fail with no recourse. In these cases the intervention may be focused on slowing the decline of the system in order to mitigate the effects of the eventual collapse or to buy time for alternatives to emerge or evolve. The palliative model may appear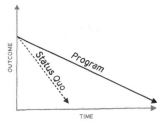

to show a negative relationship between the intervention and the outcomes—that the program is actually doing harm—unless we consider the historical trendline. *Conservation example:* mitigating the effects of global warming or sea-level rise.

Guidance for Understanding Your Overall Impact Trajectory

At this point, it's a good time to sit down with your program team and partners and revisit your program purpose and situation assessment:

- **Determine your overall impact trajectory.** Think about your proposed work in relation to the six impact models described above. Which of these models most closely reflect the situation that you are in and the ultimate impact you are hoping to achieve, either with your overall program or specific strategy pathways within your program? Are you making any critical assumptions that might mean you are on one trajectory versus another? Are there any critical implications to your program design that stem from the trajectory you are on?
- **Make tough choices.** Once you and your team have determined your overall trajectory, you need to decide whether it makes sense to stay on this trajectory, particularly if you are on the stabilizing impact or palliative impact trajectory. For example, should you invest in conserving a wetland if it is likely to be drowned by sea-level rise in the near future? Or does it make sense to invest in conserving a small remnant population of an endangered species if you are only postponing their inevitable extinction by a few years? Does your decision change if you can postpone their extinction for a decade or two? A key concept to keep in mind here is the economists' concept that sunk costs are sunk costs. Having already spent substantial time and treasure on a problem does not mean you should keep spending future resources on it.
- **Ensure that key stakeholders are on board.** Before you finalize your overall trajectory, make sure that your key leaders, stakeholders, and funders are on the same page with this decision. In particular, if you are on the more negative trajectories, it is vitally important that all your program partners understand this reality.

Finding Key Intervention Points in Situation Models

This analysis involves determining where in a given situation model or pathway you can best intervene and what actions you can take to do so. As you might imagine, this is a highly iterative process. Two key concepts affect the selection of intervention points:

▸ **Leverage.** This concept comes from mechanical engineering: A small amount of effort applied on one end of a lever results in greatly magnified effect on the other end. For example, pulling the handle of an oar in a boat results in greater force in the water to propel the boat forward. Pushing the pedal on a bicycle turns the front gears, which then cause the rear gears and ultimately the rear wheel to spin at a multiplied rate, propelling the bicycle forward. Similarly, in a leveraged financial deal, you invest a small amount of your own money to get a much bigger financial return.

In conservation, you can use your situation model to find leverage points for your conservation actions. These include points along each pathway as well as feedback loops and other combinations of factors that magnify the impact of your actions. Just like a physical pry bar, intervention points that are near the target end of your pathway tend to offer lower leverage, whereas points that are on the other side of your pathway tend to have higher leverage. For example, per Figure 2.1, if you are trying to remove an invasive plant species as part of a wetland restoration strategy, a low-leverage action would be to physically pull the weed out of the wetlands in individual sites. In this case, you can affect only the wetlands you directly work in. A mid-leverage action would be to educate land managers to pull the weeds out of the wetlands under their jurisdiction. In this case, you are using a small outreach effort to affect a much larger area of wetlands. And a high-leverage action would be to develop and release a genetically modified version of the weed that would limit its ability to propagate. Here, your work could affect wetlands across an entire region.

Figure 2.1a, b, c. The trade-off between leverage and risk.

▶ **Risk.** The flip side of leverage is risk. One type of risk is the potential for the action to not be implemented or to not work, leading to no results for your investment. It is often the case that actions with higher expected leverage also have a higher probability that the action will not result in the desired outcome. In the invasive weed example, if you are pulling a weed directly out of a wetland, you can be pretty sure that your action will remove the weed from the places you are working, at least in the short term. However, if you are trying to educate land managers or research genetic technology, there is an increasing chance that your work will break down somewhere along the pathway and lead to little or no change in the wetlands in the necessary time frame.

A second and even more worrisome risk is that powerful leveraged actions can backfire and create unintended negative consequences within the system. If your oar blade gets stuck in the water, the power of the lever working in reverse can flip you out of your seat or capsize the entire boat. If you are developing a genetically modified version of the weed, it could mutate further and wreak havoc in the ecosystem when it is released.

At first it might seem as if you should look primarily for high-leverage intervention points so as to maximize your potential to change the system. But it is important to balance leverage with the risks involved. As we will discuss in Chapter 3, you probably want to develop a more balanced portfolio of actions that addresses many different intervention points, especially as you consider your scaling strategies.

Guidance for Finding Key Intervention Points in Situation Models

The starting point for identifying key intervention points is your situation model. Specifically:

- **Prioritize critical situation pathways.** In traditional conservation project-level planning, project teams typically use their situation models to analyze the viability of their target factors and the degree to which each direct threat is affecting these target factors. This analysis then becomes the basis for prioritizing which situation pathways in the overall model need to be addressed with the project team's strategies. If your program has many target or direct threat factors, you may need to undertake a similar prioritization exercise. The *Conservation Standards* and other sources provide extensive guidance on how to make these assessments.

  In many conservation programs, however, you will probably be focusing on only one or at best a couple of target or direct threat factors. Your challenge thus becomes to prioritize the situation pathways or subpathways that have the most potential to affect your focus. In many cases, if you have a good situation model, it should be fairly obvious which situation pathways are the main levers that can affect your target factors both negatively and positively. If you have a few different pathways leading to your target factors, you may have to develop a set of qualitative criteria to guide a discussion assessing which pathways make the most sense to address. And in rare cases, it may be helpful to use a structured decision-making process to develop a more formal consequences table that lists the different intervention point options and attempts to more systematically assess the relative leverage and risk of each option (see Chapter 3 for a discussion of different prioritization techniques).

- **Look for leverage points in your situation pathways.** Once you have prioritized a situation pathway, you can begin to look for leverage points. For example, say you would like to ensure that enough salmon are able to swim up key rivers to reach their spawning grounds, facing the challenges illustrated in Figure 2.2.

  Looking at the situation pathway, discuss with your team where you think you might best be able to intervene to change the situation. These intervention points could be at any spot along the pathway. For example, you might choose to try to directly increase numbers of salmon through hatchery rearing of juvenile fish (Point A). Or you could explore different options to help adults get around dams that are blocking their return to their native spawning grounds (Point B). This is probably a fairly low-leverage intervention point, but it is also less risky, at least in the short term. Or you could work to remove dams that are impeding passage of the fish (Point C). This is a much higher-leverage intervention point, especially because removing the dams would also solve the impingement (Point D) and even the sediment regime issues. But of course, it is also much more risky in that the dam might never be removed if there is not sufficient political support.

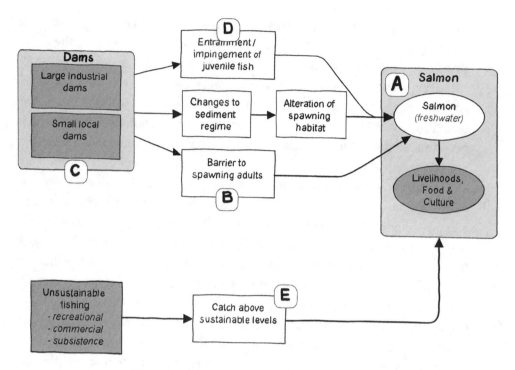

Figure 2.2. Leverage points in a situation pathway.

- **Consider alternative pathways.** Although you want to start by looking at intervention points along a situation pathway, you need to remember that you are still working in an overall system. So you need to consider other pathways or subpathways that might either contribute to the problem you are trying to solve or provide alternative intervention points. For example, in the model in Figure 2.2, although you may be focused primarily on the impacts of the dams in your system, you also need to remember that the overall salmon population is also affected by the threat of <unsustainable fishing>. So you may think about intervening on the <catch above sustainable levels> factor (Point E).

Identifying Candidate Actions

For each potential intervention point, you next want to think about candidate actions (i.e., interventions) that you can use to intervene in the system. In most cases (e.g., helping fish get around dams) there might be many different options for taking action at a given intervention (removing dams, building fish ladders, trucking fish around the dam).

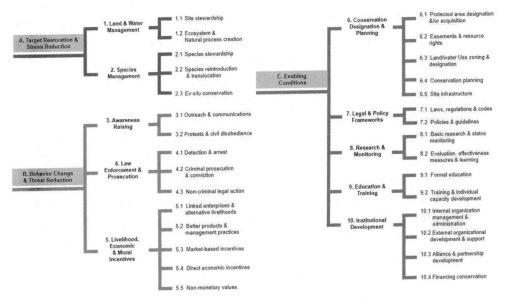

Figure 2.3. CMP Classification of Conservation Actions, v. 2.0. Source: Adapted from CMP (2014).

A wide array of potential conservation actions have been identified by the Conservation Measures Partnership (CMP) in conjunction with the International Union for Conservation of Nature (IUCN) (Figure 2.3). At the highest level, there are three categories of actions:

▸ **Direct management or restoration actions.** These actions directly affect an ecological target by mitigating a current stress or restoring damage caused by a historical stress. Many actions taken by conservation site managers fall into this category. Examples include putting up nest boxes for breeding birds, applying herbicides to control an invasive weed, using controlled burns to restore fire to a landscape, or removing dams to restore river system flows and connectivity. These direct actions tend to be lower leverage but also less risky.

▸ **Behavior change actions.** These actions change human behavior so as to either reduce threats (get people, companies, or other organizations to stop doing things that negatively affect your targets) or enhance conservation opportunities (get people, companies, or other organizations to do things that positively affect your targets). In some cases, these actions can also lead to enabling condition actions (e.g., awareness campaigns generating political support for a new policy), as shown by the bottom back-looping arrow in Figure 2.4. Behavior change actions typically focus on changing the awareness and attitudes, incentives, and abilities of key stakeholders. Examples include awareness campaigns to reduce transport of invasive weeds, enforcement patrols to deter illegal fishing, or market-based solutions to promote sustainable fishing practices.

▶ **Enabling condition actions.** These actions create the necessary conditions needed for other actions to be successful. These actions typically involve developing a regulatory environment, building capacity among key stakeholders, or developing the knowledge needed to do more effective conservation. Examples include developing policies to support fishing quotas, building the capacity of the next generation of conservationists, conducting research on key knowledge gaps, and providing funding. As shown in Figure 2.4, these actions tend to be higher leverage but also more risky; they lead to ultimate outcomes only if they enable other conservation actions.

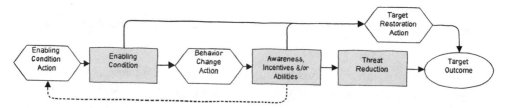

Figure 2.4. Three categories of conservation actions. Source: Adapted from CMP (2014).

Most conservation situations cannot be fixed with one "silver bullet" action. And few if any actions will work in all situations. Instead, effective conservation requires developing strategy pathways with the right combinations of actions to address the problems in any specific situation, as outlined in the next section.

Guidance for Identifying Candidate Actions

At this point, your challenge is to identify candidate actions that are worth exploring further:

• **Brainstorm candidate actions for each intervention point.** In a few conservation situations, it may be clear what action needs to be undertaken at a given intervention point, especially if you have prior experience doing similar work in that system. But in most situations, there are a range of options to consider. Furthermore, it's important not to be a prisoner of conventional thinking. Instead, you generally want your team to brainstorm as many different ideas as possible.

To this end, it may be helpful to review previous work within your project or program to see whether there are any bright spots that are worth replicating. Or to search for examples of similar programs to see what actions other teams have taken under similar circumstances. Or to review conservation evidence websites to see what they suggest. Or you might scan the classification of conservation actions to see whether it sparks any ideas.

Returning to our dam situation pathway example in Figure 2.2, you might be interested in actions to address the intervention point related to the stress put on the fish population from entrainment or impingement of juvenile fish as they pass over the dam (Point E in Figure 2.5). The dam authority is currently considering installing improved spillways to mitigate this stress. A quick search of the Collaboration for Environmental Evidence website reveals a 2020 systematic review of "What are the relative risks of mortality and injury for fish during downstream passage at hydroelectric dams in temperate regions?" The review states, "Bypasses resulted in decreased injury risk relative to controls, whereas turbines and spillways were associated with the highest injury risks relative to controls." So you then add bypasses as a candidate action. Of course, you might also want

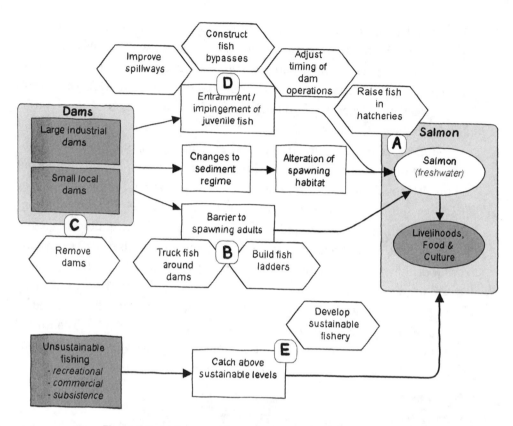

Figure 2.5. Adding candidate actions to the situation pathway.

to add dam removal as an action because doing so would also take care of the entrainment and impingement problem.

- **Quick-filter your candidate actions.** As you develop a few different candidate actions, you might want to do a quick prioritization. At this point, you are not making a final decision but rather trying to sort out the less useful or infeasible ideas from the ones that are worthy of more detailed consideration. Three common criteria used at this point to evaluate candidate actions are:

  - *Effectiveness.* To what degree will implementing this action lead to desired outcomes?
  - *Feasibility.* Is this action legally, ethically, technically, economically, and practically feasible to implement?
  - *Timeliness.* Is this the right time window to implement this action? Is there sufficient social and political support?

For example, considering Figure 2.5, you might decide that although removal of large dams could be a very effective strategy from a conservation impact point of view, it is not economically or politically feasible to undertake at this time.

Creating Strategy Pathways to Show Theories of Change

Once you have completed your initial prioritization, it's time to start developing *strategy pathways* (often referred to as *strategies*) that illustrate the theory of change for the actions you are considering. A theory of change approach refers to both the process and the product of laying out your assumptions about how taking a given action will lead to your desired outcomes through a set of causal pathways. A theory of change is often displayed in a flow diagram, although it can also be described in text, a table, sequential pictures, cash flow analysis, or even mathematical notation.

Strategy pathways are commonly used to represent a theory of change. At its simplest, a strategy pathway is an action linked to any result or outcome. Symbolically, it represents that implementing the action leads to (or, in more scientific terms, "is assumed to cause") the result or outcome. In text form, it might look like:

Implementing Action A leads to Result X.

In diagram form, it might look like this:

- ▶ **Single-action strategy pathways.** In most single-action strategy pathways, there will be a chain of results stemming from an action leading all the way to the desired outcome for your target factor. Each arrow in the chain represents an assumed causal linkage. In addition, the entire chain is itself an overarching assumption. The action may be broken down into component activities, which typically take place at different points along the pathway as shown:

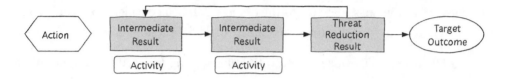

▶ **Compound strategy pathways.** Whereas a single-action strategy pathway has only one elemental action, a compound strategy pathway is composed of multiple actions that work together as part of an overall strategy, as shown:

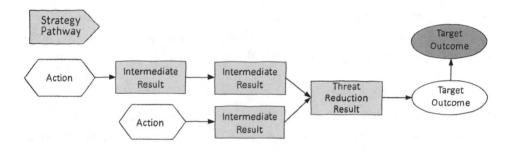

Note that although both single-action and compound strategy pathways can have multiple outcomes, typically these outcomes would need to have some relationship to one another (e.g., a species and its associated habitat; an ecological target and the human well-being outcomes that stem from it).

Guidance for Creating Strategy Pathways to Show Theories of Change

There are typically four types of source material that you can use to jump-start development of a strategy pathway for a given action:

- **Transpose your situation pathways.** As described in Chapter 1, a situation pathway typically contains a series of factors that ultimately influence your target factor. As shown in Figures 2.6a and b, you can select the relevant situation pathway and transpose each of these factors from showing the current state of the world (the problem) into your assumptions about how, if you successfully implement your action, these factors will change (your results).

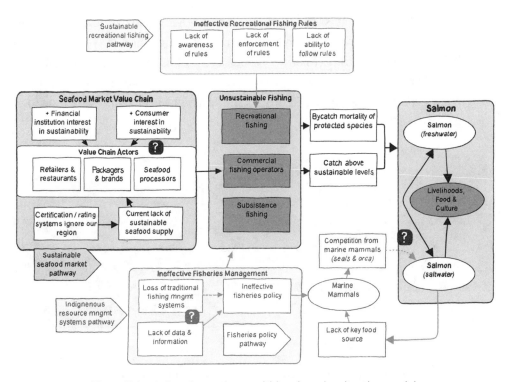

Figure 2.6a. A situation pathway within a broader situation model.

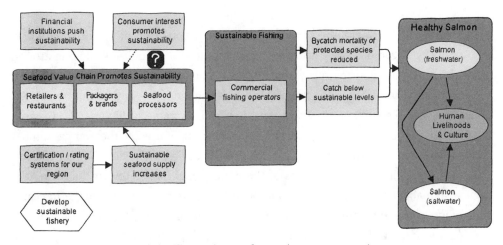

Figure 2.6b. The analogous factors in a strategy pathway.

- **Search for similar specific or generic strategy pathways.** You are probably not the first team in the world to develop a pathway involving the action you are exploring. To this end, you can search libraries of existing projects such as

Miradi's "Shared Projects" to see whether some other group has developed a specific pathway that you can copy and use as a starting point. Or you can search libraries of generic strategy pathways such as the Conservation Actions and Measures Library (CAML) to find a generic pathway that has been created and vetted by experts. For example, Figure 2.7 shows a high-level generic pathway for a market-based action.

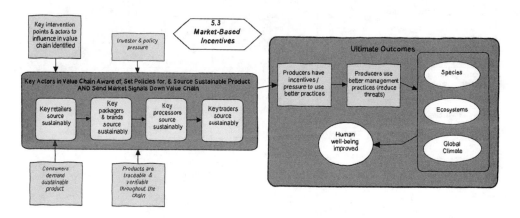

Figure 2.7. Market-based incentives generic strategy pathway.
Source: CAML Generic Single-Action Strategy: 5.3 Market-Based Incentives.

- **Find a logical backbone for your pathway.** If you are dealing with a complex pathway, it can be highly effective to find some sort of logical backbone around which to build your pathway and tell your story. For example, in market-based strategies, pathways are often built around the value chain that links end consumers to resource producers, as in the CAML example in Figure 2.7. Likewise, in most behavioral change strategies, as shown in Figure 2.8, there are a number of potential subpathways that can lead to the desired behavior change. You can (a) try to change the awareness of the recreational fishers toward following the sustainable harvest rules *(show me)*. Or you can (b) create a social marketing campaign trying to create a norm around sustainable fishing *(sway me)*. You can also (c) try to build the ability of key people to implement the desired change, such as by training the fishing guides *(help me)*. Or you can (d) provide positive incentives such as increased funding for certified fishing guides *(tempt me)*. Or you can (e) take advantage of behavioral psychology by building fish identification aids directly into boats *(nudge me)*. Finally, you can (f) use regulatory and enforcement action such as fines to motivate the desired behavior change *(make me)*.

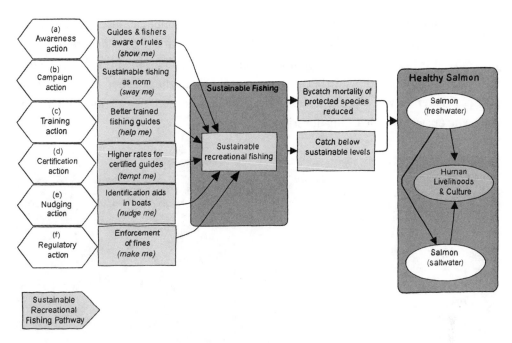

Figure 2.8. Example of behavior change pattern in a strategy pathway.

- **Use your systems thinking to factor in complexity.** Although for simplicity we may depict a given strategy pathway as a linear model, it's important to remember that each pathway is only a subsystem that takes place in the context of a larger and more complex system. As a result, you need to also consider potential dynamic relationships between factors, relevant feedback loops, and interactive effects between this pathway and other strategy pathways being implemented by your program and by other actors in the system. These interactions will occur in both predictable and sometimes not so predictable ways. So after you develop your initial pathway, go back to your situation assessment and see whether there are any additional interactive effects you need to consider.

    Whichever approach you use to start your pathway development, although you certainly want to make use of existing work to jump-start your thinking, treat this material only as an initial launching point. Your next task is to work with your team to discuss and revise the logic.

- **Use your pathways to track uncertainty and learning questions.** It is vital to remember that your strategy pathway represents your theory of change. It is not a representation of what will happen when you implement your actions but rather a model of what you assume will happen when you implement your actions. And like all models, it is likely to be wrong in some ways but can also be made more useful over time. To this end, as you develop your pathway, make sure to record any uncertainties in the form of learning questions about the presence of factors or the causal relationship between them as shown by the question marks in Figure 2.6. Later on, we will collect and analyze the data needed to test your assumptions and answer your learning questions.

Developing Your Approach for Going to Scale

At this point, you may have thought about finding the right strategy in a conceptual fashion. But as we discussed in the Introduction, you also need to think about your strategy in terms of the spatial, temporal, and social or institutional scales necessary to achieve your ultimate desired outcomes. In complex systems, increasing scale is often a nonlinear process. In addition, although there may be economies of scale, working at scale may also require additional inputs and strategies. As one example, compare removing a small privately owned barrier on a stream to removing a large publicly owned dam on a major river. Conceptually, the two actions are very similar. But the necessary time and resources and the potential impact of removing the large dam are exponentially larger.

These types of scale effects can be captured in your strategy pathways. For example, the pathway for a wetland restoration strategy (Figure 2.9a) is very simple when you think about restoring a specific wetland within the confines of a nature reserve over the course of one growing season.

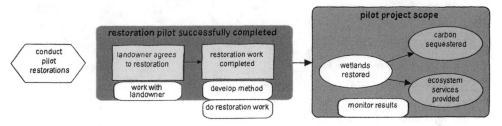

Figure 2.9a. Project-level single-site wetland restoration pathway.

But this seemingly simple action becomes much more challenging when you are trying to consider restoring wetlands over a large area that includes many sites across multiple watersheds over the long term. As shown in Figure 2.9b, this strategy requires a compound pathway that, in addition to site-level project work, requires program-level actions including conducting the pilot restorations, promoting policies to support restoration, and then managing the restorations at scale.

As you can see in this example, in thinking about how to go to scale it is often helpful to distinguish between smaller-scale project strategy pathways and larger-scale program strategy pathways, as first defined in the Introduction of this book. The right-hand side of Figure 2.9b shows the project-level strategy pathways used to implement the specific weed eradication and wetland restoration work at each site. The left-hand side shows the program-level pathways that occur at a regional or national scale to support the project-level work. The challenge lies in developing the appropriate set of pathways at the appropriate scales and at the appropriate times.

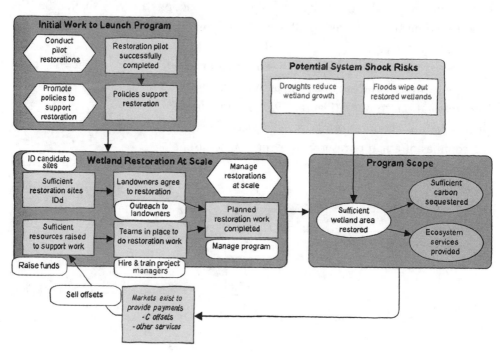

Figure 2.9b. Project-level single-site wetland restoration pathway.

Furthermore, most teams thinking about scaling up a given strategy will also instinctively propose trying new strategies within pilot projects that they then plan to take to scale over time. These pilots can be deliberately designed by the program team, or they can be "bright spots" developed by other actors in the system that the program team has discovered and would like to replicate. Either way, it can be helpful to think about five distinct approaches to taking these pilots to scale, each with its own set of activities to ensure success at the larger scale. These approaches, described below, can be used either on their own or in combination, depending on the situation.

This example starts with piloting a promising strategy in a limited number of project cases, such as restoring wetlands in two small test areas (as shown in the diagram) or working with selected restaurants to promote sustainable seafood consumption in one part of a city. Key implementation activities involved in a pilot include deciding on the strategy, planning the pilot, getting key stakeholders on board, recruit-

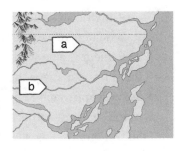

ing the pilot team, implementing the pilot, and monitoring, documenting, and sharing results.

▶ **Scaling approach 1: expanding the scope of pilot projects.** This approach involves increasing the spatial or conceptual scope of each individual project implementing the strategy. For example, you might expand the wetland restoration from the pilot sites to the entire watershed or the sustainable seafood promotional work to all restaurants in the city. This approach is most

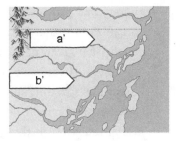

often limited by the scope of the work that a given project team can manage.

Additional activities needed to take the pilot to scale in this approach include convincing key stakeholders to expand the work, finding the resources and additional project team members to work at scale, and adapting methods as needed to operate at larger scales.

▶ **Scaling approach 2: replicating projects in programs.** This approach involves developing and managing a suite of related projects that follow the same basic template of the original project. For example, you might bring on new project teams to new sites in the same or adjacent watersheds or expand the sustainable seafood promotional work to other cities. This approach allows

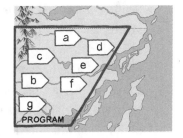

you to start new projects that build on the staff and lessons learned from your original projects. Replicated projects can be either fully owned by the implementing organization or operated under a franchise model. Either way, it's important to include resources for program-level management and maintaining quality across projects.

Activities needed to go to scale in this approach include convincing key stakeholders to expand the work, finding the resources and new project teams to implement the projects, and developing the program staff and processes needed to train and manage the new projects and ensure quality control.

▶ **Scaling approach 3: promoting dissemination of innovation.** Rather than develop new projects and programs yourself, this approach involves capturing and communicating what you have learned and then getting other organizations to adopt your strategy in their work. For example, you might publish your methods in an online library and provide consulting services to other organizations that want to replicate your watershed management work. Or you might share your outreach materials so other organizations can use them to set up similar sustainable seafood promotion work. As shown with projects h and i in the diagram, this approach can extend beyond the borders of your jurisdiction. As discussed in more detail in Chapter 6, the key is to understand how conditions vary in each site so that you can adjust the strategy as needed to succeed in these conditions. This approach benefits from an understanding the extensive literature on diffusion of innovation.

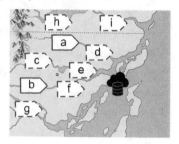

Activities needed to go to scale in this approach include investing more in documenting the results of the pilot work, determining the conditions under which your strategy will be effective, and figuring out the right messages and messengers to ensure dissemination of your innovations.

▶ **Scaling approach 4: developing higher-level strategies.** This approach involves thinking about how you might work within the system to operate at a higher and more leveraged scale. For example, instead of doing wetland restoration yourself, you might work to implement a national policy that will incentivize key landowners to restore wetlands that they manage or develop a genetic technology that will enable better control of weeds in wetlands across the region. Or you could develop a market-based strategy and partner with major seafood companies to implement sustainable seafood production.

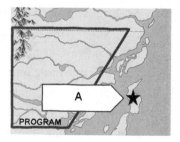

Activities needed to go to scale in this approach include using what you have learned in the pilot to credibly develop higher-level strategies and raise the necessary resources and build the program team needed to implement these strategies.

▶ **Scaling approach 5: transforming system intent.** Finally, building on Meadows's (2008) and Abson et al.'s (2017) systems approach, the most powerful leverage points involve changing the underlying values, goals, and mental models of the actors in the overall system. For example, you might build a stewardship ethic among all landowners and managers to conserve and  restore wetlands. Or you might work to make it socially unacceptable to consume nonsustainably harvested seafood.

It is usually difficult for any one program to develop specific and intentional strategies to make deep transformation happen. However, activities needed to go to scale in this approach might include using what you have learned in the pilot to develop and communicate the stories needed to reach and influence the hearts and minds of key influencers and stakeholders.

Guidance for Developing Your Approach for Going to Scale

Inherent in all five of the approaches above is that going to scale doesn't just happen once. Instead, it is an iterative, rolling process. Going to scale involves not just saying you will pilot a strategy but deliberately thinking about how to take early efforts and grow them over time:

- **Be explicit in your scaling approaches.** A key part of going to scale is thinking early on about which scaling approach, or combination of approaches, best fits your situation and will enable your program to ultimately reach the full scope you outlined in Chapter 1. This enables you to set up your pilots appropriately. For example, if you are planning either expand your projects in size or into a program, you might focus during the pilot on training staff who can go on to help implement or manage the future expansions. If you are planning to expand via dissemination of learning, by contrast, you may want to invest more in monitoring and documenting your results. It also allows you to make appropriate system-level interventions.
- **Build your scaling approach into your strategy pathways.** Because your scaling approach is a key part of your project or program team's work, you should explicitly build it into your strategy pathway diagrams. In complex systems,

increasing scale is often a nonlinear process. In addition, although there may be economies of scale, working at scale may also require substantial additional inputs and strategies.

In some cases, the generic theory of change inherent in a strategy pathway might be roughly the same regardless of scale. You might then be able to represent your scaling strategy in an iterative, rolling process that is similar to what business writer Jim Collins (2019) calls "creating and turning the flywheel." This process involves deliberately establishing a scaling cycle that starts to create its own momentum over time, as shown in the flywheel pathway pattern in Figure 2.10a.

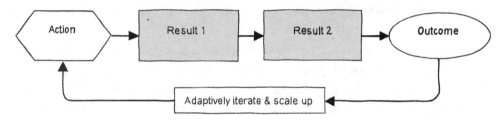

Figure 2.10a. A flywheel scaling pattern.

In most cases, however, when you get into the details of strategy implementation (e.g., developing specific objectives for key results or assigning the resources and time needed to implement actions), your pilot and implementation pathways may be very different. So rather than create one all-purpose pathway, you are probably better off creating specific versions of the pathway for different scales (Figure 2.10b).

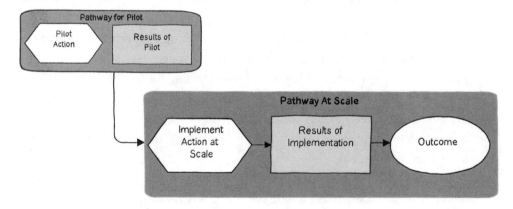

Figure 2.10b. A pilot to program scaling pattern.

- **Use systems thinking in designing your pathways.** As you develop your strategy pathways, it's important to think about factors in the system that can either promote or hinder your ability to get to scale. Business writer Peter Senge (1990) describes the utility of creating positive reinforcing feedback loops while also making sure to reduce the limits to growth imposed by balancing loops within the system. As one simple example in the wetland restoration work described in Figure 2.9b, the development of markets that provide payments for carbon offsets or other ecosystem services can help raise the resources needed to support this wetland restoration work. But conversely, your ability to get to scale may be slowed down as the obvious and cheap restoration sites get completed and you have to shift to more expensive sites; in effect, the system is pushing back and imposing limits to scaling that you need to overcome.

- **Make your models more coarsely grained as you increase scale.** As you change scale, you generally need to make your pathways more coarsely grained or you will drown in the detail. As an analogy, think about looking at an online map of the neighborhood where you live. This map will typically show every road and creek as a thin line. Now imagine zooming out to your entire city or region. If you keep the same local road and creek layers visible, then the sum of all the thin lines in these data layers will completely cover the screen in digital ink. So you need to hide that detailed layer and show only the bigger roads and streams. And if you were to zoom out to the entire country, then you need to again hide the regional detail and only show the largest highways and rivers. The detail is not removed from the system, but it is hidden as you move to a coarser scale, only to reemerge when you zoom back in to a finer scale.

  The same principle applies when you are shifting scales in your problem and strategy pathways. For example, as shown in Table 1.1 in the previous chapter, ecological targets become coarser when you move from a local project scale to a regional or national program scale. Likewise, the threat factors identified in a situation model also need to become coarser as we shift scales (Table 2.1). For example, at the project site level, the local program team might identify a particular privately owned dam that is blocking fish passage on a key stream. By contrast, the regional program team might instead list more generic <tributary dams> as a threat and then subdivide them into abandoned dams versus active dams of different types, following the general principle that you should split threat types when they are caused by different actors and require different types of actions. Finally, at the national level, the program team might track different kinds of dams and barriers that pose threats to free-flowing rivers. Likewise, we can see a similar

---

Table 2.1. Threats and actions become coarser at higher scales
(This is a continuation of Table 1.1.)

Examples of Factors	Programmatic Scale		
	Local Project (e.g., small watershed)	Regional Program (e.g., large bay)	National Program

Direct threats	Salmon Creek Dam
	Overfishing of salmon
	  Our community
	  Neighboring communities
		Tributary dams
		  Abandoned
		  Active flood control
		  Active hydropower
		Overfishing of salmon
		  Indigenous communities
		  Recreational
		  Commercial
			Dams and barriers
			  Private
			  Industrial
			  Public
			Overfishing
			  Stock A
			  Stock B
			  Stock N

Strategy pathway Actions	Remove Salmon Creek Dam
	  Get family agreement
	  Raise financing
	  Get county permit
	  Hire contractor
	  Remove dam
		Remove tributary dams
		  Prioritize candidate dams
		  Engage landowners
		  Set financing mechanism
		  Select projects to fund
		  Follow-up monitoring
			Promote "Wild Rivers"
			  Use pilots to make case
			  Pass legislation
			  Raise awareness
			  Create info hub
			  Track "Wild River" status

coarsening of factors when we consider strategies at different scales. For example, at the project level, one strategy pathway might focus on removing a specific dam on a specific stream tributary. At a regional level, however, the strategy pathway might focus more generally on removing tributary dams. And at the national level, the strategy pathway might involve setting up "Wild Rivers" across the country, providing a generic template for more specific work done at local levels.

- **Nest subfactors to accommodate detail.** If you are using coarser factors as you increase scales, you can still preserve more detailed information as needed, but you can nest it in the higher-level factors. For instance, in Table 1.1 the focal ecological targets from the local project have moved one level down as nested targets in the regional project (e.g., the <*rivers target*> has <*tributary streams*> and <*river mainstems*> as its subtargets). Likewise, the detail of the local project-level action <*remove Salmon Creek Dam*> becomes only one of many similar tasks in the regional program strategy pathway to <*remove tributary dams*> in Table 2.1. By nesting this detail, you make it available to people who need to see it, but you avoid having it clutter up your pathway models, making them seem overly complex. To this end, you can also lean on standard hierarchical classifications to manage detail. For example, for actions, you might use CMP Level 3 actions at a fine scale and Level 2 actions at a coarser scale.

• **Do the math to check your scaling assumptions.** Although it can be easy to say that you plan to take a pilot strategy pathway to scale, it often can be much more challenging to do it in reality. It's thus vital to take a little bit of time upfront to check your assumptions. For example, let's assume that your organization's leaders have set an ambitious challenge goal of sequestering a half-million tons of carbon over the next decade by scaling your wetland restoration strategy. Figure 2.11 shows a quick-and-dirty analysis of the pathway for scaling the strategy shown in Figure 2.9b.

The top table in Figure 2.11a shows some basic parameters that we are using to develop our scaling model. Note that at this point during our initial analysis, it's perfectly fine to have high-level estimates or approximations for each of these values. For example, we have used a published figure that wetlands have between 200 and 400 tons of stored carbon/ha (row 6) to then estimate a rough timescale over which a wetland could sequester that much carbon (rows 7–15). We have similarly made some back-of-the-envelope calculations about how much it costs to do the restoration work in terms of carbon footprint from the restoration work itself (rows 16–18), the financial costs (rows 19–22), and the potential financial benefits (rows 24–26). Finally, we include an economic discount rate that enables us to express all financial costs and benefits in year 0 present value (PV) dollars (row 23).

Using these project parameters, we can calculate the costs and benefits of implementing this strategy pathway at a typical project site as shown in Figure 2.11b. These costs and benefits are tracked both in tons of carbon and present value dollars. This quick analysis shows us that our 10-hectare project wetland restoration strategy can expect to sequester 2,000 tons of carbon over the next twenty-five years at a cost of $5 per ton. Furthermore, if we can sell the carbon credits and maybe even other ecosystem services, we can turn a healthy profit.

Having made these calculations for an "average" project, we could now try to scale up to the program level. As a starting point, if our program goal is to sequester a half-million tons of carbon, then:

500,000 tons of C * 1 project/2,000 tons of C = 250 projects required

	Key Scaling Parameters	Calculation	
	'AVERAGE' PROJECT PARAMETERS		
	Type	Active wetland restoration	
	Habitat	Degraded Ag Land --> Estuarine or Palustrine/Riverine Wetlands	
	Average Project Size (ha)	10	Estimate
	Total Storage (tons C/ha)	200	200-400 tons C for avg wetland
	Restoration Sequestration (tons C/yr-ha)	Annual	Estimated growth curve to reach total storage
	0	0	
	1-2	5	
	3-5	10	
	6-10	15	
	11-15	10	
	>15	3	
	Cumulative Total in 25 Years	195	Sum of above * # yrs per interval
	Total tons CO2e in 25 Years	715	44 units CO2/12 units C
	Restoration Losses (tons C/yr-ha)		
	Wetland restoration	1	100 passes * 1 gallon diesel / acre plowed...
	Wetland maintenance	0.1	10 passes *
	Financial Costs (Year 0 PV $)		
	Land acquisition ($/ha)	0	land is not purchased (!!)
	Restoration costs ($/ha-yr)	750	$200-3300/acre, 2.47 acres/ha
	Maintenance ($/ha-yr)	75	Estimated as 0.1 * restoration costs
	Discount rate (%/yr)	0.05	Conservative estimate
	Financial Benefits		
	Carbon offset payments ($/ton C)	18	$5/ton CO2e * 44 units CO2e/12 units C
	Other ecosystem services ($/ha)	10	Estimate of payments for flood control, hunting

		Project Year						
Average 10 ha Project		0	1-2	3-5	6-10	11-15	16-25	Total
CARBON BUDGET (tons C)								
Carbon Expended		10	1	1	1	1	1	15
Wetland restoration		10						10
Wetland maintenance			1	1	1	1	1	5
Carbon Captured		0	100	300	750	500	300	1,950
Wetland sequestration		0	100	300	750	500	300	1,950
Net Carbon		-10	99	299	749	499	299	1,935
FINANCIAL BUDGET (Year PV $)								
Total Expenses		7,500	1,389	1,833	2,425	1,876	2,689	17,711
Land acquisition		0						0
Wetland restoration		7,500						7,500
Wetland maintenance			1,389	1,833	2,425	1,876	2,689	10,211
Total Income		0	5,195	20,701	68,612	35,370	30,370	160,247
Carbon offset payments		0	3,361	13,395	44,396	22,887	19,651	103,689
Other ecosystem services		0	1,833	7,306	24,216	12,484	10,719	56,558
Net Cash Flow		-7,500	3,806	18,868	66,187	33,494	27,681	142,536
$ per ton C (w/out income)								5.3

Figure 2.11a, b. Parameters and cash flow analysis for "average" wetland restoration project.

Obviously it might take a bit of work to set up 250 projects, but if we can earn more than $100,000 on each project as shown above, then this strategy should be a slam-dunk. Of course, this assumes that we can find 250 suitable 10-hectare wetland restoration locations within our program area. And unfortunately, this is where scaling effects come into play. As shown in Figure 2.11c, there are several additional parameters that we need to add to our cash flow model when we want to work at a program scale.

	A	B	C	D
1	Key Scaling Parameters			Calculation
27	OVERALL PROGRAM PARAMETERS			
28	Projects In Program			
29	Max # of projects initiated / year		64	Cap on the total number of project initiated
30	Ramp-up rate from 2 pilot projects		2	2, 4, 8, 16, 32, 64
31	Minor project failure rate (every x yrs)		3	Frequency of minor failure due to drought
32	% of carbon lost (annual only)		30%	Loss of annual sequestration due to drought
33	Major project failure rate (every x yrs)		10	Frequency of major failure due to flooding
34	% of projects lost		20%	Loss of project & stored carbon due to flooding
35	Costs (Year 0 PV $)			
36	Startup mngmt ($ / program-yr)		150,000	2 mid-level staff/program during initiation phase
37	Ongoing mngmt ($/manager-yr)		75,000	1 mid-level staff/program during ongoing mngmt phase
38	Number of projects/manager		32	Each manager tracks 32 projects
39				

Figure 2.11c. Parameters and cash flow analysis for overall wetland restoration program.

One key problem is that a program team can only initiate so many projects a year (row 29). Furthermore, the program needs to ramp up its ability to initiate projects from the two initial pilots (row 30). The program also has to pay for program management costs (rows 35–38). Finally, the program cannot assume that all of the projects will work out as expected. To this end, we have built in parameters that assume the program will suffer periodic minor failure events (e.g., droughts that cause a wetland to have reduced carbon sequestration in a given year) and major failure events (e.g., flooding that completely destroys a restored wetland, thus both releasing saved carbon back into the system and eliminating any future gains from that site).

To see the full version of the cash flow model, see the link in the Sources and Further Information section. But Figure 2.11d shows the summary results that emerge with the parameters set as shown above. As you can see, even fairly low project failure rates (in this case 20 percent major failure every ten years) dramatically reduce the number of active projects and bring down the total program carbon sequestration totals. Furthermore, this program requires a substantial

	H	I	J	K	L	M
7	**Summary of Program**					
8	Projects initiated					446
9	Active projects at 25 years					285
10	Total tons C sequestered					415,222
11	Total costs no offsets (Year 0 PV $)					13,559,949
12	Total costs with offsets (Year 0 PV $)					4,363,406
13	Cost/ton C no offsets (Year 0 PV $)					33
14	Cost/ton C with offsets (Year 0 PV $)					11

Figure 2.11d. Parameters and cash flow analysis for overall wetland restoration program.

cash subsidy (more than $5 million in PV$), even if the project generates income from carbon offset payments and other ecosystem services. And these calculations assume that no payments are needed to acquire or access the land, that there is no opportunity cost of converting the land to wetlands from their current usages, and that the program can manage this work on very low overhead costs. You can change these parameters in the cash flow model and see how the bottom line results change as a result of this sensitivity analysis.

Another key point that emerges from this analysis is the time frame needed to accomplish the desired outcomes. As shown in Figure 2.11e, under the current set of assumptions, after ten years, the program is just starting to generate positive returns in terms of carbon sequestration. And despite the typical ten-year planning horizon for most conservation programs, it's not until after well into the second decade of the program that even half the original goal of 500,000 tons

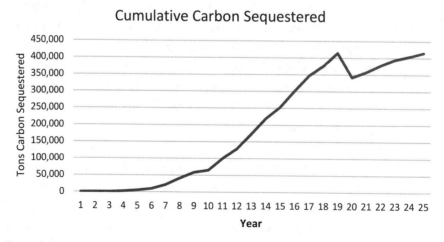

Figure 2.11e. Parameters and cash flow analysis for overall wetland restoration program.

of carbon sequestered is met. So even if this program goes well, it is not going to meet the ambitious timeline your boss already announced to the world.

Our main take-home point in this analysis is the value of doing this level of upfront work to consider your scaling assumptions. The point of this exercise is not to create the perfect model of your scaling plan; there are undoubtedly many holes in this model, including inaccuracies in the estimates used for key parameters, the omission of key factors, and the relatively nondynamic interactions between factors in this model. Nonetheless, it is still useful to stress-test your core assumptions and to see within orders of magnitude whether your scaling plan makes sense.

Program teams often say that they don't have the time to invest in this kind of analysis. But by developing a quick-and-dirty analysis of your scaling pathways, you may be able to find problems that you can fix, such as doubling the number of sites you are working at, finding some alternative solutions, or at least setting a more realistic goal. Alternatively, through this analysis you might decide not to undertake a program strategy that is doomed to fail. Either way, spending just a few hours upfront could save your program months, years, or even decades of wasted time and treasure. So how can you possibly justify not taking the time to do this few hours of thinking and work?

As we will see in later chapters, developing this explicit model also will greatly improve your ability to get input from experts and key stakeholders and to adaptively manage your program over time.

Determining Your Program's Investment Approach

If you are working on a program-scale strategy, your most common action is to invest in someone else's work. This is obviously something of a truism for a program strategy being implemented by a grant-making foundation or government agency, but it also holds for program strategies being implemented within conservation organizations: As a program manager, you are generally providing funding and other support to project teams that in turn can help you realize your programmatic strategies. Likewise, some backbone programs or organizations can provide financial and nonfinancial support to help coordinate and advance the collective impact of their broader partnerships.

The basic high-level strategy pathway for a funding program is shown in Figure 2.12. At its core, a good funding program needs to start with a good program design, based on the type of investment approach being used (see below). The program then needs to signal its intentions to good projects being proposed or undertaken by candidate grantees who then apply for funding and are prioritized and selected for funding support. The key result is that program funds are used to implement both more and

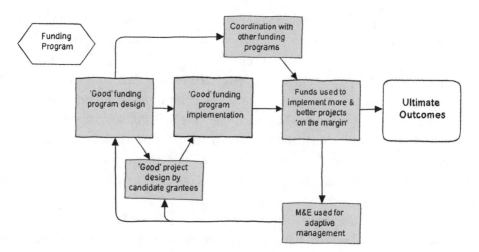

Figure 2.12. Generic strategy pathway for a funding program.
Source: Adapted from CAML, 10.4 Financing Conservation.

better projects on the margin, meaning that ideally, funds are given to grantees to support specific work and achieve results that would not otherwise take place. It is also important to monitor the projects so as to support adaptive management of both specific projects and the overall funding program. And it is often useful to coordinate with and influence other related funding programs being implemented by other donors.

Within this basic pathway, there are a number of different wrinkles depending on the specific funding approach being taken. There is a spectrum of different approaches for program managers to invest in and support project work:

▸ **More responsive investments.** One end of this spectrum involves approaches that seek to fund individuals or organizations that are doing good work, without regard to specifying particular outcomes for the work. In the donor community this is often called responsive philanthropy. At this end of the spectrum, the challenge is to identify investment opportunities where your resources can make a difference for grantees who otherwise would not have support. This in turn requires a clear articulation of your program strategy for identifying potential funding candidates. For example, in Figure 2.13, a fellowship program will typically look to fund individuals who are at a specific stage in their career trajectory. Candidates at Point A do not have a sufficient track record. Conversely, candidates at Point D have already established themselves and thus will not benefit from the additional resources of the fellowship. Thus, the theory of change is to find candidates at Point B, in the critical launch window, and give them the

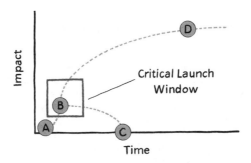

Figure 2.13. The critical launch window in which a fellowship program can boost a career. Source: CAML Fellowships Strategy Theory of Change.

resources through the fellowship to move to Point D and avoid crashing at Point C. Note that depending on the type of fellowship program, this critical launch window could be early or midcareer.

▸ **More strategic investments.** The other end of this spectrum involves approaches that seek to invest in specific actions and results needed to realize a program strategy pathway. In the donor community this is commonly called strategic (or outcome-oriented) philanthropy. At this end of the spectrum, the challenge is to find investment opportunities that can most efficiently help you realize your program strategy pathways. In this case, the <*"good" funding program design*> result in the funding approach pathway in Figure 2.12 needs to focus on developing clear program-level pathways as the basis for making subsequent investments.

Table 2.2 shows different approaches along this spectrum. Each of these approaches has its own distinct variation of the funding meta-level strategy pathway and set of activities needed to implement it. The entries in this spectrum are somewhat independent of choice of funding mechanisms (e.g., traditional grants vs. impact investments), which we discuss further in Chapter 3.

Guidance for Determining Your Program's Investment Approach

Over the past few decades, there has been a great deal of discussion about the relative merits of different investment approaches such as responsive versus strategic philanthropy. This is one of those debates for which there is no one right answer; different program managers will have different thoughts about what approach makes most sense for them. That said, it is important that everyone in your program or organization (and across your grantees or partners) understands and agrees on the investment approach you will take. Specific concepts to consider include:

Table 2.2. A spectrum of program investment approaches

Spectrum	Investment Approach	Analogy	Examples	Funder Activities
More responsive investments	**1. Support and Build Capacity of Good People and Organizations** Provide support to individuals, projects, or organizations (at various levels of experience) that have potential to do good things	Put gas in tank of cars whose drivers want to go somewhere in (almost) any direction	Genius grant awards Early or midcareer fellowship programs Organizational effectiveness grants	Determine criteria Identify or select candidates Provide grant funding Provide training and support
↑	**2. Support Good Work on Key Topics** Provide support to projects that are doing good work on relevant issues	Put gas in tank of reliable cars whose drivers are generally headed toward program decision makers' desirable destinations	Government agency programs allocating resource royalties Traditional responsive foundation grants	Select program focal topic Identify or select projects Provide grant funding Monitor legal compliance Develop shared metrics
	3. Set Program Goal but Not Strategy Select the specific scope and then challenge the community to come up with the best project pathways to achieve it	Select a desirable destination on the map and provide gas to drivers or cars who seem best positioned to get there, or offer prize money to the first driver who gets to the destination	Challenge programs to eradicate a human disease Prize competitions Large grants to lead organizations	Select program focal topic Set program goal Identify and fund project teams Monitor goal
↓ More strategic investments	**4. Facilitate Joint Program Strategies** Provide support to groups of stakeholders who develop and implement coordinated program strategy pathways	Convene drivers to agree on joint roadmap, provide gas to cars on key sections of the route	Cocreation funding programs Regional government agencies that convene stakeholder groups and serve as backbone organizations	Select focal topics Identify and fund convener Help develop program pathways Help identify or select projects Provide grant funding Monitor system compliance

Table 2.2. continued

Spectrum	Investment Approach	Analogy	Examples	Funder Activities
	5. Implement Program Strategies via Grants or Partner Support Develop program strategy pathways and provide funding to projects that can help accomplish desired results or generate learning	Develop roadmap, identify, recruit, and provide gas to cars on key sections of the route	Strategic philanthropy Nongovernment organization "offer and acceptance" initiatives	Select focal topics Develop program pathways Identify, select, or recruit projects Provide grant funding Monitor actions and results Adapt project portfolio
More strategic ↓	**6. Implement Self-Funded Program Strategies** Develop and implement program pathways and their component project pathways	Develop roadmap, buy cars, hire drivers, provide gas and specific instructions where to go	Self-implementing funder (operating foundation) programs Nongovernment organization traditional initiatives and programs	Select focal topics Develop program pathways Design or manage projects Monitor actions and results Adapt projects and program

- **Ensure your leaders articulate a clear investment approach.** Ideally, each funding organization or agency will clearly establish the investment approach (or mix of approaches) that makes most sense to them. To this end, if you are setting up a foundation or are on the board or senior leadership of a funding organization or agency, let your staff and grantees know how you would like to operate. If you are on staff of a funding organization or agency that does not have a clear approach, you may want to delicately enable a discussion of different approaches with your leadership.

- **Build your investment approach into your organizational processes and systems.** It is important to match your grant-making and reporting processes and systems to the type of approach you are taking. For example, if you are following Approach 1 or 2, then you don't need to develop specific program pathways for your work. Likewise, your monitoring and reporting efforts can focus on whether your grantees are using their resources in an appropriate and ethical fashion. By contrast, if you are following Approach 4 or 5, then you will have to invest the time and resources to develop a program-level strategy pathway and vet it with potential grantees and other stakeholders. You will also have to develop reporting systems that enable your grantees to link their project-level results to your desired program-level results (see Chapter 5).

- **Communicate your investment approach to your potential grantees.** It is also obviously important to clearly communicate your investment approach to your potential grantees or implementing partners. This is particularly critical when you are following Approaches 3 or 4, in which you need your grantee's work to fit into your program strategy, but you do not directly control this work as you do in Approach 5. To this end, some organizations have used an "offer and acceptance" process in which project teams apply to have their work fit into an overarching program. In other cases, organizations may even put out a call for proposals and then offer support to the projects that propose to deliver the highest levels of desired outcomes. Regardless of the system used, if both project and program teams have developed clear strategy pathways, then it can be a lot easier to determine how project-level results will feed into program-level results.
- **Share your investment approach with other funders and partners.** Conservation funders generally do not operate in a vacuum but instead share both issues and potential grantees with other funders. Being explicit about your funding approach enables you to better coordinate with others. For example, if you are focusing on early career fellowships, you may want to coordinate with other funders who are providing similar fellowships to ensure that you are collectively allocating your resources most effectively. It may even also be helpful to share your criteria for determining which candidates are in the key launch window. Even if you take a dramatically different approach, it is generally helpful to all concerned parties to be clear about these differences.

Sources and Further Information

(See FOSonline.org/pathways for links and updated guidance material.)

Understanding Your Overall Impact Trajectory

The material in this section was shamelessly taken wholesale (with permission!) from the following blog:

Liz Ruedy (2018), "Six Models for Understanding Impact." A brilliant and simple explanation of different potential trajectories for program impact relative to the status quo.

Finding Key Intervention Points in Situation Models

Identifying intervention points is as much an art as a science and thus hard to encapsulate in guidance. That said, some general food for thought can be found in:

Donella Meadows (2008), *Thinking in Systems: A Primer.* Chapter 6 in this book has an interesting discussion of how to use systems thinking to identify twelve types of intervention points in a system.

D.J. Abson et al. (2017), "Leverage Points for Sustainability Transformation" (*Ambio* 46: 30–39). This article extends Meadows's analysis, lumping her twelve types of intervention points into four key concepts focused on the system's parameters, feedback loops, design, and intent, with the latter options being more powerful but also less commonly addressed.

Identifying Candidate Actions

There are many resources available to learn more about different types of generic conservation actions for different intervention points:

Nick Salafsky et al. (2008), "A Standard Lexicon for Biodiversity Conservation: Unified Classifications of Threats and Actions" (*Conservation Biology* 22: 897–911). The original list of conservation actions.

CMP (2014), *Conservation Actions Classification,* **v. 2.0.** A more recent hierarchical classification of all conservation actions.

FOS and CMP (2020), *Conservation Actions and Measures Library (CAML).* A curated library of generic pathway diagrams for single conservation actions and compound conservation strategies.

There are also a growing number of libraries that provide synthesized evidence for the effectiveness of different conservation actions:

Conservation Evidence. A website and journal with expert reviews of conservation strategies.

Collaboration for Environmental Evidence. A website and journal with systematic reviews of conservation strategies.

Evidensia. A website with evidence for market-based conservation strategies.

Creating Strategy Pathways to Show Theories of Change

The theory of change concept was first developed in the 1990s in the development world by Carol Weiss and soon spread to other fields. Basic introductions include:

Richard Margoluis et al. (2013), "Results Chains: A Tool for Conservation Action Design, Management, and Evaluation" (*Ecology and Society* 18: 22). An overview of the basic concept.

Global Environment Facility (2019), *Theory of Change Primer.* A review of theories of change in different disciplines.

FOS (2021), *Planning for Conservation, Assumptions and Theories of Change: A How-To Guide.* A practical guide to developing theory of change pathways.

Miradi Software. A software system explicitly designed to support strategy pathways.

Developing Your Approach for Going to Scale

There are many different models for taking programs to scale. Some of the most helpful sources include:

Peter Senge (1990), *The Fifth Discipline: The Art and Practice of the Learning Organization.* A good discussion of how to think about scaling using a systems thinking approach.

Everett Rogers (2003), *Diffusion of Innovations,* **5th ed.** The classic work on how to spread ideas.

Michele Lee Moore, Darcy Riddell, and Dana Vocisano (2015), "Scaling Out, Scaling Up, Scaling Deep: Strategies of Non-Profits in Advancing Systemic Social Innovation" (*Journal of Corporate Citizenship* 58: 67–84). An analysis of three models for scaling social innovation.

R. Sam Larson, James Dearing, and Thomas E. Backer (2017), *Strategies to Scale Up Social Programs: Pathways, Partnerships and Fidelity.* An overview of three different approaches to scaling.

Jim Collins (2019), *Turning the Flywheel.* A monograph expanding the flywheel scaling concepts developed in his earlier works.

Damon Centola (2021), *Change: How to Make Big Things Happen.* A book describing fascinating research on how networks can be used to promote behavior change.

CAML (2021), Pathways for Scaling Approaches. Detailed pathway diagrams for each of the five scaling approaches presented in this book.

The cash flow analysis presented in this section is inspired by the method developed over decades by Glenn Jenkins and Arnold Harberger at the Harvard Institute for International Development, in particular as taught by Robert Conrad of Duke University:

Glenn Jenkins, Chun-Yan Kao, and Arnold Harberger (2018), *Cost–Benefit Analysis for Investment Decisions.* A summary of the cash flow analysis method used in this section.

FOS (2021), *An Economic Cash-Flow Model for Taking Nature-Based Climate Solutions to Scale.* The cash flow model example presented in this section.

Determining Your Program's Investment Approach

Some of the more helpful discussions of different approaches to philanthropy include:

Paul Brest and Hal Harvey (2018), *Money Well Spent: A Strategic Plan for Smart Philanthropy,* **2nd ed.** Suggestions for improving the strategic philanthropy approach.

John Kania, Mark Kramer, and Patty Russell (2014), "Strategic Philanthropy for a Complex World" (*Stanford Social Innovation Review*). Suggestions for improving the strategic philanthropy approach.

The William and Flora Hewlett Foundation (2016), *A Practical Guide to Outcome-Focused Philanthropy.* A good intro to these concepts.

Key Learning Questions

1. How can we develop more systematic guidance for determining the types of actions to use at different leverage points within a situation assessment?
2. How can we develop and promote use of a shared conceptual and spatial information system for tracking specific conservation actions and strategies being implemented around the world?
3. How can we build a more complete library of generic scaling pathways? Of specific scaling examples?
4. How can we develop cash flow model templates for analyzing the costs of different actions at scale?
5. Given unequal power dynamics, can we more effectively and equitably reconcile and connect funder program goals and strategies with those of implementing organizations?

3

Operationalizing and Implementing Your Program

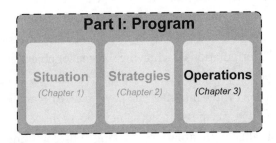

Now that you and your team have planned out your strategy pathways, your need to figure out how to implement them. Key analyses in this process include:

- Setting SMART goals and objectives
- Analyzing trade-offs and conflict
- Turning your strategic plan into an actionable work plan
- Assembling a programmatic investment portfolio
- Awarding contracts and grants that enable adaptation

Setting SMART Goals and Objectives

One of the key steps in any planning process involves specifying longer-term goals and intermediate objectives that describe in some detail what you are trying to achieve. In the *Conservation Standards*, goals are the desired future state of your target factors (the oval shapes in the diagrams that collectively represent the program's ultimate purpose), whereas objectives are the desired state of your intermediate results (boxes in our diagrams). You can substitute any terms your organization or program team prefers for *goals* and *objectives*; the critical thing is to distinguish between the ultimate ends and the intermediate achievements you need to accomplish to get to these ends.

You may be familiar with the SMART mnemonic: Goals and objectives are supposed to be Specific, Measurable, Achievable, Results-Oriented, and Time-Limited. In some formulations of the SMART acronym, the *R* stands for *realistic*. However, we find that this overlaps with *achievable* and that it is more important to be *results-oriented* (or *relevant* in some SMART formulations); achieving the goal or objective represents achieving a key result in your theory of change. As an extreme example, you could set an objective that "in the next three minutes, you have to take off and put on your left shoe three times," which is specific, measurable, achievable, realistic, and time-limited—but also utterly trivial in almost all situations. Making your goals and objectives results-oriented instead helps ensure that they represent meaningful accomplishments in the context of your theory of change.

Creating SMART goals and objectives helps ensure that your work is focused on what your team *needs to* accomplish rather than what your team *could* accomplish. For example, let's say that you are trying to set up whale watching ecotourism businesses to provide an alternative livelihood to people who are currently operating unsustainable fishing trawlers. A typical non-SMART objective might be to:

Establish viable whale watching businesses.

If you consider this objective in the context of your theory of change as shown below, you would realize that you are using a behavioral change strategy. The key result in this pathway is that to reduce the threat of unsustainable fishing, each boat operator would have to take home at least as much money from their new job in the whale watching business as they currently do from running their fishing boats in order to incentivize them to change their livelihood (Figure 3.1). To this end, a SMART objective might read:

Within three years, each current fishing boat operator makes at least as much money annually from employment in a whale watching business as they would from fishing.

As you can see, going through the discipline of developing SMART objectives forces your team to think hard about the strategic pathway you are using and question some of the key assumptions you are making. For example, key questions include:

- How many fishing boat operators are there today? And thus, how many whale watching jobs do we need to create? Is it even possible to create this many jobs?
- What annual salary is needed to entice people to stop fishing and work for the whale watching operation? Specifically, is whale watching easier or safer work so that people would be willing to switch for less income than their current fishing income? Or, by contrast, is it viewed as economically more risky or not a "respectable" livelihood in the local culture so people would require more money to switch?
- What's the possibility that fishing boat owners will switch to working for the whale watching enterprise but still bring in their cousin to run the fishing boat on the side? Or what's the possibility that other boat owners will move into the vacated fishing space?
- What are the potential negative impacts of whale watching on the whale populations?

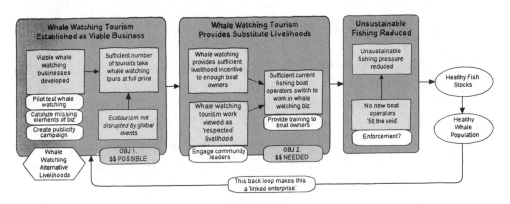

Figure 3.1. Whale watching alternative livelihood strategy pathway.

Developing SMART goals and objectives thus forces your team to focus on key results, figure out whether your proposed strategy pathway is feasible, and, as we will see later in Chapter 5, create a more specific and testable hypothesis.

When working at large scales and in complex systems, it is more important than ever to develop SMART goals and objectives. However, you also need to think about adapting these criteria:

▶ **Specific versus scale-appropriate.** In traditional project planning, goals and objectives are supposed to be specific about what you need to accomplish, such as having at least fifteen adult salmon per hour travel past a counting station during peak migration season or reducing toxin levels below 5 parts per million in the water. The idea here is that you have to clearly articulate what success is going to look like. When operating at large scales, however, it may not be possible to define such specific targets. For example, each watershed might have its own unique target level of salmon per hour. Or you might have to think about an average amount of the toxin across the program scope. The key is to focus on getting the underlying concept right and then translating it into a scale-appropriate objective.

▶ **Measurable.** In traditional project planning, goals and objectives also need to have a measurable indicator baked into their formulation, as shown in the two examples above (more than fifteen salmon per hour traveling past a counting station, or less than 5 parts per million of chemical toxin in the water). As discussed in detail in Chapter 5, when operating at large scales, it can be a more challenging or expensive task to collect reliable data, and you may have to adapt your indicator accordingly or use a proxy indicator. You may also have to roll up indicators from project strategy pathways to program strategy pathways, as discussed in Chapter 5.

▶ **Achievable versus results-oriented.** In traditional project planning, there is a tension between setting goals and objectives that accomplish the needed result in your theory of change and setting goals and objectives that are feasible given available resources. If you need to give every boat operator $25,000 per year to get them to switch to being tourism guides, but your business projections show that you can pay only $10,000 per year, then your tourism guide strategy is unlikely to be successful, and you should consider a different approach. Dealing with this tension is particularly important when you are trying to scale up a pilot project to a much larger program. For example, in the wetland restoration work described in Chapter 2, you need to calculate how much money you might need to raise in order to put enough restoration projects in place to achieve your goal of sequestering 500 million tons of CO_2 over a ten-year period. You may find that your desired result may not be achievable given current resources. In addition, whereas in project planning your team can (at least sometimes) undertake all the work needed to achieve a goal (e.g., restore a specific wetland area), when working at a larger program scale it is much more likely that your work will only contribute to an overarching goal or even intermediate objectives that will require work by many different people and organizations (e.g., restore wetlands across the region or enact a national policy). You thus need to be comfortable with setting an ambitious results-oriented goal or objective but then recognizing that achieving it may not be fully within your control.

▶ **Time-limited.** Finally, in traditional project planning it is important to understand the time sequence of your different objectives leading to your goal. This sequencing is even more important when working at scale. For example, if your stated goal is to sequester 100 million tons of CO_2 over a ten-year period and it takes at least three years for restored habitat to start putting carbon into the soil, then you have to have a sufficient area replanted by Year 7. And if it takes three years to get projects permitted and the work done, then you have to have sufficient projects ready to go by Year 4. Which means that you have to have your funding lined up well before that time.

Guidance for Setting SMART Goals and Objectives

One of the big advantages of using strategy pathways is that they greatly facilitate the process of creating SMART goals and objectives. If you are starting from scratch, it's often hard to figure out exactly how to focus your goals and objectives. But if you have a pathway showing the key factors in your strategy, then most of the work is already done for you (this is why in the *Conservation Standards* we coach teams to first develop the concept in the target factor or intermediate result and then later turn it into a goal or objective):

- **Develop goals and objectives at critical points in your pathway.** As a rule, you do not need to develop SMART goals and objectives for every factor in a given pathway. Instead, as discussed in more detail when we come to monitoring in Chapter 5, you want to focus on critical factors in the hypothesis represented by your pathway diagram; you can think of them as "pulse points" where you know you are going to want to check your progress over time. These can either be critical results that need to be tracked and reported on or uncertainties that require assessments and potential adaptation. Even without looking at the content of a pathway diagram, there are certain obvious places where you are probably going to want to develop goals and objectives. For example, in Figure 3.2, you would probably develop a goal for each of the target factors. You probably also want to develop an objective for the threat reduction result. And finally, it probably makes sense to develop objectives at key confluence points where subpathways come together within each group box.

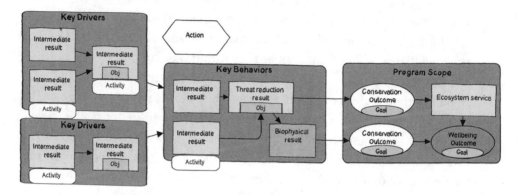

Figure 3.2. Generic pathway diagram showing goals and objectives.

- **Apply the SMART criteria one-by-one.** It is often challenging to write a good goal or objective on your first attempt. So a more practical approach is to develop an initial draft concept and then use the SMART criteria to guide a series of edits to this draft. Start with the core concept in a key result. In the example shown in Table 3.1, you might start with the threat reduction result *<reduce toxics pollution>* in row 1. You then apply the SMART criteria in succession as you move down the table, editing the initial concept in the factor to get your final SMART objective statement in row 6.

- **Focus on results you need to accomplish, not what you can accomplish.** Many teams when developing their objectives tend to focus on what they can potentially accomplish. For example, in the whale watching example above, they might state as their objective, *"Within three years, a profitable whale watching business is created."* Or in the toxic pollution example above, they might have as their objective, *"Within five years, reduce heavy metal levels in freshwater ecosystems by 50 percent."* Both of these objectives meet the criteria of being specific, measurable, achievable, and time-limited. Unfortunately, however, they are not sufficiently results-oriented. In the case of the whale watching business, the ultimate point of this strategy is not just to establish a profitable business but rather to have this business provide sufficient income to people who are currently operating unsustainable fishing boats. And in the case of the toxic pollution example, the key is not just reducing the heavy metal levels but reducing them to whatever

Table 3.1. Example of refining a draft objective by applying the SMART criteria

Row	Draft Version of Objective	SMART Criterion
1	**Threat reduction result:** Reduce toxics pollution	
2	**Objective:** Reduce toxics pollution *in freshwater ecosystems*	Results-oriented?
3	**Objective:** Reduce ~~toxics pollution~~ *heavy metal levels* in freshwater ecosystems	Measurable?
4	**Objective:** Heavy metal *maximum* levels in freshwater ecosystems never exceed *[fish spawning limits] or [5 ppm government standards]*	Specific?
5	**Objective:** Heavy metal *maximum* levels in ~~freshwater ecosystems~~ *all major river systems* never exceed *fish spawning limits*	Achievable?
6	**Objective:** *By 2030,* heavy metal maximum levels in all major river systems never exceed fish spawning limits	Time-limited?

level is safe for fish spawning, which might be 5 percent or 50 percent or even 95 percent of current levels.

There is thus often a tension between making an objective results-oriented (what you need to accomplish) and realistic (what you can accomplish). For example, a project team might find that it is beyond their power to reduce heavy metal levels to a level that is safe for fish spawning given current resources within a short time frame. In these cases, the difference between what you can accomplish and what you need to accomplish signals that you have to go back to the drawing board and figure out how you can adapt your strategy, your scaling approach, or your time frame to ultimately accomplish what is needed to achieve your goals. You will probably have to consider developing partnerships with other programs and organizations that can contribute to reaching your overall objective or goal.

- **Develop approximate measures of exact concepts.** In many cases you may not know the precise value for a specific objective or the specific time frame for achieving it. It's okay to be uncertain about the value, but you want to be as clear as possible about the underlying concept. For example, building on the above toxics example, it is far better to have a qualitative but conceptually clear objective (*"reduce heavy metal levels below the limits that inhibit fish spawning"*) that guides your thinking and work than a quantitative but non–results-oriented objective (*"reduce heavy metal levels by 10 percent"*) that is essentially meaningless. You can also use algebraic placeholders or question marks to denote missing or estimated specific values that you hope to be able to fill in later as you acquire more data and evidence (*"reduce heavy metal levels below xx ppm, which is the maximum limit for fish spawning"*).

- **Do the math for outcomes at scale.** As discussed in Chapter 2, it's often helpful when trying to scale up your work to do some basic estimation to see whether your scaling approach is at the right order of magnitude. These calculations are particularly useful in trying to see whether a series of objectives along a theory of change pathway will lead to the desired ultimate outcome. Continuing with the whale watching alternative livelihood pathway from above, let's assume there are about 1,000 people currently working in unsustainable fishing operations in a given region for whom you would like to find alternative livelihoods. Each of these people is currently taking home an average of $25,000 per year. So you can figure you need to bring in at least:

$$\$25,000/\text{person-yr} * 1,000 \text{ persons} = \$25 \text{ million}$$

Even if you assume that working on a whale watching tourism boat is less demanding than fishing, people may still need to make at least 80 percent of their fishing income in order to switch. So is raising this amount of money through whale watching feasible? Figure 3.3a shows some rough parameter estimates that are then used to make the *Estimates of Key Objectives* in Figure 3.3b.

Notice that in this estimate, we are not trying to figure out the profitability of a whale sightseeing cruise and attempting to factor in costs such as boat payments, fuel, and insurance. Instead, we are making a simplifying assumption that the only expense that really matters for this strategy pathway is the fraction of income from ticket sales that accrues to the employees. Framing this analysis is the embodiment of the art of "approximate answers to exact questions." If we assume that the employees will get 50 percent of the revenue, then as currently shown, the whale watching business will raise only 10 percent of the funds needed to induce the people fishing to switch their behaviors. So at this point, assuming that your estimates are at least in the right ballpark, you have a few choices:

- Figure out how to scale the whale watching by an order of magnitude (e.g., run 4,000 trips per year!),

	A	B
1	Factor / Parameter	Estimate
2	OBJ 1. $$ POSSIBLE to Raise from Whale Watching	
3	Number of boat trips (#/yr)	400
4	Passengers / boat trip	100
5	Cost per passenger ($)	100
6	% of revenues going to employees	50%
7	OBJ 2. $$ NEEDED to Incent Switch from Fishing	
8	Total number of people in fishing industry (#)	1,000
9	Current average take home pay ($/yr)	25,000
10	% of income needed to induce switch	80%

	D	E	F	G	H	I	J	K	L	M	N	O	P
12	Estimates of Key Objectives												Total
13	OBJ 1. $$ POSSIBLE to Raise from Whale Watching												
14–15	400	$\frac{\text{boat trips}}{\text{yr}}$	*	100	$\frac{\text{passengers}}{\text{boat trip}}$	*	100	$\frac{\$}{\text{passenger}}$	*	50%	$\frac{\$ \text{ to}}{\text{employees-yr}}$	=	$ 2,000,000
16	OBJ 2. $$ NEEDED to Incent Switch from Fishing												
17–18	1,000	$\frac{\text{people}}{\text{fishing}}$	*	25,000	$\frac{\$}{\text{yr}}$	*	80%	needed to switch				=	$ 20,000,000
19										Ratio of POSSIBLE : NEEDED			10%

Figure 3.3a, b. Estimating objectives needed to assess feasibility of alternative livelihoods pathway.

- Figure out additional livelihood substitution activities to complement whale watching,
- Decide that having even 10 percent of the people currently fishing switch their livelihoods is still a useful outcome, or
- Find a new strategy altogether to solve the unsustainable fishing problem. This means going back to your situation assessment and potential intervention points.

The one thing you don't want to do is naively develop a whale watching business hoping that it will by itself solve the unsustainable fishing problem because even if the business works as expected, it will not come close to solving that problem. And this doesn't even factor in risks such as a global pandemic that puts a halt to most ecotourism businesses.

Analyzing Trade-Offs and Conflict

One of the key benefits of using strategy pathways is that they can help frame some of the critical sources of conflict that underlie most complex conservation situations. Much of this conflict is rooted in the fact that from the perspective of the natural world, an increase in human alteration of an ecosystem almost by definition leads to degradation of natural world well-being (the primary curve in Figure 3.4). At small scales (as shown by the inset), it may be possible to find conservation actions that also result in an increase in natural world well-being (the win–win solutions). For example, we might be able to set up a whale watching ecotourism business that provides income for local communities while reducing fishing pressure on the salmon that the whales depend on. But, especially when we are operating at larger scales, we are much more likely to be in win–neutral or win–lose situations where gains in natural world well-being (i.e., conservation outcomes) come at the expense of human well-being, at least in the short term. For example, it's hard to imagine that the market would support enough whale watching to replace the entire fishing industry in a given region. This in turn puts the project team in the uncomfortable position of having to pick winners and losers in the system.

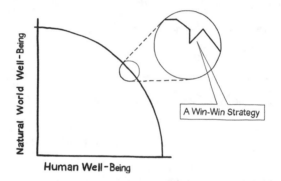

Figure 3.4. Trade-offs between the natural world well-being and human well-being. Source: Adapted from Salafsky (1994).

As one example, let's look at the process of setting salmon harvesting quotas. Let's say that the existing fishery management system currently allocates one third of the harvestable salmon stock in a given management area to recreational fishing, one third to indigenous communities, and one third to commercial fishing. A recent credible scientific study determines that to maintain the fishery at a long-term sustainable level, the current harvest rate would have to be reduced by 25 percent overall. In effect, this is an intergenerational equity issue; to preserve future generations' rights to salmon, we collectively have to forgo or at least reduce our consumption of the salmon today.

Furthermore, under the federal Endangered Species Act, the study determined that the total fishing level needs to be reduced by 50 percent overall to ensure the long-term survival of seal and killer whale populations in the region that depend on salmon as their principal food source. Now this is not just an intergenerational human equity issue but also an interspecies equity issue. Analogous issues arise in other resource allocation situations such as water rights, in which scarce water resources must be allocated not only between various human water uses such as agriculture, municipal water systems, and power generation but also for endangered fish populations or wetlands and other water-dependent ecosystems.

So the question is how a systematic adaptive management approach using pathways can help navigate this complexity and make these difficult trade-off decisions. It's probably obvious at this point that if we are going to reach any kind of sustainable fish harvesting system, some hard choices are going to have to be made that cause pain to one or more parties; it's unlikely we are going to find a win–win situation at scale. These decisions are often not scientific but rather political; they are in the realm of what Kai Lee (1993) has called the gyroscope of politics. Which of course also brings in justice and equity issues as well.

In the 1950s, James Thompson and Arthur Tuden (as described by Lee) developed a useful heuristic to think about conflict situations by looking at whether different stakeholders agree or disagree on both their preferences about outcomes (the desired end of a decision) and their beliefs about causation (either in the problem analysis in a situation assessment or in the proposed means of how to reach the desired ends as expressed in a strategy pathway). As shown in Figure 3.5, there are four quadrants:

- ▶ **Computation quadrant.** If there is agreement on both these axes, then the situation merely requires using available science and evidence to clarify the exact nature of the decision. This should presumably be part of the regular management bureaucracy.
- ▶ **Bargaining quadrant.** If there is agreement on causation but disagreement on outcome preferences, then your pathways become a model for at least understanding the position of each stakeholder and then using a political process to agree at some level on the desired outcomes.
- ▶ **Judgment quadrant.** If there is agreement on the outcome preferences but disagreement on the causation, then pathways can potentially help narrow the disagreement over causality, assuming that there is sufficient good faith to at least consider each other's models of the system.
- ▶ **Conflict quadrant.** Finally, if there is disagreement on both these axes, then you have to try to use your pathways to move toward the judgment quadrant or settle based on a purely political exercise involving bargaining and compromise.

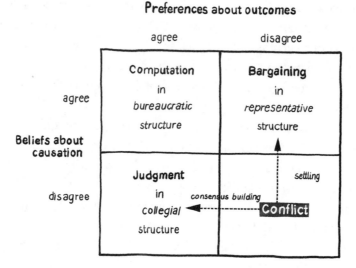

Figure 3.5. Four quadrants in which to consider stakeholder conflict.
Source: Adapted from Thompson & Tuden (1959), in Lee (1993).

Guidance for Analyzing Trade-Offs and Conflict

If you find yourself in a situation in which different stakeholders are potentially in conflict over, for example, limiting resources in the system, you need to think about managing these issues and developing appropriate trade-offs:

- **Diagnose your situation.** Managing trade-offs and conflict starts with understanding the issues at stake. Going back to your situation assessment, what is the limiting resource at the root of the conflict? Who are the various stakeholders in this resource, and what share of the available resource does each currently have versus what they want? In particular, are there any stakeholders who have been marginalized or shut out of the current resource allocation system (including nonhuman stakeholders such as key species or ecosystems)? And finally, do these different stakeholders (or their representatives) share a reasonably common set of beliefs about the situation? Do they agree on the outcomes of how the resource should be allocated?

  Looking at the four quadrants in the Thompson and Tuden diagram, it's pretty clear that if your situation is in the right-hand column, in which parties are disagreeing about preferences (i.e., values) of outcomes (e.g., who should get what share of the available salmon resources), then resolving the conflict is going to be largely a political exercise that requires political analyses and solutions beyond the scope of this book. However, if your situation is in the left-hand column, and in particular, in the lower left judgment quadrant, then there is potential for the types of systematic analysis outlined in this book to be of use in resolving the conflict.

- **Develop the right mix of strategies.** If you are in the judgment quadrant, then you need to work with your partners to explore finding the right mix of conservation strategies to address the issues you are facing. Different strategies have different theories of change as to how they might help solve these conflicts, each with its own benefits and challenges. Some common examples include:

  - *Improving resource management.* One classic set of strategies involves directly improving the management of the critical resource so that there is more of it to go around. For example, your program could remove dams or assist salmon in their migration so that there are more fish to catch, thus allowing each stakeholder group to maintain current absolute harvest levels while still providing enough fish for the seals and whales and to maintain long-term salmon populations. Likewise, you could invest in fixing water transport infrastructure to reduce losses due to leakage or evaporation. In effect, these strategies are shifting the curve in the trade-off diagram in Figure 3.4 outward. However, these strategies can also lead to an intensification of the focal resource at the expense of other conservation values in the system. For example, setting up fish hatcheries may increase the total number of salmon available, but they may swamp the native salmon and also bring disease and other problems into the system. They are also on a slippery slope that leads from hatcheries to fully enclosed aquaculture production of salmon.

  - *Setting and enforcing resource use limits.* A second common set of strategies involves restricting resource use to try to keep it below some predetermined sustainable cap level. These restrictions can be based on quotas or on gear, effort, or timing restrictions. For example, fishing may be restricted to certain seasons or certain days of the week, allowing some salmon to complete their annual migration to the spawning grounds. These approaches obviously require good enforcement to be effective. They also often inflict the most hardship on resource users who are politically or economically unable to compete for the resources that are made available.

  - *Creating voluntary market-based incentives.* This set of strategies entails using market pressure for sustainable resource production to provide incentives to resource producers who can demonstrate that they are producing resources using appropriate practices. For example, in the sustainable fishery pathway diagram in Figure 2.6b, the seafood value chain may signal fish producers by (at least in theory) offering a premium price or greater market share for sustainably harvested fish. These approaches require reliable traceability and verification processes to ensure that unsustainably produced products do not leak into the system. As a rule, most incentive programs have discovered that there is little or no price premium for sustainable products. Furthermore, this approach typically has to focus on demand from companies in the value chain rather than consumers themselves. Finally, there is a great deal of discussion as to what the appropriate unit is for ensuring sustainability (the producer, the fishery or sector, or the jurisdiction).

- *Providing long-term rights and incentives to resource users.* Another set of strategies for managing resource conflicts involves providing long-term resource rights to specific stakeholders under the assumption that they will then have the incentive to manage the resource sustainably, or in economics parlance, internalize the externalities. For example, various organizations have tried to provide fishing communities with territorial use rights for fishing (TURFs) or catch shares. Other organizations have tried to develop linked enterprises in which the long-term success of the business depends on maintaining the ecological targets (e.g., setting up a whale watching business that obviously depends on having whales and a healthy marine ecosystem, as shown by the feedback loop in Figure 3.1). As discussed above, these types of win–win strategies are often limited in the number of stakeholders they can support and thus may not work to resolve conflict at scale in situations in which human demand for resources far outstrips supply.

- *Direct payments.* This set of strategies involves having society (either through the government or via foundations and nongovernment organizations [NGOs] that make up civil society) make direct payments to current resource right holders to forgo their use of the resources and thus effectively transfer those rights to ecological targets in the system. For example, the government might provide payments or alternative livelihoods to fishing boat owners, or an NGO might purchase water rights that are then used to support freshwater-dependent ecosystems. As shown in Figure 3.6, this approach (assuming it is enforceable) has the potential to both reduce the overall harvest level and minimize the cost of forgoing resource use. However, it depends on having an external source of funds from society for the payments. It may also be difficult to meet the goal of maintaining traditional fishing livelihoods and culture.

- *Equitably sharing the costs.* A related set of strategies involves using various market-based mechanisms to allocate scarce resources. For example, under a cap-and-trade market strategy, various resource rights holders are allocated a quota of the resource in question. If there is a gradient in economic value derived from their use of their quota, then the parties can trade their rights to others who can presumably derive more benefit from exercising them. Market trading can minimize the hardship inflicted by the quota (in economic terms, it enables us to find a Pareto-optimal allocation of the fish resources, meaning that we have maximized the total benefit in the system across all stakeholders). But, as shown by the dotted arrow in Figure 3.6, this market approach will not contribute to sustainability unless the cap is set at a meaningful level and enforced.

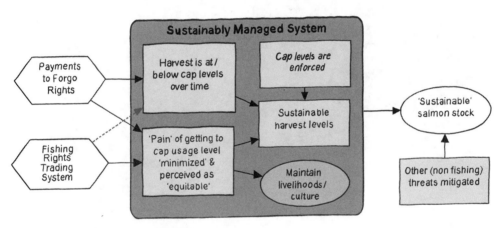

Figure 3.6. Excerpt from a strategy pathway market-based trading system coupled with payments.

Turning Your Strategic Plan into an Actionable Work Plan

At this point, your team might have a fleshed-out strategic plan that shows the major strategic pathways you will use at both project and program levels. Although this is a major accomplishment, you are unfortunately not done yet; it's like trying to construct a building but having only the high-level concept designs from the architect. You still need to get the architect to develop a set of construction drawings that your builder will use to construct the building, ideally on schedule and within the allocated budget.

Work planning thus involves taking your strategic plan and breaking it into a series of activities and tasks that your team and your partners can actually implement. Each activity and its nested tasks will typically have a time frame over which it must

be completed and certain milestones that must be reached by a certain date. These time frames collectively create the calendar for your team's work. Work planning may involve identifying dependencies across activities and tasks; for example, you might need to get permits in place before you begin physical wetland restoration work. It also involves budgeting the time and treasure needed to complete each of these activities and tasks and determining where these resources will come from. Finally, work planning involves tracking the progress of implementation over time and then adjusting the plan as needed. At a program scale, work planning is almost inevitably coarser grained than when working at a project scale.

There is a spectrum of work planning approaches roughly defined by two endpoints:

► **Waterfall planning.** One end of the spectrum involves developing in great detail all the work you will need to do to fully implement your strategy pathways. The term *waterfall* comes from software engineering in which product managers need to specify in great detail all the requirements for the system they are building. They then pass these requirements on to the designers, who plan the system and then pass the plans to the engineers who write the code. At each handoff, the process "goes over a waterfall," at which point it becomes expensive to go back and make changes in the earlier step. In a similar fashion, in waterfall work planning, a team will specify in great detail a sequence of tasks that have various dependencies on one another (Figure 3.7a). As a result, the team can set an exact calendar needed to achieve critical milestones and estimate the resources needed to accomplish these tasks. Waterfall planning also supports critical path analysis, which enables managers to optimize completing the project by a given date or minimizing cost, or other factors. If completion of a task slips, then it is necessary to adjust all the subsequent tasks. A waterfall approach is best used when you have a good understanding of the system and the tasks you need to accomplish. It's especially useful in the shorter term, for example if you are trying to plan a specific event that is set to occur on a given date or complete a specific restoration project.

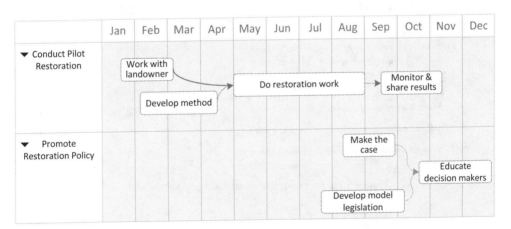

Figure 3.7a. An excerpt from a waterfall style work plan.

► **Agile planning.** The other end of the spectrum involves being more iterative in planning work. Under an agile planning approach (Figure 3.7b), you might develop only a very high-level work plan for a three-year strategy. You could then plan each quarter in more detail on a rolling basis, taking time to adjust and adapt the high-level plan as the situation changes. As part of agile planning, you also assign activities and tasks to people on your team and develop budgets for each planning period on a rolling basis. It's worth noting that agile planning is not a license to do whatever you want; good agile planning actually requires as much or even more discipline than waterfall planning to ensure that you are deploying available resources on the most important tasks and not letting key tasks fall through the cracks.

Item	Who	Year 1				Year 2	Year 3	TOTAL
		Q1	Q2	Q3	Q4			
Wetland Restoration		15	100	75	25	975	1390	2580
Conduct Pilot Restorations		15	100	65	5			185
Work with landowner	Pilot team	5						5
Develop method	Science team	10	10					20
Do restoration work	Pilot team			90	60			150
Monitor & share results	Felix			5	5			10
Promote Restoration Policies				10	20	25		55
Make the case	Ali, Che			10	10			20
Develop model legislation	Ali, Che				5			5
Educate decision makers	Dana, Jane				5	25		30
Manage Restoration at Scale						550	390	940
ID candidate sites	Science team					120		120
Raise funds	Development team					40		40
Outreach to landowners	Program team					10	10	20
Hire & train project managers	Program team					90	90	180
Manage program	Eddy					260	260	520
Sell offsets	Greta					30	30	60
project 1 wetland restoration	project 1 team					400		400
project 2 wetland restoration	project 2 team						600	600
project 3 wetland restoration	project 3 team						400	400

Figure 3.7b. An excerpt from an agile style work plan.

As discussed above, in some situations it might make sense to take a more waterfall-based approach to your work planning. For example, if you are building infrastructure such as a bridge (or, conversely, removing a dam), then your work allocation problem involves optimally deploying a team of, say, fifty people to complete ten major activities and their associated tasks in a fairly strict sequential order. Furthermore, as described in the "Awarding Contracts and Grants That Enable Adaptation" section below, certain funding mechanisms may also require more detailed waterfall planning.

In general, however, when working in complex systems and at scale, it will generally be more helpful to take a more agile approach to work planning. As opposed to the bridge builder's problem, the typical work allocation problem for most conservation programs is to deploy a team of five to ten people to accomplish fifty activities. Furthermore, although there may be some rough dependencies among these fifty activities, for the most part they just need to get done more or less concurrently during some window of time. So the manager's challenge is not to find the critical path but rather to avoid overallocating any one team member at any given point in time while still ensuring that critical work gets done.

An additional problem is also that conservation teams face a great deal of uncertainty. You might be able to predict with some certainty what you need to do over the next month or the next quarter. But trying to develop a specific work plan for project activities scheduled to take place in two years or more is probably an exercise in futility; undoubtedly your project team composition will change, or your strategies will change, or the underlying situation will change.

Guidance for Turning Your Strategic Plan into an Actionable Work Plan

Your organization will probably have existing procedures and systems for doing work planning that you probably need to follow. However, in multipartner programs, you need to reconcile different procedures used by different organizations. Furthermore, some key points to keep in mind when doing work planning for complex strategies at scale include:

- **Involve both program and admin staff.** In many conservation organizations, there seems to be a large gap between the program staff who are typically responsible for the content of the work and the administrative staff who are typically responsible for supporting the work. Good work planning could benefit from bringing these two groups together to develop a solid plan that is fully supported by your organization.
- **Start with your strategic pathways.** The starting point for any work planning effort should be your strategic plan. In particular, you will want to look at the actions and specific activities that you have identified as necessary to each of your strategic pathways.
- **Determine feasibility in light of limited resources.** It is important to look at your work plan and see what it will cost in terms of time and treasure to implement

your planned activities. You will often find that even rough budgeting estimates will reveal that you don't have nearly the staff or money needed to implement your activities at the necessary scale—and thereby achieve your desired goals and objectives in your strategy pathway. As a result, you may have to go back and revisit your strategic plan and figure out how to adjust it in light of these realities. Or alternatively, you will have to figure out how to get the resources needed to scale up your work.

- **Do work planning on a rolling basis.** As discussed above, conservation work planning takes place under great uncertainty, especially over longer time horizons. As a result, there's not much point in doing detailed planning for work that is going to take place far in the future. Instead, it's much better to do detailed planning for the upcoming two to four quarters and then only higher-level planning for subsequent years as shown, in the agile example above. You would then meet every six months to reflect on the work to date and then do the detailed work planning for the coming six months.

- **Develop activity-based accounting codes.** Traditional work planning systems have relied on developing a chart of accounts that contains codes that categorize different activities. But for some reason, these codes tend to categorize expenditures by standard accounting classes such as staff time, consultant time, facilities, equipment, and travel. But when it comes time to use these data for management purposes, why does it matter how many trips your team has taken or pencils you have bought? Instead, it could be much more useful to track expenditures in relation to your specific actions and tasks and from there use your strategy pathway to tie these expenditures to your results and ultimate outcomes.

- **Use the right tools.** There are dozens of software systems that support work planning. However, most of these systems are designed to support waterfall-style planning efforts focused on discrete and shorter-term task management. Some tools (including Miradi Software and some of the tools used to manage computer software program development) are designed for more agile style planning. In addition to forward-looking work planning tools, it's helpful to ensure that your backward-looking time tracking systems are using the same chart of accounts. This enables you to assess the accuracy of your planning estimates and improve them over time.

Assembling a Programmatic Investment Portfolio

At this point, your team may have developed one or more strategy pathways for your program. Each strategy pathway will have a number of results you need to achieve, and you will probably have multiple actions that you could invest in to achieve each result. So how do you and your decision makers choose where to invest your scarce time and treasure across all these options?

In the world of financial planning, investors typically don't make just one investment but instead put together a custom portfolio of different investment options that varies depending on their financial situation. Similarly, whether you are the leader of an NGO, agency, or funding program, you and your team need to think about a programmatic portfolio of investments of time, treasure, and other resources that considers several key trade-offs:

▶ **Cost versus your investment budget.** In building a standard financial portfolio, investors first need to consider the absolute cost of a given investment in relation to their available investment budget. For example, an average individual investor probably can't consider purchasing an entire downtown apartment building. Along similar lines, conservation program teams need to think about the scale of their investments relative to their available resources. You don't want to undertake a massive program that far exceeds your ability to make it happen. Part of the art of program design obviously comes in setting a program scope that is ambitious but not too ambitious in relation to your available budget. But a large part of the art also comes in having an approximate but realistic understanding of what a given investment or portfolio of investments will cost. To this end, the work planning described above is critical to come up with cost estimates that can inform your portfolio design.

▶ **Risk versus return.** In constructing standard financial portfolios, investors typically pay a great deal of attention to the risk–reward trade-off. For example, young people at the start of their careers are encouraged to invest in riskier stocks that have the potential to deliver a high return on investment. In comparison, older people nearing retirement who need the money for living expenses in the short term are encouraged to shift their investment allocation to safer and more stable bonds that will offer a more secure albeit lower return. Other investors may also choose to have a more balanced and diversified portfolio that includes a mix of higher and lower risk–reward ratios.

In constructing a programmatic investment portfolio, similar concepts apply, although typically the return is measured in programmatic results rather than monetary terms. You and your organizational decision makers will have to decide what proportion of your investments you want to make in risky "moon shots" that could transform your system of interest versus safer investments that make solid but incremental progress toward your goals. Keep in mind that several smaller but solid investments may pay off in the long run much more than one risky "moon shot" that ends up not working out. On the other hand, unlike a retiree living on a pension, maybe your organization can also tolerate the risk of having that "moon shot" fail. That is the calculus you have to make.

▶ **Diversification versus redundancy.** Again, in a standard financial portfolio, investors are encouraged to think about diversifying their investments across a broad range of assets to help mitigate risk. You don't want to have all of your eggs in one basket. Even if a real estate investor could afford to purchase an entire apartment building, they probably would not want to put their entire investment fund in that one asset.

When building your program, however, you should also decide as part of your risk calculation what level of redundancy you will build into your investment portfolio, not just for the portfolio as a whole but also for each key result within your overall theory of change. This is especially important when later results are contingent on achieving earlier ones. This decision depends on both the probability of success (what are the chances the investment will work out as planned?) and the cost of failure (what are the consequences if you do not achieve the desired results from the investment?). If you have a great deal of certainty that a given investment will pay off or the consequences of not achieving the desired result are not high, then you don't need to waste resources by investing in backups. However, if there is much less certainty or there is a high cost to not achieving the desired result, then you may want to invest in multiple redundant approaches to achieving this result, in much the same way as aircraft designers build redundant systems for key safety features.

This calculus can be particularly challenging when you are facing potential black swan events: threats or opportunities that are very rare and unlikely to occur but have potential to dramatically change the system. As one example, should the government fishery program invest in buying and maintaining emergency cleanup equipment on site to respond to the very unlikely event of a major oil spill in the adjoining offshore ocean shipping corridor? Or would the funds used to purchase and store that equipment be better spent on more likely and pressing conservation needs?

Developing backup or contingency plans can also be challenging in conservation programs because it can send the wrong signals to both your partners and your opponents. For example, if your NGO is advocating to stop the building of a large mine on the grounds that it will do irreparable damage to the local species and ecosystems, then it can be counterproductive to simultaneously also plan for amelioration of the mine's impacts in the event it were to go forward. In these cases, it is often useful for different organizations to take on complementary strategies as part of an informal or formal coalition arrangement.

▶ **Urgency versus longer-term payoffs.** In constructing standard financial portfolios, investors are encouraged to think about the time horizon for both their investments and their anticipated returns. For example, young people at the start of their careers might be investing for their retirement, which is decades away, whereas middle-aged parents who are facing imminent college tuition payments might be counseled to invest at least the tuition funds in a liquid and safe investment account. In a similar fashion, conservation program teams need to think about the timing of both their investments and their desired outcomes. As shown by the years along the top of Figure 3.8, a strategy pathway typically has an implicit or even explicit timeline associated with it, as reflected in the time-limited dates in each of its goals and objectives. Each action takes place over a defined time interval that includes both a start date and an expected end date. Less obviously, each result also has an associated time interval. For example, if you are using mechanical removal to manage invasive weeds in a wetland, one removal action may clear the weeds for only a single growing season, and the action will have to be repeated annually. If you are using chemical control to kill the plants including the roots, the weeds may be controlled for several years. And if you are using biological control, then it may be effective for many years, and you will have to repeat the action only once a decade. The circle in the diagram thus represents the temporal footprint of a given conservation action.

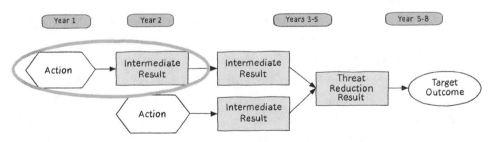

Figure 3.8. Generic strategy pathway being rolled out over time.

One of the classic clichés of planning is "Don't focus on the urgent problems at the expense of the important problems." And as a rule, you will probably be more effective if you can focus on effecting system change rather than putting out short-term fires. But this advice also ignores one of the most fundamental challenges of conservation: the inherent temporal imbalance between actions and threats. Conservation almost always involves defensive action to stop our ecological target factors from being degraded or destroyed by a vast array of threats. If just one of these threats breaks through our defenses just one time, then a species population or an ecosystem can be wiped out and take decades, centuries, or even millennia to recover, if ever.

For example, say your program is focused on keeping a large mine from being built in critical salmon spawning habitat. Through extensive advocacy work, you have gotten the current federal administration to agree not to provide permits to develop the mine. Unfortunately, however, you cannot just mark the problem as solved and then go on to the next problem. The valuable metals are still in the ground, and there's nothing to stop the next administration from reversing policy and permitting the mine. And once that mine is built, that habitat will be lost for generations. You have to win every year or at least every political cycle just to keep the status quo. But if you lose just once, you will effectively lose forever. Admittedly, this fundamental imbalance is daunting and depressing! But it's also reality that you need to address head-on with your work.

In a similar fashion, consider a situation in which a wetland is threatened by shoreline development in the short term but also by sea-level rise in the long term. Your team has to decide whether it is worth investing in saving the wetland not just now but also as sea level rises in the coming years. If it is not feasible to provide a future migration path for the wetland as the waters rise, it may not be worth conserving that particular area of wetland in the short term by limiting shoreline development.

Finally, in some pathways there is also the concept embodied in the old saying that "a stitch in time saves nine." As one example, if you can stop a new invasive plant or insect that is emerging in a small area, then you can save huge amounts of effort to try to eradicate the invasive species later on once it is more widespread and established. But if you spend all your time trying to fight short-term problems, you will never achieve lasting systemic change, such as changing the laws to reduce import of new potential invasive species. The key is to use your situation model and strategy pathways to figure out the right balance.

▶ **Steady-state versus entrepreneurial growth.** The final calculation involved in setting up your portfolio of investments relates to your overall program's growth strategy. Some programs, such as a grant fund that is based on spending the income from a capital endowment, are pretty much fixed in terms of the resources they have to allocate. As shown in Figure 3.9a, these steady-state programs need to end one investment before they can free up resources to make a new investment (although see the discussion of declining payments in the "Awarding Contracts and Grants That Enable Adaptation" section below).

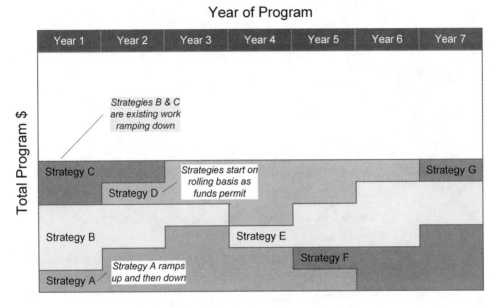

Figure 3.9a. A steady-state program portfolio.

Other programs are able to increase in size by attracting additional sources of revenue to fund their work. As shown in Figure 3.9b, in these entrepreneurial programs, it is often useful to use initial funds to make a number of pilot investments that you then hope will attract funding and grow into long-term self-funded strategies. Under this model, however, you have to be prepared to cut funding to pilot strategies that are not working out as planned, which may of course affect the careers and lives of the people involved in these strategies (see the section on "Exiting Responsibly" in Chapter 5). This model is thus often uncomfortable for staff who are used to working in a more traditional NGO culture.

Guidance for Assembling a Programmatic Investment Portfolio

In traditional project planning, allocating your time and treasure across your candidate investment options is generally a fairly straightforward process of developing a list of candidate strategies, developing a set of assessment criteria, and then applying the criteria to the list of candidates to arrive at your preferred options. When working

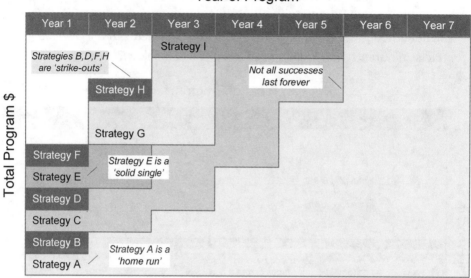

Figure 3.9b. An entrepreneurial program portfolio.

at a program scale, however, this allocation process is typically more complicated and as much an art as a science. In particular, you need to simultaneously think about the options along a given strategy pathway and across strategy pathways. Some key tips to keep in mind include:

- **Frame the context for your investment decisions.** Assembling an investment portfolio for a given program starts with clearly articulating the scope and target factors of your program (per Chapter 1), your overall impact trajectory (Chapter 2), and your overall investment approach (Chapter 2). All of these are primarily values-based rather than strategic decisions. It also helps to determine what level of resources you have to allocate and whether this level will be constant or can grow over time. Once you have made these decisions, the next step is to develop your candidate strategies and prioritize your investment options. As a rule, you are not looking for the optimal allocation of resources so much as you are looking for a good allocation of resources.

- **Select the appropriate comparison approach for each decision.** Approaches for comparing investment options range along a spectrum from more qualitative to more quantitative. Each of these approaches requires having developed a list of candidate strategies. Ideally, these strategies should be at roughly the same conceptual level and have comparable information about each of them. They also require that you have agreed upon the specific criteria that you will use to compare your candidate options, as discussed above.

- *Purely descriptive comparisons.* These approaches involve describing the strengths and weaknesses of each candidate option, often in relation to a situation assessment, some set of criteria or decision nodes, or each other. There is no attempt to rank or quantify the differences between options. One example is a pros and cons table, which presents a list of options with the positive and negative reasons for selecting each option. Another example is the use of a SWOT table, which analyzes strengths, weaknesses, opportunities, and threats for each option. A third example is a decision tree, which helps a team think about the conditions under which a given option might be more or less appropriate.
- *Criteria-based comparisons.* These approaches involve rating each candidate option across a set of criteria. Typical criteria might include the potential impact, scalability, feasibility (financial, technical, moral), risk, cultural fit, and gap (is there an open niche relative to other actors?) of each candidate. These criteria can be applied through relative (ordinal), categorical, or absolute (cardinal) ratings. One common way of doing criteria-based comparisons is by using categorical scale rating tables. In this approach, respondents qualitatively rate each option against defined criteria (Table 3.2a).

  A similar approach uses relative rating tables. In this approach, respondents rank all the options against each other for each criterion (Table 3.2b). This approach is useful to force more of a spread across the options, but it gets hard to do when you have more than a dozen candidate options.
- *Constrained-choice comparisons.* These approaches involve selecting a portfolio of strategies given a binding constraint such as total amount of funds or time available. A simple example is dot voting, in which a workshop facilitator gives each participant a limited number of actual or virtual sticky dots to allocate across a set of candidate strategies listed on a flip chart or virtual table. This approach can be useful if you need a quick-and-dirty assessment across a limited handful of candidate choices.

  A slightly more complex approach is point allocation, in which candidate strategies are listed in a spreadsheet and each team member gets 100 points that represent the total amount of time and treasure available to the program over the time frame being considered. Each team member then allocates their points across the different candidate strategies (Table 3.2c). One

Table 3.2a. Example of categorical scale ratings

	Criterion Weights (0 = exclude)						
	2	1	1	1	1		
	Criteria						
Candidate Option	Impact	Scalability	Feasibility and Risk	Cultural Fit	Gap	Weighted Sum	Weighted Average
Option C	4	4	3	3	4	22	3.7
Option E	2	4	4	4	4	20	3.3
Option H	2	2	3	4	3	16	2.7
Option F	4	3	2	2	1	16	2.7
Option G	2	3	3	3	2	15	2.5
Option A	3	1	1	2	3	13	2.2
Option B	1	1	2	1	2	8	1.3
Option D	1	3	1	1	1	8	1.3

Each criterion is on scale: 4 = very high, 3 = high, 2 = medium, 1 = low.
Weights can be used to explore how ratings change if criteria are emphasized or excluded.

Guide to Criteria
Impact: To what degree will this work contribute to our overall strategy?
Scalability: What is the potential to scale up this work over time?
Feasibility and Risk: To what degree is this work financially, technically, and morally feasible?
Cultural Fit: To what degree does this work fit with our history and culture?
Gap: To what degree is this option an open niche not filled by other investors?

advantage of this approach is that it enables participants to judge not just whether a candidate strategy is a good investment but also how much investment is needed. If each team member assigns their points independently (or in small groups), it also enables an assessment of consensus by looking at the variation in points allocated for a given strategy across the team members and rich discussions in which people who made outlying assessments (substantially more or less investment than the average for a given strategy) can explain their rationale.

Another useful approach to constrained choice investing uses knock-off tables in which candidate strategies are stacked vertically in a spreadsheet and their estimated cost in terms of the limiting resource is cumulatively summed up (Table 3.2d). You can then draw a cutoff line that represents the total amount of available resources so that strategies above the line will be funded

Table 3.2b. Example of relative scale ratings

Candidate Option	Criterion Weights (0 = exclude)					Weighted Sum	Weighted Average
	2	1	1	1	1		
	Criteria						
	Impact	Scalability	Feasibility and Risk	Cultural Fit	Gap		
Option C	7.5	8	6	5	6.5	41	6.8
Option E	4	7	8	8	8	39	6.5
Option H	5	3	5	7	5	30	5.0
Option F	7.5	6	3	4	1.5	30	4.9
Option G	3	5	7	6	4	28	4.7
Option A	6	2	2	3	6.5	26	4.3
Option B	2	1	4	2	3	14	2.3
Option D	1	4	1	1	1.5	10	1.6
Total	36	36	36	36	36		

Options are put in rank order for each criterion from highest (8) to lowest (1). Weights can be used to explore how ratings change if criteria are emphasized or excluded.

Guide to Criteria
Impact: To what degree will this work contribute to our overall strategy?
Scalability: What is the potential to scale up this work over time?
Feasibility and Risk: To what degree is this work financially, technically, and morally feasible?
Cultural Fit: To what degree does this work fit with our history and culture?
Gap: To what degree is this option an open niche not filled by other investors?

and those below the line will not. Candidate strategies can then be moved up or down the list to arrive at the final allocation. This approach requires having at least a high-level estimate of the cost of each candidate strategy but is generally fairly effective in forcing teams to make trade-off decisions.

In any of these constrained choice approaches, there is inevitably a temptation to shave down the allocation to the various options in order to squeeze more needed work under the constraint. It is important to not go too far down this path, however, or you will end up with a portfolio of strategies that don't have the resources they need to reach the desired results.

• *Consequence comparisons.* These approaches involve developing a consequences table that shows the candidate strategy options crossed by different management objectives (Table 3.2e). The team then uses the cells of the

Table 3.2c. Example of point-based allocation ratings

Candidate Strategy	Points Allocated by Program Team Members											Total	Average	S. D.
	Ali	Betsy	Che	Dana	Eddy	Felix	Greta	Hank	Ida	Jane	Kiran			
Option C	30	25	30	25	25	25	30	40	20	25	30	305	28	5
Option E	20	25	25	20	25	25	25	25	20	20	25	255	23	3
Option H	10	10	10	15	10	15	20	20	10	10	15	145	13	4
Option F	10	15	10	10	15	10	5	0	15	10	10	110	10	4
Option G	20	10	15	5	10	5	10	0	15	10	5	105	10	6
Option A	5	10	10	5	15	10	0	15	10	15	10	105	10	5
Option B	5	0	0	15	0	5	0	0	5	10	5	45	4	5
Option D	0	5	0	5	0	5	10	0	5	0	0	30	3	3
	100	100	100	100	100	100	100	100	100	100	100			

S. D. = Standard Deviation

Allocate 100 points representing our program's total time and treasure over the next 5 years. Shading highlights responses that are substantially above or below the group average; it would be good to ask these people why they voted this way.

table to explore the consequences of each option in relation to each objective, as shown in the following example. One key is to make sure that the entries clearly distinguish between facts (which come from experts) and values (which come from all stakeholders). One advantage of the consequences table is that it allows you to consider the effects of different substrategy pathways on key results in your overall strategy.

- *Quantitative model-based comparisons.* These approaches involve establishing a mathematical model that helps determine the optimal set of decision variables (in our case strategy selection) given a defined objective to be maximized or minimized, objective function coefficients that model how decision variables lead to the objective, and a set of constraints.

One example is benefit–cost targeting, in which strategies are ranked by an estimate of the total benefit per dollar spent. The project team then selects the top-rated projects until their funds are exhausted. Binary linear programming extends this type of analysis by optimizing the selection process, taking into account various constraints.

Table 3.2d. Example of knock-off table

	Portfolio A			Portfolio B	
Candidate Option	Option Cost ($)	Portfolio Cost ($)	Candidate Option	Option Cost ($)	Portfolio Cost ($)
Option C	700,000	700,000	Option C	700,000	700,000
Option E	100,000	800,000	Option E	100,000	800,000
Option H	200,000	1,000,000	Option H	200,000	1,000,000
Option F	500,000	1,500,000	Option G	400,000	1,400,000
Option G	400,000	1,900,000	Option B	100,000	1,500,000
Option A	300,000	2,200,000	Option F	500,000	2,000,000
Option B	100,000	2,300,000	Option A	300,000	2,300,000
Option D	700,000	3,000,000	Option D	700,000	3,000,000

The cutoff line for this program is $1,500,000. Options below the line are not being funded. Portfolio B swaps out Option F ($500,000) for Options B ($100,000) and Option G ($400,00), pushing Option F below the cutoff line.

Table 3.2e. Example of consequences table

Result or Objective	Evaluation Criteria	Option A	Option B	Option C
Viable enterprise created				
Financial	% Subsidy required in years 1–5	10%	40%	60%
Risk reduction	Chance that enterprise will fail	20%	30%	50%
Alternative livelihoods	Number of jobs created	200	500	1,000
Social support	Level of community support	Moderate	High	Low
Environmental side effects	Potential to disturb whale populations	Low	Medium	Medium

This example compares three options for implementing the whale watching alternative livelihood strategy.

Economic benefit–cost analysis involves establishing a model of investment in a strategy that shows both the inputs and the expected outputs under different parameters (see for example the wetland carbon sequestration models in Chapter 2). These models can then be used to calculate the net present value (NPV) or internal rate of return (IRR) for a project under different parameter conditions.

As a rule, these quantitative model-based comparisons can be very effective if you are just looking at the financial returns of an investment because both costs and benefits can be expressed in a common currency: money. It becomes more challenging to undertake this kind of analysis when the desired outcomes are not measurable in strict financial terms. In other civil society sectors, there have been some efforts to develop common outcome metrics. For example, in the medical and public health sector, the concept of quality-adjusted life years (QALYs) has been advanced as a way of comparing different project investments. The basic concept is that one year of any human life at a given level of health is a fundamentally equivalent unit. Therefore, if Intervention X that costs \$10,000 would save the lives of 1,000 sixty-year-olds (who have a life expectancy of eighty healthy years) whereas Intervention Y that costs \$20,000 would save the lives of 1,000 newborn babies, then we can calculate the following returns to each investment:

Intervention X: 1,000 people * 20 years/person = 20,000 QALYs/\$10,000 = 2 QALYs/\$

Intervention Y: 1,000 people * 80 years/person = 80,000 QALYS/\$20,000 = 4 QALYs/\$

So in this case, Intervention Y has twice the return of Intervention X.

As you might imagine, there are many assumptions baked into even the simple calculations shown above. But this approach fundamentally depends on the assumption that a year of human life is a "standard currency" anywhere in the world. Similarly, tons of carbon (or CO_2 equivalent) could serve as a standard currency for assessing carbon sequestration strategies. Unfortunately, it's much harder to imagine coming up with some equivalent standard metric in biodiversity conservation. This challenge relates to the discussion of defining success in conservation described above. Is saving a hectare of tundra the same as saving a hectare of rainforest or coral reef? Is saving the last population of a beetle the same as saving the last population of a rhino? Is saving fifty insects the same as saving two birds? And this is even without trying to factor in all the knock-on effects of intertwined ecosystems, not to mention the human benefits from biodiversity.

As a rule, quantitative comparisons are most feasible and useful in more narrowly defined situations in which it is possible to develop measurable indicators of both the costs and the outcome benefits of different intervention options along comparable axes. For example, if you are trying to decide which wetland restoration parcels to invest in restoring, then you can make reasonable apples-to-apples comparisons in terms of a bottom-line outcome metric in dollars per ton of carbon sequestered or even hectares of key wetland habitat conserved. These approaches are less useful in situations in which you are comparing strategies with radically different outcomes, such as saving whales versus conserving migratory birds. In these cases, it's probably no less precise to use a more qualitative approach, which also has the benefit of not implying a false level of precision.

- **Use your comparison approaches to develop your initial investment portfolio.** As you develop your portfolio, remember that you are not looking for the optimal allocation of resources so much as you are looking for a good allocation of resources. As you might guess by now, you should select the simplest comparison approach you can that enables you and your team to arrive at a portfolio of investment options. In particular, in order to harness the wisdom of the crowd it is probably better to use a simpler aluminum-standard approach that enables lots of different people to provide their input, rather than a more sophisticated gold-standard approach that is understood by only a few people. You may also find that you want to use one approach to compare one set of options and a different approach for another set. And at the end of the day, it's important to remember that selecting the right investments is as much an art as a science. Just document your assumptions so that you can go back and test them later.

Awarding Contracts and Grants That Enable Adaptation

In a small site-specific conservation project, most work is typically done by project team members and other key stakeholders. In larger-scale projects and programs, however, it is often necessary to develop contracts, grants, or investments to carry out the work plan. Although the specifics of contract and grant types and agreement language may seem like trivial administrative matters, unfortunately, as discussed in more detail below, traditional contracting or grant-making processes and mechanisms can often be a major barrier to good program implementation and adaptive management. And conversely, use of appropriate mechanisms can greatly enable effective programs.

There are several commonly used ways of awarding contracts in which a sponsoring funder provides money and other resources to an implementer, who is responsible for providing agreed-upon deliverables, which can include both goods and services:

▶ **Competitive award.** A competitive award involves the funder tendering a request for proposals from potential implementers. The funder typically also states the criteria by which proposals will be assessed, which can include both quality of the deliverables and costs. In some cases, the award process can take the form of an open or sealed bid auction. As a rule, competitive awards are useful when the desired deliverables (both quantity and quality) can be easily defined and understood by all parties so that potential implementers are competing primarily on price, as is more typical in shorter-term waterfall-type planning situations. Competitive awards can also seek to address diversification and equity issues by offering preferences for bidders that fit into certain desired categories, such as firms owned by small businesses or by indigenous peoples.

Within the category of competitive awards, typically two main types of contracts can be awarded:

- **Fixed price.** A fixed-price contract details specific deliverables that the implementer will produce for a predetermined price. This type of contract is often described as being more encouraging of innovation because it does not specify how the implementer should do the work but only that they deliver the agreed-upon result by the agreed-upon date. As a result, the implementer has an incentive to develop better and more efficient ways of fulfilling the contract requirements. It also provides the funder with more budget certainty, putting the risk of completing the work if it is more difficult or costly than anticipated on the implementer. Fixed-price contracts are often harder to develop, however, because the implementer has to invest substantial effort in ensuring they are making a feasible bid.

- **Time and materials.** A time and materials contract involves paying the implementer for actual time and expenses that they incur when doing the work, typically at some agreed-upon charge-out rate for time spent or at cost plus a negotiated fee. This type of contract is more forgiving of uncertainty from the point of view of the implementer, but obviously it has the disadvantage of not incenting the implementer to become more efficient and cheaper at their work and leaves open the possibility that funds will be expended without achieving the desired outcomes.

▸ **Sole source award.** A sole source award involves the funder developing a contract with a specific implementer that they believe is best suited to deliver the desired outcomes. Although private entities generally have more latitude to give sole source awards, public agencies generally have to meet certain internal criteria to use them. Note that sole source awards can use either fixed-price or time and materials contracts. If there is a set of sequential work that has to take place, a sole source award can also be used to establish a master service agreement that sets the general framework for a series of more specific task orders. There are also more hybrid models between sole source and fully competitive awards, such as cases in which implementers go through an initial open competitive process to then become part of a small handful of organizations qualified to bid on specific contracts. Sole source awards are often faster to develop, but they can lead to cronyism, in which funders end up favoring the same "usual suspects" at the expense of a more diverse set of implementers.

▸ **Cooperative agreement.** A cooperative agreement is an arrangement between a sponsoring public agency or other funder that provides an implementing organization with funds in support of a defined public purpose. Cooperative agreements are typically more flexible than contracts, and there is often a great deal of latitude for the sponsor and the implementer to agree on the scope and the activities of the work. From an accounting point of view, however, cooperative agreements generally require the implementer to use charge-in rates (what you pay your staff) rather than charge-out rates (what you bill other organizations for your staff) to account for their staff costs, which is either a benefit or a limitation depending on which side of the equation you are on.

Grants differ from contracts in that rather than purchasing a specific service or deliverable, they involve the funder providing resources to the grant recipient that the funder believes will pay off in terms of different outcomes from the grant. Grants thus function more like an investment in which the funder is either lending funds and expecting to get paid back with interest or with some kind of equity ownership in the ongoing venture. Unlike in a traditional financial investment, however, at least some of the payback is in the form of social rather than financial returns. Indeed, different grant and investment types can be put into a spectrum depending on the relative proportion of social to financial returns:

▸ **Implementation grant.** Under a pure implementation grant, there is no expectation of funds being paid back. Success of the investment is measured solely in terms of social return (e.g., a grant to restore a specific wetland that pays back in terms of providing biodiversity habitat and carbon sequestration, or a grant to fund a fellowship that pays back in terms of the ongoing accomplishments of the fellow over the remainder of their career).

▶ **Catalytic grant.** Here again, there is no expectation of funds being paid back. But there is a pathway that assumes that if an initial investment is made, the strategy will become self-sustaining over time (e.g., providing a grant to a linked eco-enterprise that will eventually generate revenue to pay for ongoing conservation). Note that this type of investment can pay off even if the enterprise is not 100 percent self-financing; even if the enterprise can cover only 50 percent of its costs, then this at least frees up 50 percent of funds that could be used to then start another enterprise project.

▶ **Soft loan or program-related investment.** In this case, the funder provides a loan to a grantee that may not otherwise get access to needed capital. The funder may charge a lower interest rate, offer a longer-term payback period, or accept a higher degree of risk that the loan will not be paid back, but in return also hopes to achieve some degree of social return related to their program goals (e.g., providing microcredit loans to small businesses or providing loans to fishing boat operators who want to invest in more sustainable fishing gear).

▶ **Socially screened loan or investment.** In this case, the funder's main goal is to maximize their financial return. However, the funder may put limits on the type of investments being made so as to either promote certain desirable activities or limit undesirable activities (e.g., decarbonizing an investment portfolio by avoiding stocks of oil and gas companies).

▶ **Commercial loan or investment.** Finally, under a commercial loan or traditional equity investment, the expectation is to maximize financial return, regardless of social benefits (e.g., attracting investors to a solar or wind energy project that is expected to deliver competitive returns compared with fossil fuel projects or to a carbon sequestration program that is expected to generate revenue from offset payments).

Many conservation organizations and especially government agencies have contracting and grant-making procedures and mechanisms rooted in traditional procurement systems in which both the quantity and quality of desired deliverables can be clearly defined and specified and in which work plans are developed via a waterfall planning approach over limited time frames (see "Turning Your Strategic Plan Into an

Actionable Work Plan" section above). These more fixed approaches may work for some conservation programs. For example, consider a commercial carbon mitigation program that is looking to invest in organizations that will restore and maintain wetlands for their carbon sequestration benefits over at least a ten-year time frame. The program could use a competitive bidding process to award fixed-price contracts to organizations that agree to deliver parcels of restored and maintained wetlands at the lowest cost per hectare. Or the program could provide loans that would then be paid off as the implementer sells accumulated carbon credits. Presumably, risks such as those posed by periodic droughts or flooding could be calculated and appropriate insurance or other risk hedging tools could then be factored into the investment calculus on both sides.

But these more fixed approaches tend to be challenging to use in conservation and other civil society work in which there is often a great deal more uncertainty regarding the production of desired outcomes, especially using agile design over longer time frames. As a result of this uncertainty, it is difficult for both the funder and the implementer to accurately project costs and benefits, as would be required in a fixed-price contract or a loan arrangement (e.g., think about a program that is looking to work with different indigenous communities along the coast to develop natural resource management plans). The program theory of change calls for developing outreach efforts to build connections to these communities and then working with the communities to develop their management plans. Given that there are probably only a handful of people with the skills and social connections to reach each community, and given that it is impossible to predict whether it will take a week, a month, a year, or a decade to gain the trust of a given community, it is difficult to imagine using a competitive contracting or even grant-making process to fund this work.

In addition to the uncertainty in the award phase, more fixed procurement approaches also have a major downside when it comes to the inevitable need to adapt a program during implementation. As an obvious example, let's say your agency has tendered a large contract to restore degraded wetlands that was awarded through a highly competitive bidding process. The winning bidder has now committed to deliver 10,000 hectares of restored wetland in a certain watershed over a ten-year period. In Year 2 of the project, however, new scientific research emerges that shows most if not all of the wetland locations will be flooded by rising sea levels within twenty years. If you have a fixed-price contract, it may be difficult or expensive to get the firm to agree to stop the current project and rework it to focus on different lands that are less likely to be affected by the rising sea levels. More agile contracting approaches, on the other hand, might allow you to work with the implementer to adapt the work as needed.

Guidance for Awarding Contracts and Grants that Enable Adaptation

Obviously, when it comes to awarding contracts and grants, you absolutely need to follow all relevant procedures and regulations of your organization or agency. But that said, it is important for both program and administrative staff within an organization or agency to work together to figure out how to use (and ideally adapt over time) these procedures and regulations to best support agile and adaptive contracts and grants that maximize your collective programmatic impact:

- **Use your strategy pathways to be as explicit as possible about required work assumptions.** As discussed above, it is often a challenge in the environmental and social sector to precisely define the deliverables for a given contract or grant. Although they are not a panacea, having explicit and shared strategy pathways at least allows all sides to have a common understanding of what work is being proposed as part of a specific contract or grant, what results are anticipated, and what could go wrong. Your strategy pathways will also provide good clues as to whether this work will fit better under a more fixed waterfall implementation approach or a more agile approach and thus which contract or grant mechanisms might be most appropriate.
- **Select contract or grant types that enable appropriate levels of adaptation.** In selecting a contract or grant type, start by thinking about your organization's funding approaches, as defined in Chapter 2. If you are taking a more responsive approach, then you may want to consider contracts or grant types that give more flexibility to the implementing organization to use funds as they see best. However, if you are taking a more strategic approach, you may want to consider contracts or grant types that enable the funder to have more say and closer oversight in how funds are allocated and spent. In either case, however, it is generally better to have contract or grant types that enable adaptation as you collectively learn more about the situation and the successes and failures of your strategies.
- **Set contract or grant time frames to best support adaptation.** Following on the previous point, it is also important that the time frames for your contracts or grants enable change over time. To this end, if you have to use fairly rigid procurement mechanisms, you may want to keep your contracts shorter so that you can issue new contracts to deal with changing circumstances or even write a series of task orders under a master services agreement. This need for short-term mechanisms is particularly important when you are piloting strategies that

you then hope to take to scale, where you might want to use planning grants. By contrast, if you are able to use more adaptable mechanisms, you can issue longer-term contracts or grants that can be adjusted over time as needed.

- **Work closely with your organization's administration to mitigate risk.** Boards, managers, and legal and financial departments in many organizations and agencies are often very cautious in avoiding any activities that might entail financial risk, trigger audits or legal action, or jeopardize the tax status of their organization. As a result, some people in these positions tend to steer program staff far away from what they perceive as unsafe investments that could cross the line into financially risky returns or audit-triggering activities that could then come back and cause problems for the grant-making organization. Unfortunately, however, many of these more risky investments are also those that have the greatest potential social payoff, such as investing in a small local startup NGO that might have trouble completing necessary grant reporting in the short term but could become a major player in your system over time (in the U.S. tax system, an expenditure responsibility grant). To this end, it is helpful to work with these departments in your organization so that they are aware of why these investments might be important and so that they can help your program mitigate risks so as to get as close to this line as needed without going over it.

- **Pay out multiyear grants in declining payments.** If you are a funder making multiyear grants or allocations of resources (e.g., three years), the natural inclination is to divide your grant payments into approximately equal tranches, as shown in Table 3.3a. From the grantee's point of view (and assuming this is an ongoing project strategy), this equally allocated grant payment schedule creates a "cliff" at the end of the grant period that the grantee then has to scramble to cover. Furthermore, from the funder's point of view, allocating all your budget in year 1 means that you have no money to make additional grants in Years 2 and 3. You have to wait until all your payments are completed before you can make new grants in Year 4, as shown by the "New $ awarded" row at the bottom of the table.

  To this end, using declining payments involves paying out a higher proportion of your available grant funds in the first year of a multiyear grant as shown in Table 3.3b. From the grantee's point of view, they get more money to spend upfront (or assuming your contracting mechanism allows it, to put in the bank) and do not hit such a large cliff at the end of the grant. More importantly, the funding program has new money to award new grants every year and spreads out the work of researching and awarding grants more evenly over the three-year cycle. In this approach, however, you do have some extra funds in Years 1 and 2

Table 3.3. The advantage of declining multiyear grant payments

a. Equal Multiyear Grant Payments

Program Year	1	2	3	4	5	6
Grant A	200	200	200			
Grant B	200	200	200			
Grant C	200	200	200			
Grant D				200	200	200
Grant E				200	200	200
Grant F				200	200	200
Total $ spent	600	600	600	600	600	600
New $ awarded	1,800			1,800		

b. The Martin Method: Declining Multiyear Grant Payments

Program Year	1	2	3	4	5	6
Grant A	300	200	100			
Grant X1	200	100				
Grant X2	100					
Grant B		300	200	100		
Grant C			300	200	100	
Grant D				300	200	100
Grant E					300	200
Grant F						300
Total $ spent	600	600	600	600	600	600
New $ awarded	600	600	600	600	600	600

of the funding program, but these can often be used to support pilot grants, as described in more detail above.

• **Ensure that your contract language promotes appropriate information sharing.** Many organizations reflexively include boilerplate legal language in contracts and even in some grant agreements that treats the contract as work-for-hire and thus asserts copyright ownership of intellectual property created as part of the contract or grant. This language then legally limits the ability of the implementing organization to share their findings with the wider community and promote learning. To address this issue, you can put in legal language that allows joint nonrival ownership of all relevant intellectual property, or you can agree to use an open source licensing agreement such as the various Creative Commons licenses, giving all parties rights to use and redistribute materials under certain conditions of providing credit and sharing alike.

Going a step further, you can even use your contract or grant language to actively promote information sharing. In particular, you can use your contract or grant negotiations to develop and agree on language about how results of the work will be appropriately shared with the rest of the world. As we will discuss in Chapter 6, developing the global evidence base for conservation requires getting as many projects and programs as possible to share their results—both their successes and failures. If your organization is providing funds to support implementation of a strategy pathway, then this is your opportunity to include language that states that certain key results will be reported into your organization's outcome database or, better yet, into the appropriate public shared data library. Ideally, this reporting language would become your organization's new standard boilerplate in all similar contracts and grant agreements!

Sources and Further Information

(See FOSonline.org/pathways for links and updated guidance material.)

Setting SMART Goals and Objectives

There is a long history in the business and social sector world of setting goals and objectives:

Peter Drucker (1954), *The Practice of Management.* A foundational work in this field that introduced the concept of management by objective.

Peter Senge (1990), The *Fifth Discipline: The Art and Practice of the Learning Organization.* One of Senge's core disciplines involves creating shared vision.

Jim Collins and Jerry Porras (2004), *Built to Last: Successful Habits of Visionary Companies.* Emphasizes the concept of Big Hairy Audacious Goals as a way to chart a path to success.

FOS (2021), *Planning for Conservation, Develop Objectives: A How-To Guide.* Contains a practical guide to setting goals and objectives in conservation work.

Analyzing Trade-Offs and Conflict

There is a large body of study and practice on conflict resolution that is beyond the scope of this book. Two sources for this chapter:

Kai Lee (1993), *Compass and Gyroscope: Integrating Science and Politics for the Environment.* A good overview of combining the compass of adaptive management with the gyroscope of politics for managing bounded conflict in dealing with large-scale messy ecosystems.

Nick Salafsky (1994), "Ecological Limits and Opportunities for Community-Based Conservation," in *Natural Connections: Perspectives in Community-Based Conservation.* The source for the analysis between natural world and human well-being trade-offs.

Turning Your Strategic Plan into an Actionable Work Plan

A recent Conservation Measures Partnership (CMP) working group review found dozens of guide books and software systems that support waterfall-style work planning (e.g. Asana, Monday.com, Microsoft Project). There are also a number of systems that support more agile task-oriented software development planning (e.g., Jira). Unfortunately, there seems to be a major gap in systems that link strategic planning to agile work planning. This working group is currently exploring extending Miradi Software to help fill this gap.

There are nascent efforts to develop standards for recording conservation actions and costs. For example:

Gwen Iacona et al. (2018), "Standardized Reporting of the Costs of Management Interventions for Biodiversity Conservation" (*Conservation Biology* 32: 979–988). Proposed data fields for capturing the costs of actions.

Assembling a Programmatic Investment Portfolio

There is a wide literature on different methods for prioritizing options:

R. Gregory, L. Failing, M. Harstone, G. Long, T. McDaniels, & D. Ohlson (2012), *Structured Decision Making: A Practical Guide to Environmental Management Choices.* A useful overview of structured decision making; Chapter 8 provides a comprehensive guide to consequences tables.

Kent Messer & William Allen (2018), *The Science of Strategic Conservation.* If you want to go there, this book provides a detailed introduction to various mathematical model-based decision tools.

CMP (Forthcoming), *Making Strategic Planning More Strategic.* A review of different criteria and tools for comparing and selecting strategies.

Awarding Contracts and Grants That Enable Adaptation

The concept of declining payments came from Dan Martin, who ran the MacArthur Foundation's Environmental Program for many years. It is part of a broader approach to the craft of philanthropy that Dan taught all of his program officers that was centered around "the moving spotlight" in which a program (e.g., the Asia-Pacific Region) would focus on three subprogram areas (Melanesia, Southeast Asia, South Asia) over the course of a three-year cycle, making a package of three-year grants in the first area in Year 1, the second area in Year 2, and the third area in Year 3, and then repeating the cycle. This had the benefit of allowing the program officer and the foundation decision makers to devote their travel and attention to one region in a given year, which also fit Dan's preferred funding approach of having funding programs "put gas in the tank of reliable cars whose drivers are generally headed towards desirable destinations."

Key Learning Questions

1. How can we coach teams to be able to quickly estimate objectives at scale?
2. How can we use these analytical tools to more usefully frame and solve conflicts between stakeholder groups?
3. Can we better integrate work planning into the more conceptual analyses of the program cycle?
4. Can we develop and share better cost estimates for key conservation actions in different conditions?
5. How can organizations and agencies (especially larger ones) develop more adaptable contracts while still conforming to required procurement regulations?

PART II

Using and Expanding Your Evidence Base

Part I of this book focused on the actions your program is taking within your system of interest. This work is captured in your evolving situation assessment, strategies, and operations. But your program does not exist in a vacuum. Instead, it is surrounded by your program's ever-growing evidence base, which contains the relevant data, information, and knowledge that can help you and your partners better design and manage your work. Part II of this book is about how you use and expand this evidence base to inform key decisions about your pathways to success.

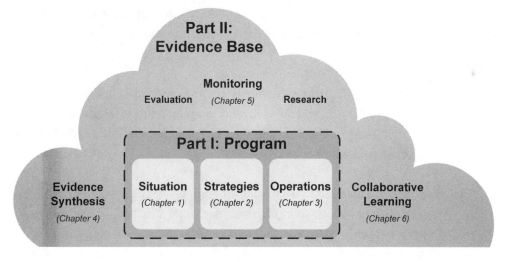

Figure IIa. Sources of evidence.

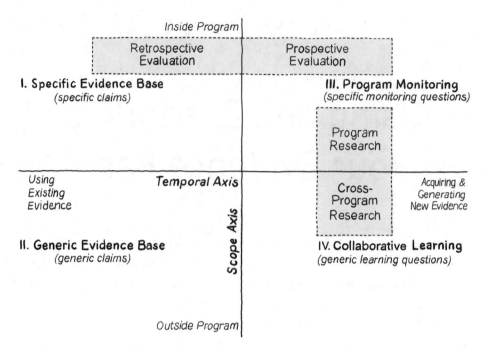

Figure IIb. Sources of evidence.

As shown in Figure IIb, your program's evidence base comes from a number of distinct sources of evidence that can be used to meet a program's analytical needs. These include:

▶ **Existing evidence (Chapter 4).** Available data and information used to support claims you are making as you develop your program's situation assessment and design your strategies. They include both scientific and traditional knowledge and are synthesized from two sources:

I.   **Specific evidence base.** What your program team, partners, and stakeholders already know about your program's particular situation and strategies

II. **Generic evidence base.** What the rest of the world knows about similar situations and strategies

▶ **Future evidence (Chapters 5 and 6).** The data and information you need to collect going forward to answer questions (formulated as hypotheses) needed to adapt and learn from your program. They are generated from two sources:

III. Program monitoring. How you plan to answer questions about your program's situation and strategies through monitoring, evaluation, and research

IV. Cross-program learning. How you plan to answer questions about your program's situation and strategies through collaboration with similar programs

Although many people use the term *claim* synonymously with *hypothesis*, in Figure IIb and throughout this book we are deliberately reserving *claim* for use with existing evidence. We are using *hypothesis* to refer to an assumption that needs to be tested as part of a future monitoring or learning question.

4

Synthesizing Existing Evidence

Quadrants I and II in your program's evidence base involve synthesizing existing evidence to assess the claims needed to inform your program's situation assessment and strategy development. Key analyses in this process include:

- Determining investment in evidence based on burden of proof
- Identifying critical claims requiring evidence
- Compiling evidence sources and assessing claims

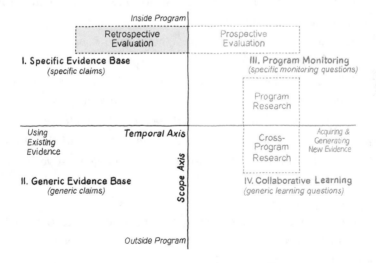

Determining Investment in Evidence Based on Burden of Proof

Before talking about evidence itself, we need to first take a detour to establish a framework for thinking about how much to invest in acquiring and analyzing evidence. A key theme that has run throughout this book involves determining when you need to invest in more sophisticated and resource-intensive gold-standard analytical approaches rather than simpler aluminum-standard approximations. This theme has already come up in various analyses such as:

- ▸ **Systems and situation analyses.** When might it be necessary to do a fully parameterized systems analysis rather than a basic cause-and-effect diagram?
- ▸ **Strategy prioritization.** When would it be helpful to use a mathematical decision tool rather than a stakeholder point-based prioritization exercise?
- ▸ **Work planning.** When could it be useful to develop a complete waterfall work plan that enables critical path analysis rather than a more agile rolling work plan?

In this section, this theme will again reappear when discussing:

- ▸ **Evidence use.** When might it be desirable to commission a full systematic review of the available evidence for a candidate strategy rather than a quick synthesis of locally available project knowledge?
- ▸ **Monitoring and evaluation design.** When would it be appropriate to invest in conducting impact assessments that use experimental (e.g., randomized control trials [RCTs]) or quasi-experimental (e.g., matching to a comparison group) design rather than simpler non-experimental designs (such as pre-test–post-test and time series assessments) to assess the effects of a strategy?
- ▸ **Learning.** When is it preferable to run a quantitative, statistics-driven analysis to determine the efficacy of an action rather than a qualitative assessment of a few case studies?

In each of the above examples, we are not presenting a dichotomous choice so much as endpoints of a spectrum that goes from more rigorous and precise to more cost-efficient and approximate analytical approaches. In most conservation situations, you generally want to use the least expensive approach that is good enough to get you the evidence you need to make a reasonable decision.

Going back to the graph in Figure 4.1 that we first presented in the Introduction, each of these questions is fundamentally asking, "Under what conditions is it worth

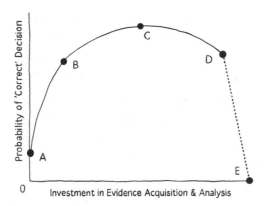

Figure 4.1. Return on investment in evidence.

moving from Point B to Point C?" Answering this overall question requires addressing three subquestions:

▶ **What is the relative cost of each approach?** If the more sophisticated analytical approaches are roughly equivalent in cost to the simpler ones (i.e., there is a narrow gap along the x-axis between Point C and Point B), then it probably makes sense to move to Point C. Or if you have an academic researcher or other partner who is willing to donate the more sophisticated approaches at no cost in time or treasure to your program budget, then again it may make sense to be more rigorous and precise (although even if the analytical work itself is donated, it may require substantial resources from your program to collect the data). But if the more sophisticated approaches require more of your program's scarce time and treasure, as is often the case, then you have to think carefully about when you need to justify this additional investment.

▶ **What is the relative benefit of each approach?** Likewise, if the more sophisticated analytical approaches deliver far more benefit than the simpler ones (i.e., there is a large gap along the y-axis between Point C and Point B), then again it may make more sense to move to Point C. Here, however, the increased benefit has to materially result in better decisions. A sophisticated decision support system may be worse than useless if the decision makers don't really understand the assumptions and limitations inherent in the system or if the system is fully operational only months or years after the decision has to be made.

▶ **What are the consequences of making the wrong decision?** Regardless of costs and benefits, the most important factor governing the choice of which analytical approach to use involves the consequences of making the wrong decision.

In a few situations where there is a high cost of being wrong, it may be necessary to invest in the most sophisticated gold-standard approaches. For example,
if you are working on the last population of an endangered species, your program will severely disrupt the lives of human stakeholders, or your action is likely
to involve expensive legal challenges, then you may have to invest in sophisticated analyses to ensure that you get to the maximum confidence level (Point C
in the graph). In most conservation situations, however, it's probably sufficient
to try to maximize the return on your decision support investment (Point B).
In thinking about the consequences of making the wrong decision in the context
of conservation actions, it is important to remember that choosing not to take
action where action is possible is in itself a decision. Thus, although no manager
wants to be responsible for having made the wrong decision when the stakes are
high, there is potentially a cost to inaction as well as action. Decision makers
need to be encouraged to act where appropriate. The concept of burden of proof
can be used to guide these decisions and help decision makers ensure that they
are making their decision according to acceptable ethical, moral, and professional
standards. In the Common Law tradition, the burden of proof is narrowly defined
as the obligation of one party in a legal proceeding to shift the accepted conclu-
sion away from an oppositional opinion to one's own position, or in effect to
prove a disputed claim (i.e., one is innocent until proven guilty). In making decisions under uncertainty, the concept has been expanded to represent the level of
evidence that a decision maker needs to meet to justify making a change from the
status quo—for example, by taking a proposed action that will have consequences
for different actors in the system.

Guidance for Determining Investment in Evidence Based on Burden of Proof

Salafsky and Redford (2013) reviewed the concept of the burden of proof in different
professional fields including law, medicine, and public safety and used the results to
develop a framework for helping conservationists determine the burden of proof when
choosing to take action within a given scenario (Figure 4.2):

- **Define your scenario.** The concept of burden of proof applies to a given scenario
  in which you are deciding to take action versus the status quo of not taking action.
  This scenario could range from an entire program that is focused on conserving an endangered seabird species to a specific project-level strategy to restore
  a small wetland. You may have different burdens of proof for different scenarios.

- **Determine your burden of proof for the scenario.** For a given scenario, you then need to answer three questions, as shown in Figure 4.2:

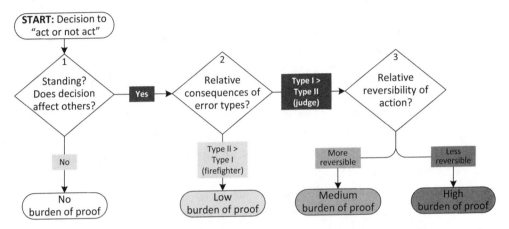

Figure 4.2. Decision tree to determine your burden of proof for taking action within a scenario. Source: Adapted from Salafsky and Redford (2013).

1. *Do you have standing, and does the decision substantially affect others?* In many professional fields, society empowers specific people to make certain decisions on behalf of others (e.g., doctors prescribing medicines, police officers enforcing laws, and pilots flying airplanes). The assumption is that decision makers with professional standing have the training and experience needed to make these decisions within their field of expertise. Similarly in conservation, park rangers, land managers, agency biologists, and indigenous landowners and managers are given authority and responsibility to take certain actions. As a rule, people who do not have professional standing should not take direct conservation management actions unless it is an emergency, in which case "Good Samaritan" rules might apply (e.g., a citizen moving a turtle out of the middle of a highway), but in these cases no burden of proof needs to be met. Likewise, there are many decisions, such as the choice of the logo for your program or whom you hire to be on your program team, that affect only you and your program and thus do not require any formal burden of proof.

2. *What are the relative consequences of different error types?* Decision scientists often talk about two types of errors that can be made in deciding whether

to take action. A Type I error involves taking action where no action is warranted, such as a judge convicting an innocent person of a crime, a firefighter responding to an alarm call when there is no fire, or a mayor ordering a hurricane evacuation when the hurricane misses the city. By contrast, a Type II error involves not taking action where action is warranted, such as a judge letting a guilty person go free, a firefighter not responding to an alarm call when there actually is a fire, or a mayor not ordering an evacuation when the hurricane ends up hitting the city. As a rule, different scenarios have different relative consequences for the two error types. For example, a judge would prefer to let a criminal go free (commit a Type II error) than falsely imprison an innocent person (commit a Type I error). By contrast, a firefighter would prefer to respond to a false alarm (commit a Type I error) than not respond to an actual fire (commit a Type II error).

If you are in a scenario like the firefighter in which there is a lower cost of taking action than of not taking action, then you have defined a low burden of proof for taking action. Examples in conservation might be capturing the last surviving population of a species facing almost certain extinction from current threats or controlling an invasive species. However, if the consequences of an erroneous action exceed the costs of inaction, you need to meet a higher burden of proof (e.g., capturing the last surviving population of a species that is not imminently threatened or releasing a genetically modified organism designed to control an invasive species).

3. *How reversible is the action?* Finally, you need to consider how easy it is to undo a given action. For example, if the punishment for a crime involves prison, then society can at least let the innocent person out of jail and compensate them for their lost time. But if the punishment involves execution, then society needs to make sure they make the right decision before carrying out the sentence because there is no going back, thus mandating a higher burden of proof. In a similar fashion, manually removing invasive species can easily be undone, whereas releasing a genetically modified organism creates a situation from which there is no return.

- **Use your burden of proof to guide your investment in evidence acquisition and analysis.** As a rule, the higher the burden of proof, the more you need to invest in evidence acquisition and analyses so you can be as confident as possible that you get the decision right. You want to get to Point C in Figure 4.1. But conversely, if you are in a lower burden of proof scenario, you need to optimize your investment in evidence acquisition and analysis, which is more likely to be at Point B. Burden of proof thus becomes a subroutine in the decision trees we present later on for investment in evidence and monitoring.

Identifying Critical Claims Requiring Evidence

A closely related concept to the burden of proof involves the evidence that is used to support a given decision. There is a growing movement in conservation and in many other disciplines toward evidence-informed practice (or evidence-based practice). Rather than exclusively rely on personal experience, anecdote, or gut feelings, practitioners make decisions and take actions that are informed by systematic and critical analyses of both their own and the world's previous experiences. Following a recent article published by the Conservation Measures Partnership (Salafsky et al. 2019), we can define:

> ▶ **Evidence.** The relevant data, information, knowledge, and wisdom used to assess one or more claims related to a question of interest.

Evidence makes sense only in the context of a claim about your program. A claim is thus the basic unit of analysis for thinking about existing evidence, as opposed to a hypothesis, which is an assumption that needs to be tested as part of a future monitoring or learning question.

There are many different types of claims relevant to conservation practice, each requiring different types of evidence. Some of these claims may be related to understanding the situation, such as the status of target species or the cause of a threat. Other claims are related to the effectiveness of an action or the conditions under which a given action might be effective. A large part of the art of evidence-based conservation practice thus involves understanding the system well enough to figure out the right set of claims to consider and the sequence in which these need to be assessed. In particular, we can define:

> ▶ **Specific claim.** A proposition about a specific case situation, typically part of your program, such as *"Rats are the primary cause of seabird nest predation on the islands within our program scope"* or *"An outreach campaign to local community members can persuade them to install rat barriers on their boats."*
> ▶ **Generic claim.** A proposition about a generic situation that is often a composite of many specific case situations, such as *"Rats are a primary cause of seabird nest predation on islands around the world"* or *"Outreach campaigns will change target audience attitudes and behaviors."*

This distinction between specific and generic claims is important because, as discussed below in more detail, a conservation program team ultimately needs to assess specific claims about its situation of interest, but most external evidence is about analogous generic claims. As we discuss in greater detail in the "Guidance" section, the shared models found in situation and strategy pathways become important tools to help program teams go through this claim generation and prioritization process.

A large part of evidence-informed conservation involves using analysis of data from specific experiences to determine generic principles about the conditions under which a given action or strategy will lead or at least contribute to desired outcomes. If researchers have a good experimental design or sufficient statistical power, they can show a significant causal relationship between implementation of Action X and achievement of desired Outcome Y without necessarily understanding the mechanism of this hypothesis. This is often how interventions in medicine are assessed. However, it is much more challenging to apply this black-box approach to conservation strategies that take place in more complex ecological and socioeconomic systems and involve multiple intermediate outcomes, long time frames, a host of confounding variables, or different combinations of actions. In these cases, if a strategy results in the desired outcome, it is hard to know with confidence that this outcome was caused by implementation of the strategy. And if the desired outcome was not obtained, it is difficult to figure out why the strategy did not work and what could be done to improve its implementation.

To solve these challenges, there is a growing recognition of the need to use theory of change strategy pathways to articulate the mechanism by which a given strategy is hypothesized to lead to intermediate results and ultimate desired outcomes. As discussed above, a strategy pathway is ultimately a set of claims that can be tested against the evidence base to determine whether and why a conservation strategy is effective.

Guidance for Identifying Critical Claims Requiring Evidence

Using evidence starts with identifying a limited set of critical claims to consider. This process is as at least as much an art as a science. Dozens or perhaps hundreds of claims can be made about any program. Your challenge is to determine which ones need to be assessed and to what degree they need to be assessed:

- **Use your situation and strategy pathways to identify claims.** The process of identifying and prioritizing claims would be difficult if you were starting from a blank slate but is much easier if you can think in terms of the critical assumptions in your situation assessment and the strategy pathways outlining your program's theories of change. Note that at this point, these are specific claims about your program.

In the situation pathway in Figure 4.3a, some critical claims relate to the status of a target factor, the threats affecting this target factor, or the contributing factors in the system. Examples of these claims include:

Overall claim: *Rats are a major threat to endangered and culturally important seabird populations:*

1. *Seabirds populations on our islands are globally important.*
2. *Seabird populations on our islands have low status.*
3. *Seabirds are a culturally important food source.*
4. *Nest predation is a major source of seabird mortality.*
5a. *Rats are the primary cause of nest predation.*
5b. *Other sources of nest predation are less critical.*
6. *Marine vessels are the major cause of rat reintroductions to islands.*

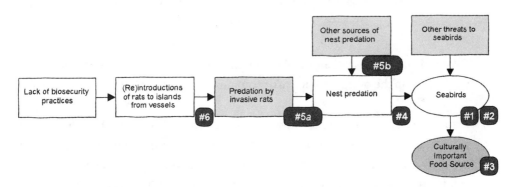

Figure 4.3a. Examples of claims within a situation assessment.
Source: Adapted from Irvine et al. (2021).

Likewise, you can develop claims in your strategy pathways (Figure 4.3b). Here the claims are regarding how you think the situation will change once you implement your actions.

Overall claim: *Rat control plus a biosecurity outreach campaign will reduce seabird nest predation to acceptable levels:*

1. *Traditional landowners will agree to rat control so we can implement control efforts.*
2. *Implementing rat control efforts will eliminate rats from key islands.*
3. *If rats are eliminated, seabird nest predation will be at acceptable levels.*
4. *If vessels implement biosecurity practices, no new rats will access the islands.*

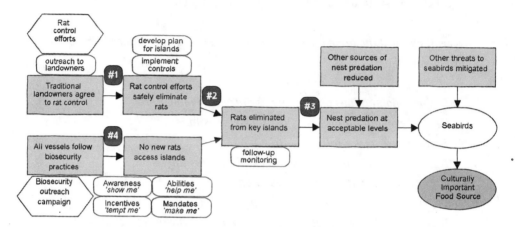

Figure 4.3b. Examples of claims within a strategy pathway.
Source: Adapted from Irvine et al. (2021).

Taken together, these claims from your situation assessment and strategy pathways make up the overall syllogism or argument for the case you are trying to make.

- **Prioritize critical claims.** Technically, every factor and every link between factors in your situation models and strategy pathways represents a claim you are making. The very act of adding a factor or a link between factors to your model means that you are making one or more claims about it. But you can't expect to need or even be able to collect evidence for every last claim. Instead, you want to prioritize the claims that are truly critical to your overall claim or argument. In particular, you want to focus on the claims that are essential to the line of reasoning in a pathway, that represent potential weak spots in your logic, that are more uncertain, or some combination of all these issues. If a claim is more peripheral to your main pathway or you and your partners are pretty confident in the claim, then you probably don't need to spend much time searching for and analyzing evidence about it. Keep in mind that almost all claims could arguably be somewhat critical; if they were not meaningful, you probably wouldn't include these factors and relationships in your models. But the art lies in knowing which claims are truly essential.

- **Develop well-formulated claims.** It is generally easier to assess the evidence for a well-formulated claim than for a vague claim. As a result, you want to try to make your claims as specific, measurable, and time-limited as possible (this is also why in Chapter 3 we advocated for SMART goals and objectives and for setting thresholds of what you need to accomplish where possible). For example, rather than assess the claim:

5a. Something is killing seabirds.

It's much easier to assess claims such as:

  2. Seabird populations on our islands have low status.
  4. Nest predation is a major source of seabird mortality.
  5a. Rats are the primary cause of nest predation.
  5b. Other sources of nest predation are less critical.

One way to arrive at well-formulated claims is to think about them in a hierarchical structure that creates an overall argument for the case you are trying to make. It's often helpful to develop a more general overall claim for a pathway and then think about the more specific claims and even subclaims about specific factors and relationships that support it, as shown in the above examples.

It is also important in developing well-formulated claims to be aware of what types of claims are amenable to evidence. Some important conservation questions, especially those related to value decisions, may not be directly answerable with evidence. For example, the question of whether nonnative salmon should be introduced to a river to provide greater ecological functioning is a values question that cannot be directly answered with data. At best, evidence might be used to validate claims that the introduced fish would potentially thrive and provide the desired ecological benefits, as well as claims that there is support from key stakeholder groups for or against this proposed action.

Compiling Evidence Sources and Assessing Claims

Evidence can be understood as a hierarchy of data, information, knowledge, and wisdom (DIKW), as represented in Figure 4.4. Building on this hierarchy, we define the following sources of evidence:

▸ **Basic data.** Raw observations about a situation of interest. These might include details about the conservation targets, threats, stakeholders, actions, or other basic data for evidence-based practice from program records, monitoring data, or key informants. They also include global data sets of target status, threats, and conservation actions.

▸ **Case-specific information.** Documentation of specific adaptive management or research efforts that describe the question, situation, analytical method, results, and conclusions of each case. These pieces of evidence can range from peer-reviewed scientific publications of RCTs to gray literature case studies or informal field notes. These studies are the core information for evidence-based practice.

▸ **Synthesized knowledge and decision support systems.** Analyses of a set of primary studies about a specific question. These range from formal systematic reviews and maps to subject-wide evidence syntheses to more informal summaries of available evidence. This category also includes decision support systems that summarize evidence and make it available to practitioners when making decisions. These can range from simple decision trees, to more sophisticated searchable online information technologies and decision support software, to traditional knowledge systems used by indigenous peoples. These syntheses and systems contain the knowledge for evidence-based practice.

▸ **Distilled wisdom.** Articulations of known evidence-based principles for a given discipline. These can range from rules of thumb to generic theories of change to codified guidance and principles. These principles ideally encapsulate the wisdom of evidence-based practice.

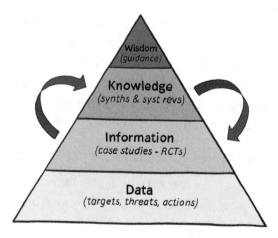

Figure 4.4. Data, information, knowledge, and wisdom (DIKW). RCTs = randomized control trials; synths = synthesized knowledge; syst revs = systematic reviews.

Some experts consider knowledge and especially wisdom to be derived from the evidence found in data and information, thus excluding decision support systems and theory from their formal definition of evidence. However, we find it more practical to compile all these sources of evidence to create:

▸ **Evidence base (for a set of claims).** The body of all data, studies, syntheses and systems, and theory being used as evidence for a particular set of claims. It is typically a subset of your program's evidence base.

Finally, within a given evidence base for a claim, we can classify different sources of evidence in terms of its relation to a system or program of interest:

▸ **Specific evidence.** Evidence from the specific system or program of interest. Examples include data from camera trap studies that show rats are the primary cause of seabird nest predation on one of the islands within our program scope or an organizational report about an outreach campaign in our program area to get fishing boat operators to adopt sustainable fishing practices (i.e., a different desired behavior).

▸ **Proximate (or neighboring) evidence.** Evidence that may not be from your specific system or program but is from a spatially or conceptually close situation that makes it potentially more relevant than evidence from the other side of the country or the world. Examples include data from camera trap studies that show rats are the primary cause of seabird nest predation on nearby islands or an organizational report about an outreach campaign in a nearby district to get fishing boat operators to adopt sustainable fishing practices. Note that the boundaries between neighboring and generic evidence can be somewhat arbitrary and fuzzy.

▸ **Generic evidence.** Evidence from the rest of the world about relevant systems or programs. Examples include a systematic review showing that rats are a primary cause of seabird nest predation on islands around the world or summaries of various strategy pathways around the world seeking to use outreach campaigns to change boat owner attitudes and behaviors about installing rat barriers.

Assessing different types of claims may require different sources of evidence, which can be categorized across four dimensions:

▸ **Direction of effect (or sign).** This dimension assesses whether the evidence supports or argues against the case for a claim. In the balance analogy in Figure

4.5, it refers to the side of balance on which you place each source of evidence (represented by the cylinders):

- Supporting (or positive) evidence builds the case for a claim.
- Refuting (or negative) evidence reduces the case for a claim.

It is vital to distinguish between negative evidence that strongly or weakly refutes the case for a claim and a lack of evidence for a claim one way or the other; often an assessment of "no evidence" refers to the latter. Similarly, "mixed evidence" refers to an evidence base in which there is a blend of positive and negative evidence.

▶ **Strength of effect (or magnitude).** This dimension assesses the degree of support for or against the claim (*strongly supports, weakly supports, mixed, weakly refutes, strongly refutes*). Note that this definition of relative strength explicitly does not include reliability or relevance. In Figure 4.5, it refers to how far away from the fulcrum you place the source of evidence:

- Strong evidence convincingly supports or refutes a claim, such as a research study that shows either a strong positive effect of poison controlling rat populations or a strong negative effect definitively showing the poison does not work.
- Weak evidence only somewhat supports or refutes a claim.

▶ **Reliability (or quality or internal validity).** This dimension assesses the quality of the evidence source or overall evidence base (*very high, high, medium, low*). In Figure 4.5, it refers to the size or weight of the solid sources of evidence:

- More reliable evidence comes from a higher-quality source or evidence base and thus has higher internal validity (e.g., a systematic review, a controlled study, or a reliable source of traditional knowledge).
- Less reliable evidence comes from a lower-quality source or evidence base and thus has lower internal validity (e.g., a single case study or an anecdote).

▶ **Relevance (or external validity).** Finally, this dimension assesses the degree to which the source of evidence applies to the specific claim being made (*very high, high, medium, low*). In Figure 4.5, it refers to whether a given source of evidence should even be placed on the balance, as indicated by the dashed lines:

- More relevant evidence addresses the claim in question and matches key enabling conditions (parameters of the situation of interest that may affect the claim, such as the local rainfall patterns or the government's land tenure policies).
- Less relevant evidence does not directly address the claim in question or does not match key enabling conditions.

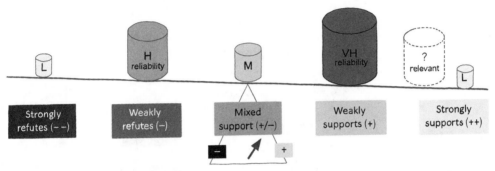

Figure 4.5. An analogy for weighing sources of evidence (represented by cylinders). Source: Adapted from Salafsky et al. 2019.

Guidance for Compiling Evidence Sources and Assessing Claims

The discipline of evidence-informed practice in medicine, conservation, and many other fields has developed an extensive literature and body of practice involved in assembling and using evidence. Some high-level guidance includes:

- **Make the appropriate investment in evidence.** Every hour and every dollar you spend on compiling and synthesizing evidence to support your conservation program is one less that you can spend on implementing your conservation program. So the key is to collect the least amount of evidence needed to make good decisions. To this end, the decision tree and matrix shown in Figure 4.6 and the sample Evidence Capture Sheet shown in Table 4.1 are designed to help you make the appropriate level of investment in collecting and analyzing evidence for a given claim or set of claims:
Start: Identify critical and well-formulated specific claims. The starting point involves determining a critical specific claim that requires evidence per the previous section. If the claim is not critical, it's probably not worth spending time on evidence for it.

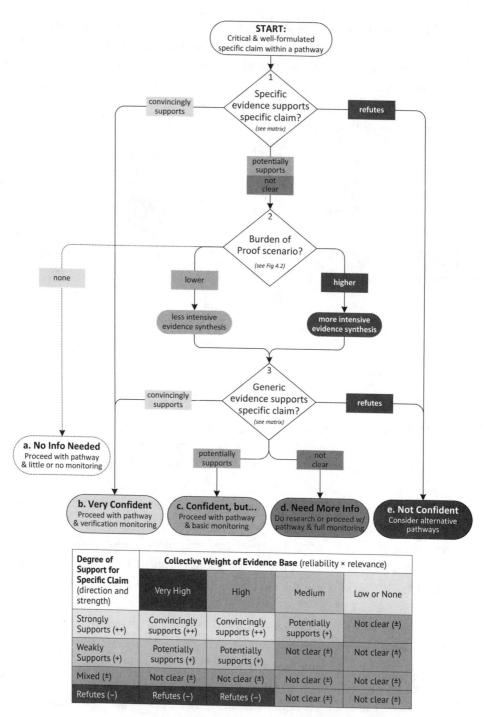

Figure 4.6. Decision tree and matrix for synthesizing evidence to assess claims.
Source: Adapted from Salafsky et al. (2019).

1. *Specific evidence supports specific claim?* The first question asks whether you have enough specific evidence in your existing evidence base to support the claim. If you know based on extensive on-site experience that rats are the main cause of seabird nest predation or if rats are eliminated, seabird nest predation will be at acceptable levels, then you should accept the claim as valid and move on accordingly. And if you know based on local experience that the claim is not valid, then you should also move on and consider alternative pathways. For example, members of your community might know that raccoons are also a main source of nest predation. The bottom line is that if you are truly sure about the claim, you do not need to spend time looking for additional evidence. But if the specific evidence only potentially supports the claim or if it is not clear, then you need to consider finding additional generic evidence.

   For example, in Table 4.1, the Seabird Program team has listed the major claims they are making in their rat eradication pathway. They have then entered the available program-specific and neighboring evidence sources for each subclaim, made initial determinations of the Degree of Support and Weight of Evidence for each claim, and then used this to calculate the Initial Confidence in the Specific Claim.

2. *Burden of proof?* The second question asks about the consequences of making the wrong decision. If you are in a low-risk scenario (per the discussion of burden of proof in the previous section), then you don't need to spend a great deal of time compiling and synthesizing evidence. But if you are in a higher burden of proof scenario, then you probably need to invest more resources in collecting and weighing available evidence, perhaps even investing in doing or commissioning a systematic review. Note that if you have a hierarchy of claims, the burden of proof from a higher-level claim is inherited by its critical subclaims. This is because the subclaims are necessary for the overall claim to hold. For example, in our seabird example, because this is a critically endangered seabird species, the program team has decided this entire program is in a high burden of proof scenario.

3. *Generic evidence supports specific claim?* The last question asks you to gauge the extent to which external evidence supports your specific claim. In some situations, there may already be existing evidence syntheses such as systematic reviews and maps, subject-wide evidence syntheses, or other evidence synthesis projects, completed by specialists who have the skills and training to do this work while minimizing potential bias. If you are using these external reviews, however, keep in mind that they are almost always not evidence for

Table 4.1. Excerpt from evidence capture sheet

Overall claim: Rats are a major threat to endangered and culturally important seabird populations.

Key Subclaims	Who (Date)	Evidence Base for Claim	Degree of Support *Direction and Strength*	Weight of Evidence *Relevance and Reliability*	Confidence in Claim *Support × Weight*	Comments, Gaps, and Monitoring Questions
1. Seabird populations on our islands are globally important.	Team (Year 0)	GE: International Union for Conservation of Nature species maps show that more than 35% of the global breeding population is on 7 program islands.	Strongly supports	High	Very confident	
2. Seabird populations on our islands have low status.	Team (Year 0)	SE: Program annual quick surveys show seabird population rapidly declining on 4 of 7 islands. GE: Research shows seabirds have a low fledging rate (1.4–1.6 chicks/pair) and are thus vulnerable to fast-breeding invasive predators.	Strongly supports	Medium	Confident, but...	Need to do more intensive status monitoring
3. Seabirds are a culturally important food source.	Team (Year 0)	SE: Community elders describe traditional harvests in times of food shortage.	Strongly supports	High	Very confident	
4. Nest predation is the major source of seabird mortality.	Team (Year 0)	SE: Camera monitoring shows raccoons are spreading on islands. PE: Recent unpublished research on nearby islands shows adult seabird survival drops from 77% to 52% when raccoons are present.	Refutes	Medium	Need more info	Need to monitor presence and impacts of raccoons.

Table 4.1. continued

Key Subclaims	Who (Date)	Evidence Base for Claim	Degree of Support *Direction and Strength*	Weight of Evidence *Relevance and Reliability*	Confidence in Claim *Support × Weight*	Comments, Gaps, and Monitoring Questions
5a. Rats are the primary cause of nest predation.	Team (Year 0)	SE: Test traps have shown rats present on the 4 islands. PE: Agency records and literature review show on islands where rats are unmanaged, they have led to severe seabird population declines.	Weakly supports	High	Confident, but …	It's clear rats are a cause but not clear they are the primary cause.
5b. Other sources of nest predation are less critical.	Team (Year 0)	SE: Seabirds have evolved with ravens, raptors, and otters.	Weakly supports	Low	Need more info	
6. Marine vessels are the major cause of rat reintroductions to islands.	Team (Year 0)	SE: Despite prohibitions, there are reports of boats landing on islands. GE: Literature shows boats are a major source of rat introduction.	Mixed	Medium	Need more info	Need to ensure rats can't raft over from nearby islands.

GE, generic evidence; PE, proximate evidence; SE, specific evidence.
Source: Adapted from Irvine et al. (2021).

your specific claim but rather for a generic version of your specific claim. So you need to carefully consider the degree to which each of these sources is relevant to your specific situation.

In other situations, however, it may be necessary for the team to do its own search, assembly, screening, and weighting of available evidence. A range of techniques are available for each of these tasks. Fundamentally, however, these techniques involve searching for and assembling available sources of evidence. Each source is assessed in terms of its weight (relevance × reliability) and its degree of support for the claim (direction × strength of the effect), and then all sources in the evidence base are placed on the balance to arrive at a determination of the Final Confidence in the Specific Claim. There is a spectrum of five outcomes at the bottom of the decision tree in Figure 4.6:

a. *No information needed.* If you are in a scenario in which there is no or a very low burden of proof, it's probably not worth spending resources on evidence synthesis or monitoring.

b. *Very confident.* If you are very confident in your claim, you can proceed to the next claim in your analysis and ultimately to implementation of your strategy. You will probably have to invest in only minimal verification monitoring.

c. *Confident, but....* If you are confident but not absolutely sure in your claim, you can also proceed to the next claim in your analysis and ultimately to implementation of your strategy. Here, however, you will probably have to invest a bit more in your effectiveness monitoring of your strategies or the status of key factors in your situation assessment.

d. *Need more information.* If you are truly unsure about the evidence for your claim, then you need to invest in acquiring and analyzing more evidence. This could take the form of looking for additional existing evidence or conducting needed research. Or if action is more urgent, you can choose to take action, but you then need to invest in more rigorous adaptive management to collect monitoring data.

e. *Not confident.* Finally, if you are confident that your claim is refuted by the available evidence, then you should probably consider either alternative subpathways within a given model or perhaps even an alternative set of actions with different pathways. You may also want to defer action altogether. But you should not invest more in collecting evidence for this claim.

Returning to Table 4.1, the team has now compiled and rated additional external sources of evidence. These have resulted in the final confidence in the specific claim. In addition, the team notes several evidence gaps, which will become the basis for monitoring and learning questions discussed in Chapters 5 and 6.

• **Document and review your evidence.** The evidence capture sheet shown in Table 4.1 provides a living repository of the evidence associated with critical claims in your situation assessment and strategy pathway diagrams. Key columns in these tables include:

- *Claims.* A hierarchical list of the numbered key claims that correspond with the markers in the accompanying situation or strategy pathway diagram.
- *Criticality of claim (not shown in tables to save space).* The degree to which the claim contributes to the overall claim being made. Rating options include *essential, critical, less critical,* and *not critical.* As a rule, however, if a claim is not essential or at least critical, it probably should not even be entered as a row in the table.
- *Date/who.* For each claim, you need to make an assessment of the evidence. This assessment is going to be made on a given date by specific people. Over time, you can make updated assessments as new evidence is added by adding new rows to the table for a given claim. Or you can use new rows to capture different assessments by different people.
- *Evidence base for the claim.* The evidence sources that either support or refute the claim being made. They can be subdivided into specific evidence (SE) from your program or site, proximate evidence (PE) that is not from your exact program but is from a similar nearby program, and generic evidence (GE) from the rest of the world. As outlined in the decision tree in Figure 4.6, you may want to start with specific and proximate evidence and then add generic evidence only if necessary (e.g., Subclaim 3 in Table 4.1 requires only specific evidence). Sources can be directly hyperlinked or listed in a bibliography. If necessary, sources could be listed on individual lines and assessed first individually and then in aggregate, but this greatly increases the amount of work required and probably is not a good return on effort in most cases.
- *Degree of support.* An assessment of the direction and strength of the sources being assessed. Rating options include *strongly supports, weakly supports, mixed, refutes, too early to know,* and *not clear.* (Note that we don't find it helpful in practice to distinguish between *strongly* and *weakly refutes.*)
- *Weight of evidence.* An assessment of the reliability and relevance of the sources being assessed. Rating options include *very high, high, medium, low,* and *none.*
- *Confidence in claim.* Your overall confidence in the claim being made based on the sources shown here. It is calculated by combining degree of support with the weight of evidence from the matrix in Figure 4.6. Rating options include *very confident, confident but . . . , need more info,* and *not confident.*
- *Comments, evidence gaps, and questions.* A place to note comments and identify evidence gaps that might need to be addressed through additional acquisition and synthesis of existing evidence or questions that could be answered through future monitoring, research, or learning.

In some situations, it may also be helpful to have outside parties assess your evidence analysis. In these cases, it can be helpful to add additional columns (not shown in diagram):

- *Review assessment.* The degree to which the reviewers agree with the overall assessment. Rating options include *agree, conditionally agree, disagree, insufficient info presented, we lack expertise to assess,* and *divergent opinions in group.*
- *Criticality of claim.* The degree to which the reviewers think the claim is critical. Rating options include *essential, critical, less critical,* and *not critical.*
- *Review comments.* Comments from the reviewers.

Over time, you can revisit this sheet, updating it with new rows that hold new evidence and revised assessments, or even new claims.

- **Include all relevant forms of evidence as appropriate.** There are many potential sources of both specific and generic evidence for a given claim. These include both scientific knowledge and indigenous or traditional knowledge. But it can be challenging to draw a sharp dichotomy between these two types of evidence when in reality they are at best on a fuzzy spectrum. And it's also important to differentiate the person with the knowledge from the type of knowledge. Maybe at each end of the spectrum one might occasionally find the stereotype of a scientist in a white lab coat consulting a dusty stack of journal articles in a library, or the tribal elder telling an ancestral story that describes how to manage fish harvests. But in the vast middle, it's far more likely to find indigenous land managers who use the scientific method and consult or contribute to the scientific literature. And good Western scientists ideally use all available evidence, including relevant observations by local communities or indigenous peoples. The key is to make sure you include all relevant forms of evidence in your analysis.
- **Be aware of limits to using evidence in decision making.** Although evidence-informed conservation has great potential to lead to better decisions and ultimately more effective and successful programs, it is not a panacea. There are certainly times when sufficient evidence may not be available or affordable. But for some questions that are more about values, evidence may be less relevant. Furthermore, there are cases in which decision makers might choose to ignore or even distrust evidence. Many people may have cognitive or cultural biases that make them less receptive to rational arguments and instead rely on different decision-making heuristics. Even in these cases, however, people may vary in

their willingness to accept evidence based on the type of question being asked. For example, if you are asking purely empirical questions, skeptical people might be more likely to accept scientific evidence:

Q: How many adult salmon are returning to spawn up this stream this season?

Q: How has the average annual stream temperature changed?

By contrast, if there are questions that involve mixtures of empirical data and values, it might be harder to get skeptics to accept evidence:

Q: What is the sustainable harvest limit for species X from this stream?

Q: Should we invest in stream shading efforts to reduce climate change impacts?

And finally, if there are questions that are primarily values-based, there may be even less of a role for evidence in decision making:

Q: Should we stock salmon in this lake system where salmon have never existed before?

Q: How big of a seal population should we support?

The key is to understand who the decision makers are and what evidence they need to make their decisions.

Sources and Further Information

(See FOSonline.org/pathways for links and updated guidance material.)

Determining Investment in Evidence Based on Burden of Proof

This section is directly adapted from a paper that Nick wrote with Kent Redford developing the framework for determining the burden of proof for a program:

Nick Salafsky and Kent Redford (2013), "Determining the Burden of Proof in Conservation" (*Biological Conservation* 146: 247–253). This work also greatly benefited from numerous conversations with Lash LaRue, professor emeritus at Washington and Lee Law School.

Identifying Critical Claims Requiring Evidence

This section is directly adapted from work that Foundations of Success (FOS) has been doing with Parks Canada to identify and vet evidence for key restoration strategies:

Foundations of Success and Parks Canada (2021), *Assessing the Evidence for Adoption of a Conservation Breeding Strategy to Enable Recovery of Southern Mountain Caribou Populations in Jasper National Park.* Evidence capture sheets developed for a multistakeholder workshop review of a critical caribou restoration strategy.

Robyn Irvine, Becky Graham, Paul Harper, André Laurin, Christine Persohn, Kent Prior, Jean-François Bisaillon, Lalenia Neufeld, Judy Boshoven, and Nick Salafsky (2021), *A Practical Approach to Developing the Evidence Base for Conservation and Restoration (CoRe) Projects in Canadian National Parks.* Evidence capture sheets for different strategies. Our seabird nesting example is a fictionalized adaptation of a real-world program developed by Robyn Irvine.

Compiling Evidence Sources and Assessing Claims

Chapter 2 has links to some of the most useful libraries of synthesized conservation evidence. Other sources for this section include:

Nick Salafsky et al. (2019), "Defining and Using Evidence in Conservation Practice" (*Conservation Science and Practice* 1: e27). The source for much of the material in this section.

Collaboration for Environmental Evidence (CEE). This website has a wealth of information including guidance and standards for evidence synthesis.

Glenn Suter (2016), *Weight of Evidence in Ecological Assessment.* A helpful guide to weighing evidence.

Natalie Dubois and Andrés Gómez (2018), *Evidence in Action: Using and Generating Evidence about Effectiveness in Biodiversity Programming.* A useful overview of using evidence in U.S. Agency for International Development work.

Michael Lewis (2016), *The Undoing Project.* A highly readable summary of the work by Daniel Kahneman and Amos Tversky on cognitive non biases and heuristics used in decision making.

Key Learning Questions

1. How can we help program teams identify and test claims routinely within the program cycle? Specifically, how can we:

    1a. Coach practitioners to identify the most critical claims for a given strategy?

    1b. Coach practitioners to get the minimum of evidence needed to test these critical claims?

    1c. Help teams determine when they have sufficient evidence for a claim?

2. When is it necessary to invest in full systematic reviews rather than quicker and simpler evidence syntheses?
3. How do we promote use of evidence in the face of growing evidence that people often rely on internal decision rules (i.e., heuristics) to make decisions?

5

Monitoring and Adapting

Quadrant III in your program's evidence base focuses on the questions you need to answer in the future through monitoring and more formal evaluation and research efforts. A key tenet of good program management is that you integrate monitoring and analysis with implementation to iteratively adapt and improve your work over time. Key analyses in this process include:

- Developing your monitoring plan
- Monitoring your strategy effectiveness
- Defining and measuring long-term program success
- Analyzing data and using the results to adapt
- Reporting to your team and stakeholders
- Exiting responsibly

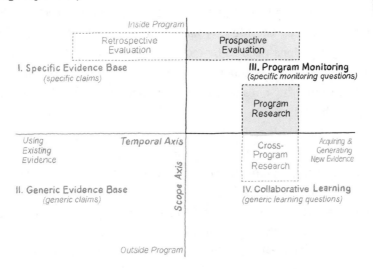

Developing Your Monitoring Plan

In Part I and again in Chapter 4 in more detail, we described how you can use existing evidence as part of your program's overall evidence base to help you develop your situation assessment and strategies (Quadrants I and II in Figure IIb). At the time, however, we also noted that you may identify evidence gaps that will require collecting and analyzing additional data about your situation and proposed strategies. You will probably want to collect additional data about the ongoing implementation of your program's strategies. Your monitoring plan thus summarizes the data you intend to collect in the future through monitoring, evaluation, and research (Quadrant III) to answer your monitoring questions which take the form of hypotheses. As a rule you should develop your monitoring plan concurrently with your strategic plan. The evidence you generate and acquire as you implement your monitoring plan is then added to your ever-growing evidence base, expanding your understanding of your program and the system in which it operates. Key elements of a monitoring plan include:

▸ **Monitoring questions.** The sole point in collecting and analyzing data about your program is for it to be used by somebody for some management or learning purpose. Developing your monitoring questions thus starts by working with your program's decision makers and stakeholders (collectively audiences) that you identified in Chapter 1 to determine what monitoring questions they need answered. Some examples of high-level monitoring questions for typical program decision makers and stakeholders are shown in Table 5.1.

Each of the decision makers and stakeholders you have identified will have their own set of monitoring questions that they need to have answered at different points during the life of your program. In order to be answered, these monitoring questions need to be more specifically articulated as the currently unsupported hypotheses inherent in your situation assessment and strategy pathways. Monitoring questions come from both your situation assessment and strategy pathways:

• *Monitoring questions in your situation assessment.* During the initial design phase of your program, many of your questions will be related to the status and relationship of key factors in your situation assessment, including targets, threats, and contributing factors. In many cases, these questions will be answerable with existing evidence (Quadrants I and II in Figure IIb), as described in Chapter 4. But in some cases, you may have to collect additional primary data to answer these questions. So you need to add the relevant monitoring questions to your monitoring plan.

Furthermore, over the life of your program you will need to come back and revisit these monitoring questions every so often to make sure that your original analysis still holds and no adjustments are needed. In particular, you might want to look for early warning signs of new threats or contributing factors that might be emerging and require attention. There may also be precipitating events that necessitate changes to your monitoring plan out of the normal cycle. If there is a political event, an economic crisis, or a natural disaster that imposes major shocks to the system, then you will want to revisit your strategic plan and your monitoring plan as needed to account for these changes.

- *Monitoring questions in your strategy pathways.* During the design phase of your program, you may also need to fill gaps in the existing evidence base you are using to develop your proposed strategy pathways. For the most part, however, your strategy pathway questions will focus on assessing the effectiveness of your actions over time so that you can then manage and adapt as necessary.

▶ **Factors and indicators.** Answering each monitoring question will require collecting data about one or more factors in your situation assessment or problem pathways. Indicators (or metrics) are the variables that describe the specific data you plan to collect and analyze about each relevant factor. When used to assess progress toward goals or objectives, indicators are sometimes called key performance indicators (KPIs) in the business world. Indicators are generally categorized as:

- *Quantitative indicators.* Includes both continuous variables (measured by decimal numbers) and discrete variables (measured by integers or other limited sets of numbers).
- *Qualitative indicators.* Includes both ordinal variables (categories that are in some order such as *very high*, *high*, *medium*, or *low*) and nominal variables (unordered categories such as species type).

Another way to think about indicators includes dividing them into:

- *Natural (or direct) indicators.* Direct and usually quantitative measurements of a variable of interest (e.g., <*hectares of wetland restored*>, <*average household income*>).

Table 5.1. Key audiences and their high-level monitoring questions

Decision Makers and Stakeholders	Examples of Their High-Level Monitoring Questions
Program team	Does our program team adequately represent our stakeholders? Is our understanding of the situation correct? Can we reduce uncertainty in key gaps in this understanding? Is a given strategy on track? Are the individual projects we support achieving expected results? Is a given strategy effective? How should we adapt a given strategy? How should we adapt our overall portfolio of strategies? Are we achieving long-term durable success?
Organization leader or investor	Are the reported results of this program credible? Are our resources being used appropriately and efficiently? Does this work contribute to our organizational strategies? Should we continue to invest in this work? Are we achieving long-term, durable success?
Government agency	Is this work in accordance with our policies and aims? Are taxpayer dollars being used wisely? Should we continue to authorize and support this work? Are we achieving long-term, durable success?
Local stakeholders	Is this program affecting our lives? Are proper social safeguards in place? Should we continue to support this program? Are we achieving long-term, durable success?
Conservation community	What lessons can we apply from this program to our work?

- *Proxy indicators.* Indirect and usually quantitative measurements of a variable of interest (e.g., *<numbers of sightings of wetland-dependent birds>* as a proxy for wetland health, *<household consumption of rice>* as a proxy for income).
- *Constructed indicators.* Assessments of a variable along a rating scale or through some type of index (e.g., *<an index of wetland health>*, *<ratings of household income along a 1–5 scale>*). Although constructed indicators are typically treated as qualitative data, in some cases they can be analyzed via quantitative data analysis techniques.

Building on the criteria in the *Conservation Standards*, good indicators meet the criteria of being:

- *Measurable.* Able to be recorded and analyzed with quantitative or qualitative data.
- *Precise.* Defined the same way by all people (e.g., specifying *<number of adult birds>* so that it doesn't get confused with *<number of breeding pairs>* or *<number of adults and juveniles>*).
- *Consistent.* Not changing over time so that it always measures the same thing (e.g., using *<present value currency>* so that you can directly compare the relative amounts of money year over year).
- *Sensitive.* Changes proportionately in response to the actual changes in the condition being measured (e.g., if you are using household rice consumption as a proxy indicator for income, that rice consumption actually increases in the same proportion as income).
- *Understandable.* Both the indicator and its underlying concepts can be clearly communicated and understood by different people.

▸ **Monitoring design and methods.** The data needed to answer a given monitoring question can often be collected through a range of approaches that draw from evaluation design. At its core, monitoring always involves measuring indicators to make some sort of comparison within or between groups of individual monitoring units drawn from a defined population.

In evaluating the effectiveness of a strategy, you first have to choose the type of comparison:

- *Comparing a group affected by your intervention to itself over time (i.e., non-experimental design).* This type of comparison involves measuring how the indicators for one or more factors in a strategy pathway change in only the units affected by your interventions. The comparison can be a simple pre-test–post-test design in which you measure your indicators before you start the intervention and then again after the intervention. Or you can use a time series design in which you measure your indicators at multiple intervals both before and after the intervention. These comparisons do not necessarily establish causal relationships but are often both technically and ethically easier to do and rigorous enough to determine whether your interventions are working.
- *Comparing a group affected by your intervention with a group not affected by your strategy over time (i.e., quasi-experimental or experimental design).* This type of comparison involves measuring how the indicators for one or more factors in

a strategy pathway change in those affected by your interventions compared with those not affected by your interventions. The gold standard for this type of comparison is an experimental design (i.e., randomized control trial [RCT]) in which you randomly assign individual units to a treatment group (those affected by your interventions) and a control group (those not affected by your interventions). You then measure your indicators in the treatment and control groups before and after the intervention to determine whether there is a difference. Or you can use a quasi-experimental design in which you match comparison group individuals to treatment individuals on important characteristics, thus attempting to make their exposure to the intervention the only difference between the two groups. Finally, you can use various statistical control techniques to analyze the effect of the treatment on different individual units. These comparisons are the best option for establishing causal relationships, but experimental design in particular tends to be expensive and subject to various ethical questions. Quasi-experimental and statistical control designs are often more cost-effective approaches to measuring impact, but they can be very difficult and complex to implement correctly.

A second set of considerations has to do with how you choose which individual units within your population to measure:

- *Censusing.* In a few cases, you can monitor the entire population of interest, such as the total number of hectares of wetland restored or the average income of all of the households involved in your sustainable fishing strategy. If you can monitor the entire population to an acceptable level of precision, then you do not need to worry about statistical analyses because by definition your monitoring group represents the entire population.
- *Sampling.* In many other cases, especially when working at larger scales, you cannot reasonably monitor the entire population. In these cases, you need to develop a sampling frame and then use statistical analyses to determine how confident you can be that your result from the sample truly represents the entire population. There are many types of sampling frameworks, such as stratifying the population to be sampled (into various subgroups) or using random versus purposeful selection of the units to measure. As a rule, bigger samples reduce the level of uncertainty more than smaller samples but are usually more expensive and time consuming to collect.

Finally, you need to think about the specific data collection methods you will use to collect data for each indicator. Each type of indicator will probably have one or more candidate methods associated with it. For example, you might directly measure hectares of wetland restored by *<compiling project records>*, *<conducting ground surveys>*, *<conducting aerial surveys>*, or *<downloading and analyzing satellite imagery>*. You might measure average household income by *<conducting a household survey>*, *<analyzing available tax records>*, or *<estimating through direct observation of household economic activities>*.

Building on the criteria in the *Conservation Standards*, good methods meet the criteria of being:

- *Accurate.* The data collection method has little or no margin of error.
- *Reliable.* The results are consistently repeatable; each time that the method is used, it produces the same result.
- *Cost-effective.* The method does not cost too much in relation to the data it produces and the resources the program has.
- *Feasible.* The method can be implemented by people on the program team.
- *Appropriate.* The method is acceptable to and fitting within cultural, social, and biological norms.

There are entire books and university courses that focus solely on monitoring design, sampling frameworks, and data collection methods, so providing detailed guidance here is beyond the scope of this book. Overall, as discussed in more detail in the "Guidance" section below, you want to select the least expensive monitoring design, sampling framework, and methods that will give you an acceptable level of certainty for the decision you are making. That said, in almost all cases, the single best monitoring method is to use existing data (collected by someone else for some other purpose) instead of collecting new data, assuming these data are available and fully meet your needs.

▸ **Adding monitoring activities to your work plan.** Once you have developed your candidate list of monitoring questions and their associated indicators and methods, you need to figure out who will actually collect and analyze the data. Any monitoring, even just harvesting data from the internet, requires some expenditure of your team's scarce time and treasure and must be tracked to ensure it gets done when needed. To this end, you need to explicitly build your monitoring activities into your ongoing work plan, including assigning specific tasks for people to complete in specific time frames and allocating the level of team effort and other resources to this work. Once you have completed your initial monitoring work plan and have assigned work to your team and calculated the total costs of this work, you may well be facing sticker shock. You may have to revisit your plan and decide where you can economize by using cheaper methods or even deprioritizing certain questions or indicators for data collection, keeping in mind, of course, your burden of proof requirements. Finally, as you implement and track your work plan, you should also track implementation of your monitoring plan, updating and adapting it as needed.

▸ **Monitoring data information system.** A key part of your monitoring plan involves determining how you will collect, store, clean, analyze, and back up your monitoring data. These tasks are greatly facilitated by incorporating these data into your program's overall information system. You typically will need to have different information subsystems for different types of data. For example, you might store survey data in one type of database and spatial mapping data in another. Often these systems will not be unique to your program but will be shared across multiple programs within your organization or even across organizations. Ideally, however, these subsystems will be sufficiently integrated to enable easily combining different data as needed for analyses and reporting. The key is to have a common data framework so that each subsystem shares the same objects (i.e., units of analysis or data records) and attributes of these objects (i.e., data fields), thus allowing integration.

Guidance for Developing Your Monitoring Plan

Each type of monitoring question and its associated indicators and methods requires its own specific guidance that is beyond the scope of this book. But some general points for developing monitoring plans for programs include:

• **Make the appropriate investment in monitoring.** Every hour and every dollar you spend on monitoring your conservation program is one less that you can spend on implementing your conservation program. So the key is to have the simplest, most efficient monitoring plan you can develop that gets you the evidence needed to make good decisions. Per the previous section, a given monitoring question can usually be answered in a number of different ways. For example, if you need to understand whether rats are the main cause of seabird nest predation on an island, you could look for signs of rat teeth marks on broken eggshells at a few seabird nests. Or you could set up an elaborate controlled experiment in which you exclude rats (but not other winged predators) from some nest areas and then compare predation rates with those of control sites where rats still have access.

As you might suspect by now, this is yet another case where gaining additional certainty in your decision making typically requires an increasing investment of resources in evidence acquisition and analysis, as shown in Figure 0.8 in the Introduction. It's fairly inexpensive to look for rat teeth marks on a few eggshells, but even if you do so, you can't say for sure whether rats are the main cause of predation. On the other hand, although the controlled experiment excluding rats should give you more confidence in your hypothesis that rats are the main predation source, it also takes a lot more time and treasure. Some monitoring questions are inherently cheap to answer with complete certainty (e.g., how many people did we train in the workshop?), but most others require making a decision about how much to invest in getting an answer.

As shown in more detail in the decision tree in Figure 5.1 and the examples in Table 5.2, deciding how much time and treasure to invest in monitoring for a given question related to a conservation action depends on the following:

- *Criticality of the monitoring question.* The starting point for deciding on how much to invest in monitoring is the utility of the monitoring question. How useful is the evidence that will come from answering the question? To be blunt, if there is no decision maker or stakeholder who will use the data from monitoring, then there is not much point in doing the monitoring.
- *Confidence in the existing theory and evidence base for this question.* If you have high confidence that your diagnosis of the problem is correct and that your proposed action will work in your program's context, then you don't need a sophisticated monitoring design. You can just go ahead and implement your actions at scale and then do a minimal amount of verification monitoring to confirm that the actions have indeed been implemented and verify that the expected outcomes are being achieved over time. However, if you have lower confidence in your understanding of the situation—and the mechanism of change from your intervention to the desired outcome—then you need to think about the consequences of your decision to take action.
- *Burden of proof.* If you are in a low-risk situation (per the discussion of burden of proof in Chapter 4), then again you generally don't need a sophisticated monitoring design. But in this case, given that you have less confidence in

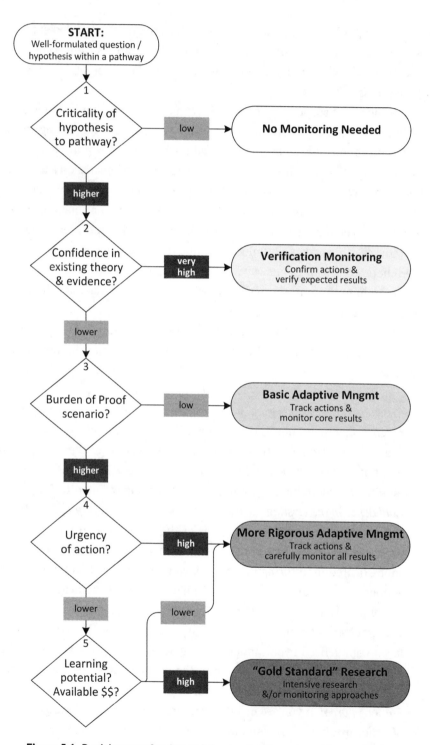

Figure 5.1. Decision tree for determining level of investment in monitoring.

your understanding of the situation, you may want to invest in a basic adaptive management approach that involves monitoring of relevant results along your strategy pathway to ensure that your actions are on track. However, if you are in a higher-stakes situation such as working on an endangered species or on actions that will disrupt people's livelihoods, then you next need to think about the urgency of action.

- *Urgency of action.* If there is high urgency to take action, then you can't afford to wait while you study the problem. Instead, you need to take action under a more rigorous adaptive management approach, ensuring that you allocate sufficient resources to carefully track not just the anticipated results of your actions itself but also any related results in the system so that you can quickly react if there are unexpected consequences of your actions. However, if there is lower urgency to take action, then you need to consider your available resources and the learning potential in your situation.

- *Learning potential and available resources.* Finally, if there seems to be high collective learning potential *and* you have the necessary resources, then it may be appropriate to take the time to invest in high-quality gold-standard research so that you can reduce your uncertainty as much as possible. But if you don't have the resources, you may have to revert to an adaptive management approach at the level of rigor you can afford.

- **Articulate specific hypotheses.** As stated above, collecting and analyzing both existing evidence and future monitoring data are much easier when you have specified exact questions in the form of specific claims or hypotheses that can be tested and falsified. The first column in Table 5.2 shows the specific hypotheses that need to be tested to diagnose and treat various medical conditions and the resulting actions and monitoring. In an analogous fashion, the middle column shows specific hypotheses involved in diagnosing the threat to common and endangered nesting seabirds. And the third column shows specific hypotheses about a coastal zoning strategy to enable wetland migration over the long term in the face of climate change. These specific hypotheses combined with the riskiness of the situation and your level of certainty govern what you need to monitor and how much you need to invest in this monitoring work.

- **Bring in formal evaluation only where necessary.** As shown in Figure IIb, we are defining formal evaluation as being only a subset of your overall monitoring work. All monitoring work by definition involves evaluative thinking such as that described in the "Analyzing Data and Using the Results to Adapt" section below.

Table 5.2. Examples of different levels of investment in monitoring

Medical Analogy	Diagnostic Hypothesis in Situation Pathway	Action Hypothesis in Strategy Pathway
High Confidence in Existing Theory and Evidence → Verification Monitoring		
Situation: Hairline fracture in arm (shown in x-ray) **Hypothesis:** Immobilizing arm for 6 weeks will heal arm **Action:** Cast arm **Monitor:** Proper application of cast, quick check of arm functioning	**Situation:** Eggs of a common seabird being eaten by predator **Hypothesis:** Rats are the main cause of nest predation (clear existing evidence) **Action:** Eradicate rats **Monitor:** Rats killed, seabird nesting success	**Situation:** Jurisdiction has strong permit system **Hypothesis:** New coastal zoning policy will cause no new buildings built in areas enabling wetland migration **Action:** Develop and enact new policy **Monitor:** Policy enactment, building permits issued for sensitive areas
Lower Confidence and Low Burden of Proof → Basic Adaptive Management		
Situation: Compound fracture in arm with possible infection **Hypothesis:** Immobilizing arm for 10 weeks will heal arm **Action:** Cast arm and prescribe antibiotic **Monitor:** Proper application of cast, track arm functioning, core body temperature, and wound healing	**Situation:** Eggs of a common seabird being eaten by predator **Hypothesis:** Rats are a possible cause of nest predation **Action:** Eradicate rats **Monitor:** Correlation of rat density and damaged eggs, seabird nesting success	**Situation:** Jurisdiction has weak permit system **Hypothesis:** New coastal zoning policy will cause no new buildings built in areas enabling wetland migration **Action:** Develop and enact new policy and enforcement **Monitor:** Policy enactment, building permits, presence of new buildings in sensitive areas
Lower Confidence and Higher Burden of Proof and High Urgency → More Rigorous Adaptive Management		
Situation: High fever of unknown origin **Hypothesis:** Possible bacterial infection? **Action:** Prescribe antibiotic and continue diagnostic work M**Monitor:** Temperature, blood work, and chest x-rays	**Situation:** Eggs of endangered seabird are suddenly being eaten by predator **Hypothesis:** Rats are a possible cause of nest predation **Action:** Eradicate rats and continue diagnostic work **Monitor:** Correlation of rat density and damaged eggs, other possible predators, seabird nesting success	*Example not relevant because coastal zoning in the face of climate change is not urgent.*

Table 5.2. continued

Medical Analogy	Diagnostic Hypothesis in Situation Pathway	Action Hypothesis in Strategy Pathway
Lower Confidence and Higher Burden of Proof and Lower Urgency → Gold-Standard Research		
Situation: Persistent unexplained gut pains after COVID-19	**Situation:** Eggs of endangered seabird are occasionally being eaten by predator	**Situation:** Jurisdiction has weak permit system, and developers will sue
Hypothesis: Possible bacterial infection?	**Hypothesis:** Rats are a possible cause of nest predation	**Hypothesis:** New coastal zoning policy will cause no new buildings built in areas enabling wetland migration
Action: None	**Action:** None	**Action:** None
Monitor: CT scan, endoscope, design experiment to test diet effects, enroll in research study	**Monitor:** Develop controlled experiment to test whether rats are cause of the decline	**Monitor:** Develop fully parameterized decision model

In this book, however, we reserve the use of the term *evaluation* for a more formal, often third-party approach to assessing program outcomes designed to help those responsible and accountable for conservation actions determine whether their interventions are working. If you need to do a formal evaluation, here are a number of different evaluation types that you may want to consider:

- *Developmental, formative, or summative evaluation.* Developmental evaluation is most akin to research and development in the private sector. It is generally used when quick answers are needed to design appropriate interventions or adjust current interventions. Therefore, developmental evaluations often occur at the beginning of implementation of a program. Formative evaluation is used to help managers learn from a program's past actions to improve future actions. Accordingly, one key element of this type of evaluation is recommendations produced by the evaluator to be applied to a subsequent implementation phase. Formative evaluations therefore generally take place during active implementation of project or program actions. Finally, summative evaluation almost exclusively concerns itself with answering the question, "Did our interventions work or not?" It is thus generally conducted at the end of the life of a project, program, intervention, or funding cycle. Although some people feel strongly about the distinctions between these three types of evaluation, real-world evaluations often are a blend of these different types.

- *Independent (or external) versus participatory evaluation.* A key goal of any evaluation is objective analysis of what's working, what's not working, and why. There are generally two camps when it comes to beliefs related to who should actively participate in an evaluation and how they should participate. The independent evaluation camp holds that for an evaluation to be truly objective, program participants or managers should not be involved in any way. The participatory evaluation camp believes that managers and those most affected by the program must be involved in order to adequately represent and analyze the program, thus leading to a more valid representation of results and a better use of the evaluation findings. There is no one right way here; it depends on the purpose and audience for the evaluation. In many cases, programs employ a mix of external and internal evaluators.

  There are certainly some monitoring situations in which you will want or even need to invest in rigorous external evaluations. For example, your funder or enabling legislation may require that your work be evaluated by an independent evaluator as a precondition for receiving current or continued funding. But in our experience (as both evaluators and evaluees), for complex conservation programs any external evaluator will inevitably have to work closely with your team and partners to design and implement the evaluation, even if it is supposed to be a third-party evaluation. To this end, you will be better off acknowledging this reality and working with the evaluator to get the evidence needed to both validate and improve your program.

- *Process audit versus impact evaluation.* A process audit is used when you are interested in knowing whether activities are being implemented according to plan or in compliance with a standard approach or policy. By contrast, an impact evaluation is used when you are interested in measuring the outcomes of your interventions.

These approaches to evaluation can be combined in ways that are appropriate to your specific program. For example, you may commission an external evaluator to help you conduct a participatory formative evaluation.

Monitoring Your Strategy Effectiveness

There are three main sets of monitoring questions that you and your team can ask about the effectiveness of a given strategy pathway, each requiring the collection of different data:

▶ **Did we do what we said we would do?** You've probably heard many times that monitoring should "focus on outcomes, not just counting actions or outputs." And results are what ultimately matter. Nonetheless, you need to monitor both actions *and* results to adaptively manage your work. One obvious reason to monitor your actions is to identify management problems that you need to address. If an action has not been implemented, perhaps there is a good reason, but this could also be a red flag that something is wrong and that some sort of management attention may be needed to correct the problem. In addition, if you are trying to determine whether your actions are effective, the first thing you need to know is whether you actually were able to implement your actions as you planned. It's hard to assess whether an action was effective if it was never implemented in the first place! More specific questions and their associated data needs include:

Monitoring Questions	Data Needs
Did we implement our actions as planned? If not, why not?	Status of actions and activities
Were these actions cost-effective? If not, why not?	Actual costs of actions and activities
Did our actions conform to relevant policies? If not, why not?	Data related to policies

▶ **Did we get the expected results?** In addition to monitoring your actions, it's important to monitor your progress in achieving key results in your strategy pathway. This will help you determine whether you are on track to achieve your desired outcomes or whether the system is behaving differently than you anticipated, thus changing your pathway to success. More specific questions and their associated data needs include:

Monitoring Questions	Data Needs
Did we see the results we expected to see? If not, why not?	Status of results in pathway
Did we achieve our desired objectives and goals? If not, why not?	Progress toward objectives and goals
Did causal relationships hold as expected? If not, why not?	Relationships between results

▶ **Were there any surprises?** Finally, in addition to monitoring the core of your strategy pathway, you may also need to track other related factors that might influence your outcomes, either in your strategy pathways or even going back to your situation assessment. This is particularly important if you are not seeing the results you expected or if you are concerned about unintended consequences for key stakeholder or under-represented groups. More specific questions and their associated data needs include:

Monitoring Questions	Data Needs
What other factors influenced the results?	Status of key factors
Were there any unintended consequences?	Indicators related to social safeguards

Guidance for Monitoring Your Strategy Effectiveness

If you have developed good strategy pathways, answering the questions described above is straightforward. There are only a few things that you need to monitor and record in order to answer all of these questions:

- **Monitoring your actions.** Monitoring actions typically does not require a complicated monitoring plan. At a minimum, a simple checklist that includes whether each action was completed may suffice. If a planned action was not carried out, you should also record why it didn't get done. For example, Miradi Software enables users to rate the progress toward each strategy, action, or activity with the following ratings:

  Completed (++): Successfully accomplished
  On track (+): Ongoing, generally on track
  Minor issues (±): Ongoing, has minor issues that need attention
  Major issues (−): Ongoing, has major issues that need attention
  Not yet (<): Scheduled for future implementation
  Abandoned (x): No longer relevant or useful
  Not known (?) - Lack of sufficient information to assess progress status

In addition to the rating, you can note important and relevant details that may facilitate corrective action. A typical report of action tracking for a strategy might look like the outline and chart in Figure 5.2.

In addition to tracking your action progress, it is helpful to track the costs of implementing your work plan. As mentioned in Chapter 3, many organizations have an existing chart of accounts that they use to track staff time and other expenditures within their financial system. Often, however, these systems tend to code activities by standard accounting categories (e.g., staff time, consultant time, facilities, equipment, travel) rather than by programmatic activities (e.g., Action A, Task 2), so you may need to work with your accounting colleagues to develop additional or substitute accounting codes that better link to your program strategies. These accounting codes can be incorporated into the timesheets that all program team members fill out and budget reports for program expenditures. Collecting and analyzing how much time and treasure you spent on each action will allow you to better track and adjust resource assignments, create more accurate, forward-looking budget estimates, and ultimately assess the cost-effectiveness of different actions.

Finally, if your organization or your funder requires you to report specific information in relation to key policies and guidelines, you need to make sure you are collecting the necessary data to complete these reports. For example, you might need to track the proportion of funds spent in different jurisdictions or whether funds were expended on prohibited items or activities.

▶ **Monitoring your program results.** In addition to monitoring your actions, it's even more important to monitor your progress along your strategy pathway, including, in particular, your objectives and goals that represent critical achievements along your theory of change. There are three main approaches to measuring progress toward results incorporated in Miradi Software:

• *Results progress ratings.* The simplest approach is to qualitatively rate progress toward a given result with the following ratings (Figure 5.3a):

Achieved (++). Desired result has been successfully achieved at the defined level.
On track (+). Desired result likely to be successfully achieved at the defined level.
Partially achieved (±). Desired result has been only partially achieved or mixture of success and failure.
Not achieved (−). Available information shows desired result has failed to be achieved or undesired result produced.

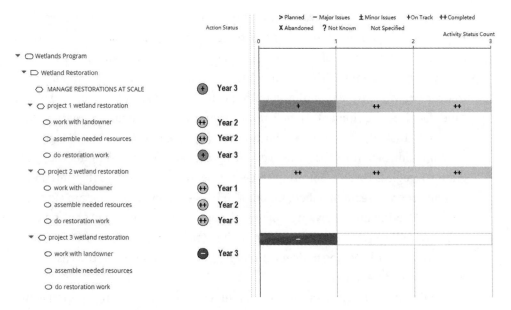

Figure 5.2. Tracking actions in Miradi Software.

Not yet (<). Too early to expect desired result.

No longer relevant (x). Result is now assumed to be not achievable or not necessary.

Not known (?). Lack of sufficient information to assess result status.

- *Progress percentage.* A second approach to assessing progress toward a given result is to report on the degree of progress toward an objective or goal (Figure 5.3b).
- *Indicator values.* The final approach is to measure one or more indicators that represent progress toward completing an objective or goal. This approach can use natural, proxy, or constructed indicators and thus provides the most valid assessment of the result (Figure 5.3c).

As discussed in more detail in the next section, each of these approaches can be used to measure program-level results, including rolling up project-level results to the program level.

- **Monitoring your strategy pathway's context.** In addition to monitoring key points along your core strategy pathway, you may also need to track related factors that could potentially affect your understanding of your theory of change. These potential confounding factors include:

- *Enabling conditions.* Peripheral factors in your strategy pathway diagram that you assumed might affect your ability to implement your strategy.
- *Other strategies.* Additional strategy pathways implemented by your team or by other actors that might affect your ability to implement your strategy.
- *Additional and newly emerging factors.* Other factors in your situation assessment (e.g., threats, contributing factors) in the overall system that either can be found or need to be added to your situation model that might affect your ability to implement your strategy.

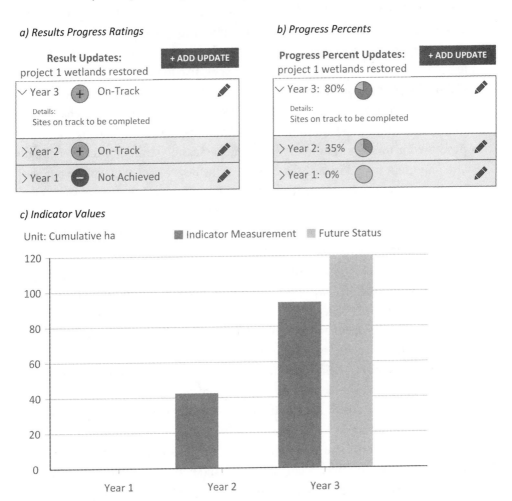

Figure 5.3a, b, c. Three approaches for tracking progress toward results in Miradi Software.

As you might imagine, there are often dozens of potential confounding factors that you need to consider. The trick is to select and monitor only the most important ones that help you understand and improve your strategies and to invest as little time and treasure as possible to get the evidence you need to make decisions.

Across all three of these elements of measuring conservation effectiveness, there are some overarching considerations to keep in mind, especially when working in large, complex programs:

- **Allow for variable project time frames.** In most programs, it's unlikely that all of your projects or strategies will be on the same time frame. Instead, especially when you are scaling up an initial pilot approach, it's far more typical that your projects and strategies will be on different time schedules. So, five years into your program, you may have a couple initial pilots that are already in their fourth or fifth years, a few more second-iteration projects that are now two to three years old, and if your scaling is working properly, a bunch of projects that have just started. Because you can't expect a two-year-old project to be as far along your theory of change as a five-year old project, you need to track and analyze results accordingly.
- **Account for unseen system effects.** When assessing strategy effectiveness, it's also important to understand the context of the larger system in which your work is taking place. In particular, always be aware that the effect you are seeing may be the result not of your work but rather of some other positive or negative force in the system. For example, maybe it wasn't your outreach campaign that actually changed people's behavior, but instead it was a government policy or some new market opening up to provide incentives.

  As a simple analogy, consider a race between two crew teams rowing along two parallel stretches of river, as shown in Figure 5.4. When the race starts at Time 0, both teams are in an equal position. But at the end of Time 1, Team A has crossed the finish line and achieved its objective, but Team B has only made it halfway to its equivalent objective. So which team has done better—and thus should receive the accolades and awards from its parent organization and society? It seems like an easy question until you get a bit more information and you realize that Team A has had a substantial current flowing in its direction so that all the crew had to do was sit in the boat and get pushed across the finish line, whereas Team B had an even stronger current working against it and had to work incredibly hard just to stay in place, let alone make any forward progress. Now which team deserves the rewards?

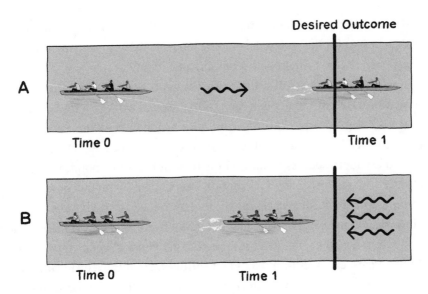

Figure 5.4. System effects: Which crew team has been more effective? Arrows represent the direction and strength of the current.

One could argue that Team A managed to achieve its objective and thus can't be faulted for having an easy trip. And if that objective is programmatically meaningful, then it's hard to fault Team A for picking a more achievable problem to work on. But if that objective is not as meaningful and thus Team A just wasted time and treasure working on a low-bar objective, it's hard to give that team too much credit. Although the rowing analogy may be simpler than most real-world cases, it makes the point that in measuring success, you have to understand the context in which a team is working. To this end, you need to use your situation assessment to identify other forces and other people's actions that could be affecting your work. Going back to the impact trajectory models we introduced in Chapter 2, a program may actually be doing great things even if it is only slowing down the loss of a habitat or species target factor.

- **Attribution versus contribution.** A related issue to the system effects problem has to do with the degree to which a given program can attribute changes in the system to its specific actions. At a small project scale, it's sometimes possible to trace results precisely back to the actions a group takes. But at a larger program scale, it's generally much harder to say that a given strategy is the sole or even the primary cause of a given outcome, especially when there are multiple organizations all taking various actions within the system. For example, if you are trying to pass a national policy, there may have been dozens of groups working on developing demonstration projects, educating key lawmakers, building stake-holder support for the policy, developing model legislation, and many other activities. So who should get credit for passing the policy?

If you have good overall situation assessments and strategy pathways that can show how different complementary strategies can work together as part of the overall strategy and you can use your monitoring data to show that key results were achieved in the order and sequence they were expected, then it may be possible to attribute success to different actors. But at some point, you might have to settle for knowing that your program has contributed to outcomes rather than claiming full credit for success. At the end of the day, if you have reasonable certainty based on available evidence that your efforts are being effective and making a difference, that should be sufficient to get you the credit you deserve.

• **Create a safe environment to detect failures.** Finally, in setting up your monitoring plan, you want to make sure that you detect and respond to complications as soon as possible. As a rule, nothing ever goes exactly according to plan. Sometimes, implementation of your actions simply doesn't play out as expected; other times, implementation results in an absolute misfire. To this end, it is vital to create a climate in which all the members of your program team feel comfortable and even encouraged to report failures. The worst thing you can have is a situation where people feel the need to hide problems to avoid getting in trouble and thus withhold critical information you could use to fix the situation and enhance learning.

Defining and Measuring Long-Term Program Success

Before you can measure the long-term success of your program, you first have to define what success looks like, which is ultimately reflected in the status of your system of interest. At first glance, success may seem fairly obvious: It involves getting your target factors that you ultimately care about to their desired status, or achieving your goals. It's about having intact and healthy ecosystems and robust species populations that can contribute to different elements of human well-being.

However, a simple thought experiment quickly reveals that defining conservation success is a bit more complicated than just measuring the status of your target factors. Imagine two identical large tracts of forest in a very remote area (Figure 5.5a). Site A has a group of indigenous people who have a small settlement in one corner of the area, and they also hunt throughout the area. By contrast, Site B is so remote that no human being has ever set foot in it, and it is pristine in every sense of the word.

"Is Site A or Site B better conserved?"

By strictly ecological criteria, by definition Site B is clearly more "natural" and in better condition. But if you then learn that Site B was recently leased to a large logging company and was scheduled to be completely cut down in six months (Figure 5.5b), then all of a sudden Site B is not looking all that good. And yet nothing has changed on the ground. All the trees and all the animals and all the ecological processes are currently there in a perfectly intact ecosystem.

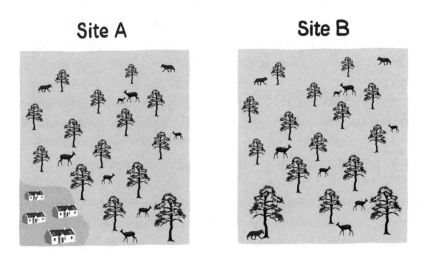

Figure 5.5a. Is Site A or Site B better conserved? The two sites today.

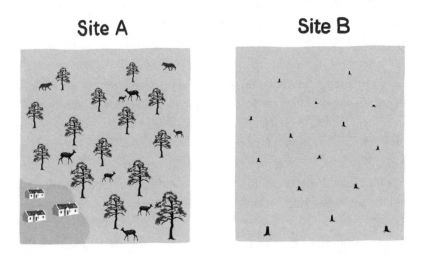

Figure 5.5b. The two sites six months from today.

As an analogy, think about how a doctor might define and assess the health of a given patient during an annual checkup. The examination starts with an assessment of broad indicators of health such as temperature, blood pressure, and blood sugar. If one of these general early warning indicators is outside the normal range, the doctor will follow up with more specific diagnostic tests to understand specifically what problem might be developing. During the exam, however, the doctor will also look for signs of potential problems that might emerge. For example, the doctor will ask the patient about their family history of disease, diet, or exposure to potentially risky situations and behaviors. If potential threats such as a family history of diabetes or colon cancer are uncovered, the doctor will then track more specific diagnostic indicators that might detect the emergence of these problems. Finally, the doctor will ideally check whether the patient has adequate insurance and medical care to deal with any future health problems.

What this example and this analogy show is that conservation success is not defined by just the health of the ecosystem at a single point of time. Instead, it has three equally important elements: the status of the ecosystem, the level of current and future threats, and the capacity to take effective conservation action:

▸ **Status of the ecosystem.** Conservation is fundamentally focused on the ecosystems, species, and ecological processes that make up the natural world and that are represented by the ecological target factors in your situation model and strategy pathways. Clearly, the health of these target factors is one important element of defining success. As we discuss in more detail in the "Guidance" section, there are well-established analytical techniques for defining both the desired future status of a given target factor and the indicators you can use to track this status over time.

What is less understood and appreciated is that the process of defining and measuring ecosystem target factors requires a blend of scientific thinking and stakeholder values. In particular, the stakeholder values are needed to set the desired future status levels for a given target, as shown in the following examples:

• Should desired seal population levels be set to some scientifically determined minimum viable population threshold? Or should they be set to precolonial levels?

• If one endangered species is preying on another endangered species, should the predator be controlled to protect the prey species? Or should the managers allow nature to take its course?

- Given that climate change is likely to radically transform the coastal environment, should program managers try to mitigate the effects to preserve the existing assemblage of species and ecosystems? Or should the managers try to preserve the biophysical stage so that different species and ecosystems can migrate across it in the future?
- And finally, if your program is interested in restoring extirpated species or degraded ecosystems, what restoration point should you aim at? Should you restore species that are functionally extinct in the wild, such as some rhino or river dolphin populations? Or species that have gone extinct in the last 100 years? Species that went extinct after first contact with colonists? Or even species that went extinct after the first contact with humans, such as saber-toothed tigers and other missing North American megafauna?

Although it may seem counterintuitive at first, conservation target factors and their desired future status are at least as much stakeholder values decisions as they are scientific questions. What is clear, however, is that your program needs to make these decisions in order to be able to move forward with your strategies.

▶ **Current and future threats.** As our thought experiment above illustrates, conservation is as much about mitigating threats as it is managing biodiversity targets. As defined in Chapter 1, threats are the human activities that directly and negatively affect biodiversity targets. As discussed in the "Guidance" section below, there are a number of tools to help in detecting and assessing the status of threats. From a status assessment point of view, there are three threat states to consider:

- *Current threats.* The human activities that are actively negatively affecting your target factors. They are typically included in threat assessments.
- *Future threats.* The human activities that are likely to affect your target factors at some point in the future. They are typically included in threat assessments over some defined window of time (e.g., in the next ten years), but you need to factor in the probability of their occurrence.
- *Historical threats.* The human activities that negatively affected your target factors in the past but are no longer active (e.g., commercial whaling). As a rule, effects of historical threats are seen in low population numbers for species and degraded ecosystems and need to be countered through restoration strategies. They are typically not included in any threat assessments because

their effects are generally no longer active and are represented in the current status of the target factor.

▶ **Capacity of people who can take effective action.** Finally, long-term conservation requires the presence of humans who have the awareness, motivation, knowledge, skills, and resources to take effective action. The third element is thus assessing the status of these human resources. Here again, there are different frameworks for making this assessment.

At the most basic level, actions are undertaken by people who value conservation and have the skills and knowledge to make it happen. At the next level, people are generally affiliated with organizations, which include nonprofit organizations, government agencies, tribal and indigenous groups, communities, for-profit firms, universities and research centers, and foundations. Within each of these categories, organizations can be further subdivided based on size and primary focus (e.g., local vs. global). Most organizations do not undertake conservation projects on their own. Instead, at the next level, they form project alliances with other organizations to implement specific projects. These alliances can take different forms including informal collaborations, contractual agreements, partnerships, and consortia. Finally, at the highest level are various networks that enable individuals, organizations, and alliances to work and exchange information with one another.

In addition to the composition of the individuals and organizations involved in conservation, it's also helpful to think about the skills and functions they have.

Guidance for Defining and Measuring Long-Term Program Success

Defining and measuring success is ultimately about assessing the status of the three elements of your system described above. It thus involves going back to your situation assessment and using appropriate frameworks and tools to track the status of the key factors that make up each of these elements:

- **Monitor target status.** Monitoring target status essentially involves establishing indicators that reflect the condition of your target factors. Although you can develop individual indicators for targets in the same way as you would for any other factor, it is often more useful to think about developing your status indicators in the context of a viability analysis framework. Essentially, this approach involves first thinking about the key attributes that define the status of a given target. Next, for each attribute you develop specific indicators that track each key attribute. For each indicator, you can also define thresholds that indicate whether the attribute is at poor, fair, good, or very good status. You can then use these indicator measurements to assess both the current status and desired future status of the target. Essentially, you are creating a model in which measuring a few carefully chosen indicators can tell you about the health of your overall system.

As many *Conservation Standards* coaches and practitioners know, viability analysis can be a black hole into which conservation teams fall, never to emerge again. Much of this problem stems from the fact that teams end up trying to measure all possible variables rather than the smallest set of indicators that will help them make good management decisions. Instead, the team should think about a limited set of meaningful indicators and thresholds for the viability ratings that will prompt conservation action where warranted.

As an example, consider a nongovernment organization program team's work on endangered toads in seasonal wetlands. Here, one critical parameter is the ability of each lake to be colonized from adjacent source populations of toads, as shown in the first column of Table 5.3. To this end, the team developed a qualitative scale for each wetland that assessed whether the distance to a source population was *Easily hoppable, Hoppable, Barely hoppable,* or *Not hoppable* due to either distance or physical barriers. Although it sounds silly, this hoppability scale tells the managers much of what they need to know. If a given wetland is not hoppable,

Table 5.3. Example of viability analysis for species and ecosystem target factors

	Species	Ecosystem	
Target factor	Toad population	Wetland ecosystem	
Key attribute	Connectivity of toad populations in wetlands	Area of wetland	Ability for wetland to migrate
Indicator	Hoppability: Distance and barriers to toad source populations	Area: % of historical wetland area	Migrability: Assessment of the spatial migration path as sea level rises
Ratings Very good Good Fair Poor	Easily hoppable Hoppable Barely hoppable Not hoppable	>90% 75–90% 50–75% <50%	Clear Mostly clear Partially blocked Fully blocked

The indicators in this table are for specific wetland sites; they would need to rolled up across all wetlands across the program scope as described in Table 5.6.

then managers know they need to take action to ensure that proper connectivity is established. The key is to use the team's ecological knowledge to find the critical attributes, indicators, and thresholds to develop useful measures.

- **Assess changes in threat status.** The second element of defining and measuring conservation success involves the absence of direct threats that currently or potentially negatively affect your target factors. The *Conservation Standards* community has developed a number of approaches for defining and assessing threats, based on various criteria such as their scope, severity, and irreversibility. For example, the Threat Reduction Assessment involves taking all your current and future threats, assessing over time the percentage change in the level of each threat, and then rolling up these numbers to create an overall index of change in threat levels.

  Here again, to make good management decisions, we may not need precise measurements of threats. Instead, it may be sufficient to assess whether a threat is declining, stable, mildly increasing, or substantially increasing in scope or severity. But there may also be some cases in which critical thresholds exist that will prompt management action. For example, if practitioners are dealing with a highly infectious disease or a rapidly spreading invasive species, then finding even one incident of the disease or invasive species in their project area may represent a critical threshold that warrants immediate management attention.

- **Track individual and program team capabilities.** The third element of defining and measuring conservation success involves the presence of people and organizations that can take effective action. There are a number of ways to think about assessing capacity across the individuals, program teams, organizations, and broader coalitions that are involved in your work.

  Table 5.4 lists some of the critical knowledge, aptitudes, and skills needed to implement the functional roles involved in the program design, management, and monitoring approach outlined in this book. Part of your challenge is to determine where across your program hierarchy these different roles are needed. Some of these skills are needed across all project sites and in central program offices, whereas for others it may be sufficient to have more centralized "circuit riders" or even external consultants who can provide these skills on demand as needed.

  Somewhat more formally, as outlined by Annette Stewart (2018), capability maturity models are tools that assist with analyzing and improving internal processes and organizational performance. The concept originated in the 1990s from efforts to improve software development processes. It has continually expanded

Table 5.4. Knowledge, aptitudes, and skills needed to perform program functional roles

Functional Role	Skill Type			
	Knowledge and Aptitudes	Programmatic Skills		Administrative Skills
Design	**Conceptualization** Systems thinking Model development Problem setting	**Situation assessment** Site assessment Capacity assessments	**Project design** Planning Scenario evaluation	**Coordination** Facilitation Partnership coordination Proposal development
Management	**Strategic thinking** Visioning Weighing alternatives	**Strategic planning** Setting targets Goals, objectives Developing activities	**Implementation** Developing work plans Setting budgets	**Organizational management** Personnel management Financial management Organizational development
Evidence acquisition	**Assumption testing** Experimental design Cause–effect thinking	**Monitoring planning** Monitoring strategy Indicators and methods	**Assess methods** Effectiveness Cost-effective-ness	**Evaluation** Performance evaluations Financial evaluations Process tracking
Analysis	**Analytical thinking** Statistics Computer skills	**Information management** Data processing Data cleaning	**Data analysis** Qualitative data Quantitative data	**Information systems** Develop and run systems Database management Cost–benefit analysis
Communi-cations	**Strategic communications** Strategic thinking Writing and design skills Conflict resolution skills	**Product planning** Audience analysis Needs assessment	**Product development** Pilot testing Production skills	**Routine communications** Internal systems External reporting Public relations

Source: Adapted from Salafsky et al. (2002).

in use and application, and models are now available for a wide variety of industries and disciplines. In this section we apply Stewart's models for conservation organizations to conservation programs.

A typical capability maturity model involves rating programs at periodic intervals against a set of criteria shown in Table 5.5 that represent the key dimensions of an effective organization. As defined by Stewart, ratings are along a five-point constructed scale:

Table 5.5. Outline of a capability maturity model

Capability	Level 1: Initial	Level 2: Developing	Level 3: Defined	Level 4: Managed	Level 5: Optimizing
Design and Implementation of Conservation Program Strategic Planning					
Strategic planning					
Program selection					
Work planning and implementation					
Information management		See Stewart (2018) for detailed criteria			
Program resourcing and management					
Measurement, reporting, and adapting					
Learning and sharing					
Organizational Business Processes Supporting Conservation Programs					
Leadership					
Fundraising					
Marketing and communications					
Financial management					
People management					
Culture					
Governance					

Source: Adapted from Stewart (2018), which has complete content for all table cells.

1. **Initial.** The program has no consistent way of performing its work. Processes are variable and localized, often reinvented for different projects. Project information is not readily accessible beyond the team; minimal sharing of information between projects and across the organization, precluding learning, measurement of results, and consistent investment decisions. Success depends on individual efforts and competencies.

2. **Developing.** Standard practices for process and information management (based on sector best practices) are adopted, but compliance is voluntary and localized. Some projects follow standard practices, recording some data in systems; project plans define expected results and measures for monitoring progress. Others continue to use ad hoc approaches with limited sharing and systematization of data, and much manual effort. Results-based management is not a key focus of the management team.

3. **Defined.** Standard practices for process and information management are used widely and consistently across the program, with strong leadership support. Most information is captured into systems and shared across the organization; enables timely, relevant, and accurate reporting and analysis of progress and performance. Manual effort has been reduced to a minimum. Projects are appropriately resourced and demonstrably delivering outcomes. The program culture values learning, sharing, and continual improvement.

4. **Managed.** Standard practices are used widely, consistently, and deeply, covering all stages of projects and programs, with most projects being adaptively managed. Comprehensive project information stored in systems informs decision making and fact-based management reviews, to ensure the right projects are being undertaken, are appropriately resourced over appropriate time frames, and are demonstrably delivering impact. The program has highly efficient workflows and shares common beliefs about the effectiveness of their processes, systems, and programs and the need for continual adaptation.

5. **Optimizing.** Portfolio investment decisions, resource allocations, and result reporting are all drawn from analysis of systematized data that is integrated across core business processes and readily available. Program finances and performance are predictable and sustainable. Funders and investors clearly see program efficiency and performance and have ready access to clear reporting of project outcomes and impacts. Impact of the investing market is being leveraged to a major extent. The program has deep capabilities to continually adapt their processes and efficiently deliver measurable conservation impact.

Here again, it requires some thought as to how to map these capabilities across your program hierarchy.

Analyzing Data and Using the Results to Adapt

Analysis is fundamentally about taking data and converting it into information and ultimately knowledge that can be used by your team and your partners to improve your program. Each type of data will have its own specific analytical approaches and techniques. For example, you can use various statistical tests to determine the degree to which quantitative data from a sample represent your overall population. You can use qualitative content analysis techniques to interpret key informant or focus group data and look for patterns. And you can use different spatial analysis tools to make sense of map-based data.

The details of these analytical techniques are beyond the scope of this book, but the real art of analysis lies not in doing a complex statistical or content analysis but rather in taking the results of your monitoring and using them to make decisions about your ongoing program strategies. The most useful high-level analytical approaches are thus directly linked to the three effectiveness monitoring questions introduced above about a given strategy pathway:

▶ **Did we do what we said we would do?** This question involves monitoring the status of actions and activities. Here, the primary analysis involves comparing your actual implementation with what you originally planned. If things are mostly on schedule and within budget, then you don't have to worry; you are on the Success Pathway (Figure 5.6a). But if you are either ahead or running behind schedule or over budget, you have to revisit your action and work plans and adjust them accordingly. And if you have not implemented key actions at all, then you are on the Implementation Failure Pathway (Figure 5.6b). You will have to look at your management systems and determine what has kept you from moving forward as planned. A lack of staff? Insufficient resources? Inability to get necessary permissions? Whatever it is, you need to solve the problem so you can take action.

▶ **Did we get the expected results?** This question involves monitoring your progress in achieving the core results in your strategy pathway. Here, the primary analysis involves seeing whether you are on track toward your stated objectives and goals. If things are going largely as you expected, then again you don't have to worry too much; you are probably on the Success Pathway. But if you notice that you have implemented your planned actions but are not achieving the desired results in the expected time frame, then you are probably on the Theory Failure

Pathway (Figure 5.6c). Something is probably wrong with the hypotheses in your theory of change, and you now need to use your analysis to debug the problem and figure out why. Some key questions that can be helpful to ask yourselves at this point include:

- Did we set the threshold for our objective correctly? For example, did getting more than 25 percent of the restaurants and retailers in the supply chain for a commodity in a region demanding sustainably harvested fish tip the producers to follow sustainable practices?
- Did our hypotheses about the causal relationships between factors hold? For example, did our awareness campaign actually lead to increased awareness in key audiences? Did the increased awareness actually lead to change in people's behaviors?

▶ **Were there any surprises?** This question involves monitoring other factors in your strategy pathways or situation assessment. It can also include tracking any potential unintended consequences of your work. If both your actions and results are going largely as expected, you probably don't have to spend much time thinking about these other factors. But if you are on the Theory Failure Pathway (discussed above) or the Total Failure Pathway (Figure 5.6d), then you need to think about the role these other factors might play by analyzing changes in these other factors. It may even require going back to your situation assessment to determine whether you diagnosed the system problems correctly and whether you selected the appropriate actions to address these problems. It is also worth considering whether you might be on the Monitoring Failure Pathway (Figure 5.6e), in which you are not getting the data you need to understand what is actually going on in the system, or worse yet, you are getting the wrong data that are misleading you about what is really happening. If you suspect you are in this latter case, then you need to carefully analyze the elements of your monitoring plan to see where you are going wrong.

Once you have analyzed your data to try to answer these three monitoring questions, two additional questions should be analyzed:

▶ **How do we need to change our strategic plan?** This question involves looking at the answers to the first three questions and using them to determine whether and how you might need to adapt your strategic plan. Your challenge is to figure

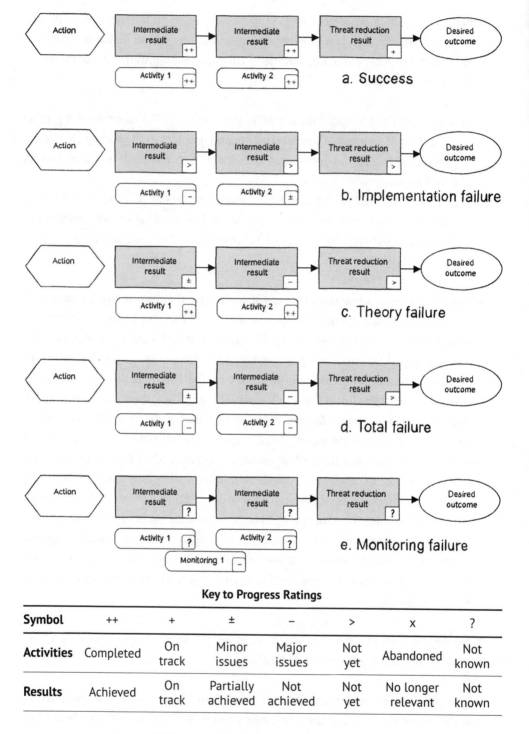

Figure 5.6. Five generic analysis pathways.

out what conclusions you can draw and what changes you need to make based on these conclusions. Change may range from slightly adjusting the timing of a few tasks, to revising your theory of change, to completely abandoning a strategy that does not seem to be working and finding a more appropriate action.

▶ **What have we learned? What do we still need to know?** This final question involves documenting what your team has learned. What worked well and why? What failed and why? A second part of this question involves identifying the gaps in understanding that you have still not filled. These gaps become the starting point for the next iteration of your monitoring plan.

Guidance for Analyzing Data and Using the Results to Adapt

As stated above, you will have to figure out the appropriate analysis approaches for each of your data sets. But some overarching considerations include:

- **Integrate basic data management into your monitoring plan.** Once you have collected your monitoring data, there is usually a great deal of basic work that has to be done to manage and prepare your data sets so that you can efficiently analyze them. This includes coding, reviewing, cleaning, transcribing, and entering data into the appropriate database. These tasks often need to be done on a continuous basis as the data come in. Accordingly, you need to make sure these tasks are explicitly laid out in your monitoring work plan.

- **Conduct periodic pause and reflect sessions.** Although the analysis of specific data sets will take place at different times as warranted, it's also good practice to schedule regular times where you bring your team together to hold pause and reflect (or after action review) sessions. The specific timing for these sessions will vary depending on the nature of your strategic interventions and the pace at which your underlying system responds. If you have a one-off action or a pilot, you probably will want to analyze the results soon after the action is completed so that the experience is still fresh and you can incorporate lessons into your next iteration of the work. If you have an ongoing strategy pathway, you will want instead to hold periodic sessions, perhaps twice a year or at least annually. And if you have slow-moving programs, might want to schedule a minor review every year and then a more intensive review every three to five years. But even in these cases, if your system suddenly changes (e.g., there is a natural disaster or a major policy shift) you may also have to convene your analytical team off cycle.

  Before each pause and reflect session, make sure your team assembles the needed data, information, and analyses regarding your actions, results, and monitoring indicators. This presession work should include analyzing both changes in the status of key factors and causal linkages between factors in your strategy pathways.

At the session itself, bring all relevant members of your team together and sit down with your strategy pathways and situation analyses. Go through the questions above and use your analysis to test key hypotheses. As you go through this process, it's important to remember that the discussion can be as important as the final conclusions. You don't need to record every conversation verbatim, but try to document how you arrived at your conclusions.

- **Focus on programmatic significance, not just statistical significance.** In analyzing monitoring results, teams can sometimes confuse statistical results with programmatic results. For example, say you are working on a strategy pathway that involves establishing a sustainable seafood production system. Your theory of change says that if you can increase income of all households working in the fishing industry by 20 percent, that will provide an incentive to get the fishing boats to switch to desired sustainable fishing practices. As part of your monitoring plan, say you decided to compare the average household income of people involved in the sustainable seafood production system to households not involved in the system. Your statistical analysis yields a p-value showing a significant difference in household income between your two groups, with the group that participated in the program earning more income. Woo-hoo! You were successful! It's time to publish your results!

  But wait: Although you can be confident that average household income has indeed increased in the households that participated in the program, the real question is whether they earned enough to change their attitudes and behaviors. What if the program led to only a 3 percent increase? According to your theory of change, you think that they need to get a 20 percent increase to adequately incentivize fishing households to adopt sustainable fishing practices. You have not yet changed the underlying system to get the desired long-term incentive; put another way, you have achieved a statistically significant increase in income but not a programatically significant increase. What you really need to be testing is not whether average household income has increased but rather whether the average income is higher than the 20 percent threshold that you predicted would need to be achieved to cause behavior change. The key is to make sure your analytical thinking is guided and testable by the theory of change laid out in your situation assessment and strategy pathways.

- **Use the right approach to roll up project-level data to a program.** In cases where your program-level strategies involve implementing or funding project (or grantee)-level work, you need to make sure you are rolling up lower-level data appropriately to determine progress in program-level objectives and indicators. Figure 5.7 shows a set of project-level wetland restoration strategy pathways that are meant to roll up to an overall program-level pathway. The overall program pathway (shown in all caps) has two main actions: promoting national policies and managing three projects that are doing actual site-level wetland restoration work. This example illustrates how factors change as you change scale. For example, *<PROG ACTIVITY R1>* (rounded box) maps directly to the entire *<proj 1 restoration action>* (hexagon). This example also shows how the lower-level project objectives and indicators are meant to add up to the program level.

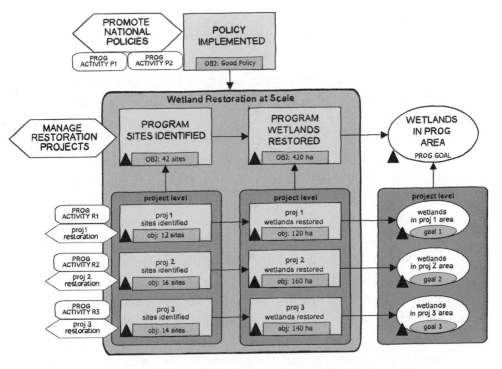

Figure 5.7. Example of rolling up project to program-level strategy pathways.

There are four fundamental ways you can roll up lower-level to higher-level results:

• *Approach A: Combine project-level objectives and indicators that have standard units.* This option involves combining, summing, or otherwise arithmetically

Table 5.6a. Approach A: Rolling up objectives and indicators in standard units

Program objective 1: Within 3 years, at least 420 ha of critical wetland habitat are restored across the program scope.

Indicator: Hectares of critical wetland habitat restored in each project.

Final year 3 measurement: The program has achieved 280 ha, or 67% of its objective.

Level	Objective (ha)	Indicator (cumulative actual ha)			Total % Objective
		Year 1	Year 2	Year 3	
Project 1	120	0	42	95	79%
Project 2	160	10	80	170	106%
Project 3	140	15	15	15	11%
Program total	**420**	**25**	**137**	**280**	**67%**

aggregating project-level data at the program level. To do this, you must also harmonize associated indicators and objectives across the project–program scale. Ideally, for data to be scalable in this fashion, collection methods and sampling must also be harmonized. For example, in Table 5.6a the program level objective and indicator ("Program total") are calculated as the sum of the project-level objectives and indicators. This approach requires that both the objective and indicator are expressed as quantitative variables that use the same standard units at both project and program levels (technically speaking, it is a subset of Approach B, in which data normalization is not required).

• *Approach B: Combine project-level indicator values to construct program-level value.* This option involves analyzing the contribution of each project to the overall program objective by combining project-level data in a logical manner to create a program-level indicator value. In this approach, project data do not need to be in the same standard units as long as your analysis normalizes the units so that you can appropriately combine them. For example, in Table 5.6b, you might weight the contribution of each project in the program by the relative size of the project in terms of area, number of stakeholders, or some other appropriate parameter. Or you might look at the average contribution of each project. This approach can be used with indicators that are expressed as both quantitative and qualitative variables. You just have to make sure you are not inappropriately combining measurements with different units unless you first normalize them.

Table 5.6b. Approach B: Constructing program-level indicator

Program objective 2a: Within 3 years, >50% of stakeholders support sustainable fishing across the program.

Indicator: Percentage of stakeholders in each project area who have support rated high or very high. In this example, to measure both breadth and depth of support, key informants are given 10 beans that each represent 10% of the stakeholder population of that project area. The respondents then put the beans in buckets representing low (L), medium (M), high (H), and very high (VH) support for the sustainable fishing system. Although it is not shown here, this exercise could be done multiple times with multiple informants and then the average allocations could be used to calculate the program-level indicator.

Final year 3 measurement: The program has achieved 69% of stakeholders supporting sustainable fishing and thus has achieved its objective.

Project Area (n = stakeholders)	Indicator (% of stakeholders at different levels of support for sustainable fishing)														
	Year 1					Year 2					Year 3				
	L	M	H	VH	≥H	L	M	H	VH	≥H	L	M	H	VH	≥H
Project 1 (n = 650)	70	20	10	0	10	50	30	15	5	20	10	0	70	20	90
Project 2 (n = 320)	90	10	0	0	0	60	20	10	10	20	50	10	10	30	40
Project 3 (n = 80)	90	10	0	0	0	80	20	0	0	0	70	10	20	0	20
Program total % (normalized by stakeholders)					6					18					69

Because this approach does not require project-level data to be in the same units, it can be used to combine data from very different systems. For example, if there is a program working on developing sustainable ecosystem management, it could combine results from Project 1 in a terrestrial area that is trying to get stakeholder support for sustainable forest management, Project 2 in an estuary trying to get stakeholder support for sustainable wetland management, and Project 3 on the coast trying to get stakeholder support for sustainable ocean management. All of these results could be combined to look at the effect of overall stakeholder support on the ability to get different ecosystems under a sustainable management regime.

However, if the program objective was written as shown for Objective 2b, with an emphasis on support in each project area rather than across the program area as a whole, then it doesn't make sense to roll up the project values to the program level because it doesn't matter that 50 percent of stakeholders on average across the program area support the sustainable fishing approach. Instead, what matters is that 50 percent of the stakeholders in each project area support the approach. This case thus becomes more like Approach C below.

Program objective 2b: Within three years, more than 50 percent of stakeholders support sustainable fishing in each project area.

Indicator: Percentage of stakeholders in each project area that have support rated high or very high.

Final year 3 measurement: In this case, only one of the projects has crossed the 50 percent support threshold, so the program has not met its objective.

- Approach C: Track projects meeting their objectives. This option involves tracking the number of projects that are meeting or on track to meet their stated objectives, expressed either as the percentage of the objective or a categorical assessment (e.g., achieved, on track, partially achieved, not achieved) as shown in the example Table 5.6c. To be effective, this approach assumes that project-level objectives are set at a programmatically meaningful level. This approach can be used with all types of indicator variables as long as the indicator and the objective are both measured in comparable units.

- Approach D: Directly assess program-level objectives and indicators. This option involves developing higher-level program indicators that directly measure program-level results in your program strategy pathway.

In some cases where the program-level indicator can be mapped back to specific project areas (e.g., remote sensing of restored wetland areas that can be intersected with a map layer of project scope boundaries), the program-level data can rolled down to determine which projects have succeeded and which are having problems. However, this attribution to projects is not always possible, in which case you will not be able to use the program indicator data to help in the management of specific projects or to assess whether your project-level actions are truly contributing to your program goals and objectives.

Program objective 4a: Within 3 years, at least 425 hectares of critical wetland habitat are restored across the program scope.

Indicator: Number of hectares of critical wetland habitat restored across the program scope as measured through remote sensing.

Final year 3 measurement: The program has achieved 280 hectares, or 66 percent of its objective.

Table 5.6c. Approach C: Track projects meeting their objectives

Program objective 3: Within 3 years, at least 9 of the 12 project areas have met at least 80% of their wetland restoration objectives.

Indicator: Number of projects that have met the 80% target.

Final year 3 measurement: In this case, only 5 out of 12 projects have met the desired target.

| Level | % of Objective Met | | | |
	Year 1	Year 2	Year 3	>80% in Year 3?
Project 1	0	10	50	No
Project 2	10	50	120	Yes
Project 3	15	70	105	Yes
Project 4	0	0	0	No
Project 5	5	30	70	No
Project 6	10	40	90	Yes
Project 7	5	45	20	No
Project 8	20	80	130	Yes
Project 9	0	20	50	No
Project 10	5	25	40	No
Project 11	10	40	85	Yes
Project 12	15	35	70	No
Program total				Yes = 5 No = 7

Program objective 4b: Within five years, there are one hundred pairs of wetland obligate raptors breeding in the program scope.

Indicator: Number of breeding pairs of raptors.

Final year 3 measurement: The program has twenty pairs, but the trend is in the right direction.

Program objective 4c: Within three years, average household income in the program area has increased by $20,000.

Indicator: Average household income in the political jurisdictions overlapping the program area (the closest easily available data).

Final year 3 measurement: Average income has increased by $14,050.

- **Value failures.** As you and your team analyze and make sense of the data about your program, you probably will find evidence that at least some of your strategies are successful and that your hard work is leading to improvements. But almost inevitably, you will also find that things did not go exactly according to plan and that some of your actions were not very effective, downright ineffective, or even counterproductive. Don't be too hard on yourself! Conservation, especially at large scales in complex systems, is really hard to do. If you don't have any failures, it's probably a sign that you are not being sufficiently ambitious in your work and that you are taking only incremental, safe actions. The key is not to try to hide your failures but rather to study them carefully and learn how you might avoid making the same mistakes in the future. It's not a problem unless you keep on making the same mistake over and over again.

  In thinking about failures, it's also important to distinguish between making a "wrong" decision and getting a negative or unexpected outcome from the "correct" decision. In Figure 0.8 way back in the Introduction, we introduced the idea that investment in evidence acquisition and analysis (the x-axis) would lead to an increased probability of a correct decision (the y-axis). But how can you measure whether a decision is correct? One way might involve asking at a later date, "If with the benefit of hindsight, you could go back in time and remake the decision, would you make the same choice?" If the answer is yes, then it was the correct decision.

  But in making this assessment, it is essential to factor in the uncertainty you were facing at the decision point. As a simple example, if you are playing cards, you often have to decide what card to play. Say there is an 80 percent chance in your favor that playing a given card will lead to your winning the hand. There is still a 20 percent chance that you will lose the hand. But even if you get that negative outcome, it doesn't mean that you made the wrong decision by going with the action that had a higher probability of success. The only thing you could have done was to try to reduce the uncertainty. In cards, this might require peeking at your opponents' cards (i.e., cheating). But in conservation, this might involve investing in getting better evidence, but only where it is feasible and has an appropriate return on investment.

- **Follow up on and fix identified problems.** Finally, after going through all the hard work of collecting and analyzing data, use your findings to revise the relevant components of your strategic plan. This includes adapting your situation assessment, your specific strategy pathways, and your overall program portfolio.

Reporting to Your Team and Stakeholders

At the beginning of this chapter, we described how monitoring starts with identifying your key decision makers and stakeholders and their high-level monitoring questions. So now that you have done all this data collection and analysis to turn your data into information and knowledge, you need to make sure that the necessary evidence to answer these questions reaches and is used by each of these audiences.

Rather than think about designing entire report documents or online dashboards, it is often easier to think about particular report elements that tell a piece of the story and feed into specific management decisions. These report elements include graphs, tables, maps, gauges, pictures, or example anecdotes could then be compiled and appear in many different information sharing products for different audiences including:

- ▶ **Team and stakeholder working sessions.** Probably the most important venue for sharing information is with your team and stakeholders as part of your ongoing management and pause and reflect sessions. The key here is to have the right report elements compiled, updated, and accessible as you go through various team discussions.
- ▶ **Management dashboards.** It's also important to feed key report elements into the decision support systems that program and organizational managers and funders use to manage the work they are responsible for.
- ▶ **Specific reports to boards, funders, or agencies.** Another critical output includes the reports you are obligated to provide to your board, funders, or regulators. Here, you need to make sure that your report elements directly address the information needs they have outlined.
- ▶ **Presentations, websites, videos, and documents.** Finally, the last main set of products involves the live and self-guided presentations and the websites, videos, and general documents that introduce and walk key stakeholders through relevant elements of your work.

Guidance for Reporting to Your Team and Stakeholders

A great deal of strategic communications guidance is available on how to best develop and share messages through each of the different platforms listed above, which goes way beyond what is feasible to address here. Some key points include:

- • **Design your report elements before you begin data collection.** As discussed above, the best time to design your report elements is when you are first starting to think about your decision makers and stakeholders and their respective information needs. At that point, it can be very helpful to sketch out on a flip chart or a whiteboard what the final report elements might look like and what information each might contain, the anticipated level of precision needed for that information, and the potential sources of that information. Ideally you would do this sketching with the users of the information or at least share your sketch with them to make sure it will meet their needs.

• **Build interpretation into your report elements.** A good report element not only presents the results of analysis but also helps the user interpret and apply them. Although this concept applies to all types of report elements, it is perhaps most apparent when thinking about key metrics displayed as gauges in management dashboards. This phrase evokes images of senior managers sitting in their command center making subtle adjustments to program strategy and tactics based on the readouts from a panel of spinning and blinking gauges. Managers are charged with moving the needle on key gauges as a measurement of the outcome of their work.

If you think about your car's dashboard as an analogy, one of the most useful components is the fuel gauge, which helps you answer a critical management question: "When should I stop driving and refuel the car?" Without this essential information, you will unnecessarily be stopping to refuel, or you will be stranded on the side of the road. Interestingly, however, what makes a fuel gauge truly useful is not the needle itself but rather the markings on the gauge that help you interpret what moving the needle actually means and then decide what actions you need to take as a result (Figure 5.8). The device measures the level of liquid in your car's gas tank, moving the needle as the tank empties. But to make sense of the needle's movements, the gauge converts them to a measurement of what fraction of your tank is filled (the markings "E ¼ ½ ¾ F" beneath the needle and

Figure 5.8. Two typical gauges on a car dashboard: fuel gauge and tachometer.

the buzzer or light that activates as you approach empty). You must then convert these markings to an assessment of how far you have left to drive before you need to take action and refuel.

By contrast, consider a tachometer that measures the revolutions per minute (rpm) of the drive shaft in your engine. Technically speaking, this mechanism is measuring the voltage generated by a magnet attached to the spinning drive shaft; the manufacturer has to invest resources in creating the mechanism to get the gauge measurement. But the observation that the needle moves from 4,000 rpm to 7,000 rpm is not that useful in and of itself. What's more important is the red line trigger point on the dial that warns you to immediately shift gears and thus reduce your rpms to avoid burning out the engine. Furthermore, if you have an automatic transmission, as in most modern cars, there is not much point in investing in a tachometer, because there are no decisions for the driver to make based on its readings. It is a waste of both the resources needed to build it and premium space on the dashboard, and it may even distract the driver from focusing on more important gauges, such as the fuel gauge. The tachometer is probably there only because it looks cool to some drivers and thus sells cars.

Developing an effective automotive gauge thus starts with understanding what the critical management decision is, figuring out the best available and affordable indicator to provide information vital to this decision, and then presenting measurements based on this indicator to the driver along with sufficient context to guide appropriate action. Interestingly, as technology changes, we can improve how gauges help drivers make better decisions. For example, modern cars are replacing the traditional fuel gauge with a digital readout of the distance you can drive before running out of fuel. Computer technology has essentially enabled car manufacturers to bypass the analog needle measuring fuel levels in the tank and present drivers with pure interpreted information to make the critical management decision about when to refuel.

So how does this link to conservation? As shown in Table 5.7, many of the status measurements we discussed in the previous section lend themselves to constructing a good gauge (e.g., the toad hoppability index or threat measurements). The key is to create a gauge that not only provides the underlying data but also helps interpret it.

- **Provide approximate yet reliable answers.** Following on the fuel gauge analogy from the previous point, if you are making a decision about when to stop and refuel, it probably doesn't make much difference if your gauge says you have about 4 liters left or that you have exactly 4.1527 liters remaining. You are not going to

Table 5.7. How viability analyses and threat ratings meet criteria for a good gauge

Gauge Element	Automotive Analogy	Viability Analysis	Specific Example
Information need for management	Distance before refueling is needed	Key ecological attribute of focal target factor	Connectivity of toad populations in wetlands
Actual measurement	Level of liquid remaining in tank	Indicator	Distance and barriers to toad source populations
Interpretive marking on gauge	E ¼ ½ ¾ F markings Light or buzzer near empty	Thresholds for very good, good, fair, and poor conditions	Hoppability ratings

make a different decision. But it does matter if you have about 0.400 versus 4.00 versus 40.0 liters left in the tank because each of these values would take you to a very different management decision. So you want the gauge to be reliable even if there is not great precision in the measurements. Analogously, in conservation it may be sufficient to assess whether a target is in good or fair status or whether a threat is declining, stable, mildly increasing, or substantially increasing in scope or severity rather than measuring the underlying indicator to three significant digits. But you certainly don't want to miss the fact that the threat is increasing.

• **Present only useful information.** Because the decisions facing a manager of a project site, the manager of a program, and the CEO of a large organization all differ, it seems as if different sets of report elements would be needed for each user. In general, project and program managers need to know how their conservation target factors are doing, whether threats are being abated, and whether their specific strategies are on track.

But especially when we jump up to the level of an organizational dashboard, it seems that most of the management decisions being made at these higher levels are about the allocation of scarce time and treasure across different parts of the organization to take on different programs. Therefore, it seems useful to have gauges that show which projects and programs are on track and which are not functioning well and need additional resources or management attention. It is also vital to monitor current and projected levels of key financial, human, and other resources so that managers can ensure they are available within the organization as needed.

But it is hard to imagine much else that would be useful at the organizational level including (somewhat surprisingly) measures of the status of species, eco-systems, threats, or human stakeholder well-being. At best, these measures are needed for long-term strategic reprioritization efforts, not for day-to-day or even year-to-year management work. If you were the CEO of a large organization and you saw that deforestation in the Amazon increased by 10 percent in the last five years or that the GDP of Indonesia went up 5 percent, what action would you take as a result? However, if you saw that your Amazon program was having trouble retaining key staff or meeting its agreed-upon goals, these would presumably be actionable signals.

The key to an effective dashboard—or any other report—is to collect and present data that can be interpreted and used for direct management action. Everything else is superfluous and a distraction, like tachometers on cars with automatic transmissions. The best dashboard is not the biggest and most complex one; it is the one that contains the smallest set of effective gauges needed to guide critical management decisions.

- **Standardize reporting requirements across programs.** Many conservation projects have to write multiple progress reports each year, reworking the same basic information into the many different formats requested by their home organization and their various funders. If program managers were able to agree on a standard template for reporting on the effectiveness of conservation strategies, then projects would only have to generate one main report along with perhaps a small bit of additional material unique to each funder. And if implementers and funders were using compatible information technology systems, then data from projects could be directly linked and rolled up into program-level reports. This would also enable funders to see how the work they are funding relates to work funded by others. Although realizing this vision would require overcoming some inertia and institutional barriers, the payoff is enormous potential to reduce transaction costs for both implementers and funders and to increase knowledge generation and sharing.

Exiting Responsibly

Although strategies, projects, and especially programs can be large and long-term endeavors, it is important to remember that they are not organizations that are meant to exist indefinitely. Instead, they typically have a limited lifespan. A key element of strategic planning involves recognizing and embracing this reality. The question thus becomes not whether your strategy, project, or program should end but when and how it should do so.

From a theoretical economist's point of view, a program is essentially an investment, and therefore the time to abandon your investment is at any point when future investment costs exceed potential future returns. In effect, at every given moment when you choose to continue implementing a strategy pathway, you are prioritizing that pathway over other potential pathways you could be implementing with your time and treasure. Even if you have millions of dollars invested in a strategy pathway, if you know it is going to fail (or more technically, if the next $1,000 you will invest in this pathway could be more effectively used elsewhere), then you should abandon this work. As economists are fond of saying, "Sunk costs are sunk costs."

Of course, programs aren't just theoretical concepts but are instead real-world endeavors that involve real people whose livelihoods, egos, and emotions are at stake. Therefore, it can be a challenge to make dispassionate business decisions about whether to keep investing in work that is not likely to provide a worthwhile return. These decisions are made more complex because nonprofit organizations and funders tend to have cultures that avoid conflict and hard decisions. As a result, it is all the more important to have a plan for determining when and how to exit responsibly.

There is a spectrum of approaches for exiting a given program, ranging from softer to harder transitions:

- ▶ **Move to a new phase.** With this approach, a program will bring one phase of work to an end and then start a new one. For example, a program that spent a decade restoring new wetlands might then transition to maintenance of the previously restored wetland areas for the next decade. Or a program that had a five-year funding source might start a new five-year course of work once the initial five years is completed. The formal transition to the new phase often provides a good opportunity to make necessary personnel changes or introduce new directions and new strategies and to end strategies that are no longer priorities.
- ▶ **Hand over to partners.** Under this approach, a program's implementing organization might seek to turn over control of a given strategy, a project, or even the program itself to current partner organizations. It is particularly important in this case to allow partner organizations or individuals to take increasing responsibility and gain experience operating independently before the exit.
- ▶ **Transfer to an external entity.** Under this approach, a program's implementing organization might seek to turn over control of a strategy, project, or program to an existing or new entity. Although nonprofits typically do not "sell" a line of work to another organization in the way that businesses often do, arrangements can be made to transfer responsibilities and assets. For example, an implementing organization might find another umbrella organization to manage a project. Or a funder might find other funders who can provide support to a program. In this case, it is vital to make sure that all parties are clear what staff and assets are being transferred or retained by the original entity.
- ▶ **Ramp down.** Under this approach, the managers of a program determine an end date at some point in the future and develop a plan to bring the work to an orderly close. In this case, it is particularly critical to figure out how to retain key staff needed to complete the planned work because people will have a strong incentive to leave early if they know they will be out of a job once the end date is reached. One option is to offer new jobs to these people in other parts of your organization. A second is to pay sufficient retention bonuses to people who stay through certain dates.
- ▶ **Hard stop.** Finally, under this approach, program comes to a sudden halt because of a major change in context such as the outbreak of civil conflict or a natural disaster, a sudden loss of funding or key political support, or changes in the system that no longer justify the program (e.g., some other entity is now doing it

better). It's obviously hard to plan for this kind of sudden end to a program, but you can still try to make the best of it.

Guidance for Exiting Responsibly

Exiting a program often goes against human nature and can be difficult to do. Some key things that can help include:

- **Build your exit into your initial strategic plan.** Often, the best time to think about your exit is paradoxically in your initial strategic planning. As you develop your strategy pathways, think about the critical assumptions you are making, and think about how you might test these assumptions to see whether your strategy is on track. In particular, think about the indicators that might tell you whether things are going well or need to be reconsidered. For instance, in the whale watching alternative livelihoods pathway back in Figure 3.2, if you find you can't convince fishing boat owners to give up fishing to work in the whale watching industry or if you can't keep other boats from coming in and taking over the fishing, then there is not much point in going on with this strategy.
- **Continue prioritizing options.** As discussed above, choosing to invest in an ongoing program is really no different from choosing to invest in a new alternative. To this end, as part of your regular pause and reflect sessions, you should revisit your strategy prioritization exercises with "stay the course in the current work" as one of the potential investment options. If the collective results of the analysis are not favorable to the existing work, then you may have to consider exiting.
- **Maintain transparency with key partners and stakeholders.** Throughout an exit process it is important to maintain positive relationships with partners and key stakeholders. In particular, it is helpful to clearly signal your intentions in advance. Your partners and stakeholders should be aware that you are planning an exit and actively be involved in planning for it. You should formally communicate key decisions when they are known and discuss the implications of the exit for each main strategy. You should also allow time for scaling down strategies as appropriate.
- **Treat people fairly.** In addition to supporting key partners throughout the process, consider how you will support project or program staff. For example, where people's jobs are likely to be lost as a direct result of an exit, the organizations involved should, as far as possible, provide relevant training and skill development to enable them to find new positions. As mentioned above, you may have to offer increased incentives to get people to stick around during the close-out period.

- **Consider long-term follow-up.** If possible, you might plan a follow-up evaluation of your program to take place in five to ten years or even longer. This type of assessment of long-term effects can provide a great learning opportunity.
- **Treat closure as an opportunity.** Finally, it's important to keep in mind that closure is not just the end of a program but also the start of a new opportunity. On a personal note, Nick and Richard first met while working as staff as part of a ten-year U.S. Agency for International Development–funded program. The program's long-scheduled end date provided strong motivation to finish key pieces of work that probably would have dragged on indefinitely. It also gave us the impetus to find a way to continue the work and ideas in a new form that ultimately became the organization Foundations of Success (FOS).

Sources and Further Information

(See FOSonline.org/pathways for links and updated guidance material.)

Developing Your Monitoring Plan

Some good sources to consult include:

Richard Margoluis, Caroline Stem, Nick Salafsky, and Marcia Brown (2009), "Design Alternatives for Evaluating the Impact of Conservation Projects" (*New Directions for Evaluation* 122: 85–96). A review of different monitoring designs.
FOS (2017), *Designing Monitoring and Evaluation Approaches under the Open Standards*. Another review of monitoring approaches.

Monitoring Your Strategy Effectiveness

The effectiveness monitoring approach presented in this section was developed for Miradi Software.

Defining and Measuring Long-Term Program Success

The following are some of the key references for systems for assessing ecological targets, threat reduction, and conservation capacity:

TNC (2007), *Guidance for Step 3: Assess Viability in Conservation Action Planning Handbook*. Provides a basic introduction to the theory and practice of viability analysis.
Nick Salafsky and Richard Margoluis (2001), "Threat Reduction Assessment: A Practical and Cost-Effective Approach to Evaluating Conservation and

Development Projects" (*Conservation Biology* 13: 830–841). One approach for rolling up threat measurements to create an overall index; it could be useful to update this thinking to apply to large-scale programs.

Nick Salafsky, Richard Margoluis, John Robinson, and Kent Redford (2002), "A Conceptual Framework and Research Agenda for Conservation Science" (*Conservation Biology* 16: 1469–1479). The source for Table 5.4.

Annette Stewart (2018), *Conservation Capability Maturity Model: A Tool for Assessing and Improving Performance of Conservation Organisations.* A practical overview of how to assess organizational capacity built on a framework applied in many disciplines and the source for Table 5.5.

Analyzing Data and Using the Results to Adapt

Each type of data will have its own specific analytical approaches and techniques and therefore its own set of guidance materials. One general source is:

Richard Margoluis and Nick Salafsky (1998), *Measures of Success: Designing, Managing, and Monitoring Conservation and Development Projects.* Chapter 7 explains the old-fashioned steps involved in preparing data for analysis.

Reporting to Your Team and Stakeholders

The Conservation Measures Partnership and Miradi Software have an active working group developing better reporting templates and tools to support key analyses in the *Conservation Standards*. Specifically, there is great interest in developing standard data reporting and visualization tools and building the application program interfaces linking conservation data with other types of data by using standard business information systems such as:

Microsoft Power BI
Tableau Software

Exiting Responsibly

Material in this section draws in part from:

World Wildlife Fund (2017), *Planning for Sustainability and Responsible Exits.* An overview of how to think about exits.

Key Learning Questions

1. How can we help program teams identify and test hypotheses practically and routinely within the program cycle? Specifically, how can we:
   1a. Coach practitioners to identify the most critical hypotheses for a given strategy?
   1b. Coach practitioners to get the minimum amount of evidence needed to test these critical hypotheses?
2. What is needed to develop a database of tested effectiveness monitoring indicators and methods for key conservation actions and strategies?
3. How can we cost-effectively develop shared status measures? Instead of each program having to go out and collect and analyze status measures on their own, how can we:
   3a. Create a system where all data about a species or ecosystem are shared so that we all know not just the status of species or ecosystems but also where there are gaps in monitoring and assessment?
   3b. Build shared maps of current and future human activities that pose threats to conservation targets?
   3c. Improve and operationalize the capability matrix to better assess program capacity?
4. What is the true return on investment of infrequent, expensive external evaluations rather than externally facilitated internal evaluations? Can external evaluations of large complex programs be truly objective and useful given that it is difficult for outsiders to understand large complex programs without internal guidance and analysis, there are often few truly independent sources of information for the programs, and it's more challenging for program managers to use the results of evaluations in which they have not been fully involved?
5. Most conservation projects and programs have multiple funders that each require basically the same performance report information in different formats. So how can we develop shared grant application and reporting formats that would greatly reduce transaction costs and allow information to be shared across funding programs?

6

Promoting Collaborative Learning

Learning occurs on a constant basis throughout the program management approach described in this book as you and your team acquire and analyze evidence about your program's situation and strategies. But you are not the only people who can benefit from the knowledge and understanding you gain along the way. And if you collaborate with similar programs, you can also greatly expand your learning potential. Quadrant IV in your program's evidence base (Figure IIb) focuses on the cross-program learning questions you need to answer in the future by joining forces with other conservation practitioners around the world to build the global evidence base.

Key analyses in this process include:

- Contributing to the global evidence base
- Developing collaborative learning programs
- Building the discipline of conservation

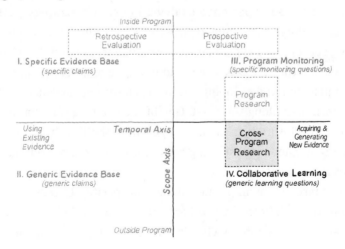

Contributing to the Global Evidence Base

As you have designed and implemented your program, you have been acquiring, analyzing, and using all kinds of evidence. You've collected and used both specific and generic evidence about key claims in your situation analysis. You've monitored critical hypotheses in your strategy pathways. And maybe you've even done a systematic review or research study to address specific information needs. Ideally, your program team has been able to learn from these analyses. But how can you also share what you've learned with others who could also benefit from your findings?

You could try to put reports about your program on your website. You could formally publish your results. Or you could try to share your program plans and outcomes with other people you know who are working on similar issues. But it's hard to put your experiences out in the world and expect people who might benefit from them to find them when they need them.

This lack of sharing is particularly unfortunate because scientific research generally depends on having replication in order to fully evaluate claims and hypotheses. But unlike laboratories or medical research in which investigators can run the same experiment hundreds of times, in many complex conservation settings it is difficult or impossible to even duplicate an action, let alone establish replicates, comparison groups, or controls. There is only so much we can learn from one site or one program. But if we combine experience from multiple sites and multiple programs, we have the potential to vastly scale up our collective learning potential, increase our sample size, and thus increase the analytical power of our learning. The key is to use your strategy pathways as the unit of inquiry and analysis for this learning:

▶ **Using specific case experience to develop generic strategy pathways.** Systematic cross-program learning (Quadrant IV in Figure 0.IIb) involves iteratively analyzing specific case experience to develop more general knowledge and ultimately wisdom (per the DIKW pyramid in Figure 4.4). As a simple example, say you are interested in developing a rotating closure management system to protect shellfish beds along the coast. One of the challenges is that people are not respecting the closure system and are poaching shellfish from the closed areas. Your program team is considering setting up a system of community resource monitors to counter the poachers.

A bit of research in an online database of specific strategy pathways reveals some comparable efforts from other parts of the world, including community patrols around pangolin sanctuaries in Africa (Figure 6.1a) and community guards on sea turtle nesting beaches in the Caribbean (Figure 6.1b). On the surface, everything about these two specific strategy pathways is different, both from each other and from your situation. Different parts of the world. Different ecosystems. Different social, cultural, and political systems. Different target and threat factors. And yet the underlying conceptual theory of change is remarkably similar. As a result, we can use these specific experiences to develop a generic pathway for a patrol and guard strategy (Figure 6.1c). This pathway can be placed into a repository of generic conservation strategies such as the Conservation Actions and Measures Library (CAML).

▶ **Determining the conditions under which a strategy is likely to work.** Although these specific pathways are conceptually similar at a high level, there are also some subtle but important wrinkles in the details. For example, we may find that in the examples in Africa, community patrols are not working in places where the poaching is being done by criminal gangs who are armed with automatic weapons. In these cases, the community guards literally don't have the firepower to confront the poachers. And maybe in some of the turtle nesting cases we find that community patrols can work to deter poachers who are coming from neighboring communities, but they are unwilling to inform on and arrest poachers who are coming from influential families in their own communities. These subtle differences are important. The question is never "Does Strategy X work?," implying that there is a yes or no answer. Instead, the question should be "Under what conditions is Strategy X likely to work?" By comparing similar actions in different situations, we can start to determine the nature of these conditions by looking at each of the subclaims in the strategy pathway (Table 6.1).

▶ **Using and contributing to generic knowledge.** Your program can use this generic pathway and analysis of the conditions under which it might work to develop your own specific pathway for the <*Community Monitoring of Shellfish Closures Strategy*> (Figure 6.1d). But of course, you should not adopt this generic strategy wholesale. Instead, you should use it as a starting point for your thinking and a guide to the objectives and indicators you can use to monitor implementation. For instance, you might decide to combine the patrols with a community outreach campaign to see whether that can increase compliance rates. You can then analyze your own data and contribute what you have learned back to the appropriate global database of specific conservation strategies, thus continuing the cycle.

Ideally, if a large number of projects and programs participate in this process and share their results, we can start to build up the replication necessary—and thus increase the power—to capture tested knowledge and even develop wisdom

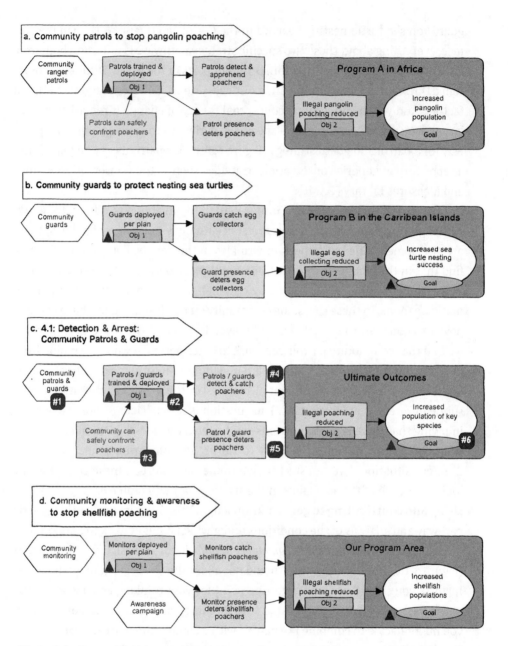

Figure 6.1a, b, c, and d. Using specific strategy pathways to develop a generic strategy pathway.

about these strategies. Figure 6.2 shows a high-level pathway for how the conservation community could collectively improve evidence generation, access, and use to build the global evidence base. This pathway hypothesizes that:

1. If specific evidence from the implementation of strategy pathways is documented and appropriately shared, then this will provide the material for cross-project and cross-program analysis and synthesis.
2. If these syntheses are appropriately shared, this will enable practitioners to find and access evidence when they need it.
3. If practitioners can find and access the right evidence when they need it, then they will use it to make decisions.
4. If practitioners appropriately use evidence to make decisions, they will implement more effective conservation programs.

Table 6.1. Key conditions related to claims about a community patrol and guard strategy

Overall claim: Community patrols and guards will reduce poaching of target species

Subclaim	Strategy is more likely to work if...	Strategy is less likely to work if...	Key Learning Questions
1. Community has economic incentive to set up patrol and guard system	Community benefits from conservation	Poachers can bribe patrols and guards	
2. Patrols and guards can be trained and deployed	External resources are available for training and salaries		
3. Patrols and guards have ability and will to safely confront poachers	Poachers come from outside community	Poachers heavily armed Poachers backed by powerful stakeholders within community	When is having the poachers come from within a community beneficial vs. a liability?
4. Patrols and guards can detect and catch sufficient poachers	Target species is located in defensible area	Target species widely spread out	
5. Presence of patrols and guards deters sufficient poachers	Patrols and guards can be deployed in nonpredictable fashion	Minimal consequences to poachers from being caught	What percentage chance of getting caught is needed to optimize deterrence?[a]
6. Target species or ecosystem is defensible	Target is contained within a defined area	Target has very high market value	

[a] Technically the ratio of the expected value of poaching to expected costs of sanctions

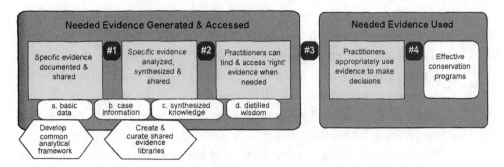

Figure 6.2. Pathway for collective evidence generation, access, and use.

To make this pathway work and build the global evidence base, we collectively need to undertake two major activities:

▶ **Develop a common analytical framework.** To efficiently share and compare conservation work around the world, we need to have a number of elements of a common analytical framework in place:

- *Common units of analysis.* First, we need a shared way of describing both the work we are doing and the system in which this work is taking place. The situation analysis and strategy pathway tools described in this book are the ideal units for these kinds of analyses. Going back to Figures 0.1 and 0.2 in the Introduction, projects and programs are too coarse a unit because they often combine various unrelated elements of work. Actions, disassociated from outcomes, on the other hand, are too fine a unit. They really don't capture the necessary details and wrinkles, especially when multiple actions are combined in one strategy pathway. Strategy pathways and their associated situation analyses are the Goldilocks "just right" units to use.
- *Common elements.* Next, we need to have a shared set of building blocks in each unit of analysis. To this end, the factors defined by the *Conservation Standards* such as target factors, threats, intermediate results, and actions provide a good set of basic elements to capture and describe conservation work.
- *Common classifications.* It is also essential to have common classifications for each of the different factor types. As an analogy, think about the very early days of medical research. If each doctor had a different name for the parts of the body, the diseases they were seeing, and treatments that they were using, it would be very hard to determine what interventions worked. Similarly, in conservation it's useful to have a common way of naming the target and threat

factors and the different conservation actions per the various International Union for Conservation of Nature (IUCN) and Conservation Measures Partnership (CMP) classifications described in Chapters 1 and 2. Ideally, there would also be common terms to describe contributing factors, although that is a much more challenging proposition.

- *Common data and metadata standards.* It is likewise necessary to have standardized ways of capturing and recording data and information about conservation work. This includes how you capture data about each factor and relationship. It also includes how you spatially map factors, track expenses, and record monitoring data. And it would ideally also include standard metadata about your various data elements, such as who collected them and how they were collected, and an assessment of the data quality and its limitations.
- *Shared intellectual property rights agreements.* Finally, to make data maximally useful, it's important that each data set be shared with clear use rights agreements. The open source licenses produced by the Creative Commons are generally good starting points for these types of agreements.

This common framework would both enable people engaged in evidence synthesis to find the case information they need to do their reviews and also enable practitioners to easily search and find the evidence they need to inform their work.

▸ **Create and curate shared evidence libraries.** Another necessary ingredient to efficiently share and compare conservation work around the world is having four types of libraries, each containing a different kind of evidence:

- *Libraries of basic data.* Repositories of unfiltered basic data about key factor types. Examples might include the presence or status of key species, the status of key ecosystems, the location and current and projected intensity of different threats, and the presence of key threat drivers.
- *Libraries of case experience.* Registries of specific conservation strategies that have been or are being planned and implemented. Each entry would ideally describe the situation in which the work is taking place, the actions being taken, the resources needed to implement the actions, and the results of the work. Although they are typically organized by projects, ideally they would be organized by strategy pathway.
- *Libraries of synthesized knowledge.* Repositories of analyzed evidence about conservation actions. These include evidence syntheses, systematic reviews,

and other decision support systems such as those found in the various evidence sites described in the "Sources and Further Information" section at the end of this chapter.

• *Libraries of distilled wisdom.* Repositories of generic theories of change (and, to the extent possible, the specific examples used to derive them) and other associated materials that represent the state of the world's knowledge about a given strategy. One example is CAML.

We do not need to create one all-encompassing database of all conservation experience. Instead there can be multiple instances of each library type, perhaps focused on conservation work on different themes or in different parts of the world. But it would be most helpful if all libraries were interoperable; each library would be compatible and allow seamless exchange and integration with the others. For example, people recording case experience might want to start with a generic theory of change for a given strategy so that they can be sure to capture the same factors and use common indicators. People who are conducting systematic reviews would ideally be able to draw on the libraries of case experience to inform their studies.

Guidance for Contributing to the Global Evidence Base

Some practical tips for sharing your data and results with the rest of the world include:

• **Use common templates.** As you design your strategies and your monitoring plans, make sure you consult with existing libraries such as CAML to see whether there are generic templates for the type of work you are doing. These templates will enable your team to jump-start your thinking based on the collective knowledge and experience of managers from around the world. But just as importantly, it also means that the data you collect about your experiences will be compatible with the data being collected by other people using this template.

• **Manage and document your data with an eye towards sharing.** As you and your team collect data about your situation and your strategies, make the little bit of extra effort needed to annotate and document your data. This includes not only describing the data's context and limitations but also providing sufficient metadata so that other people can easily know whether your data set is relevant to their analyses. By doing so, you will ensure that your data are findable and usable by both your team (even if current team members have moved on) and people from the rest of the world who can benefit from it. It's also important to separate out potentially sensitive data that can't be shared from data that can be shared. All too often, if sensitive data are mixed in with shareable data, then none of it ends up getting shared.

- **Report both successes and failures.** There is a natural human tendency to trumpet our successes and try to cover up our failures. And yet from a learning perspective, we can benefit as much or even more from understanding our failures as our successes. As a result, rather than hide your failures, study them and to publicly share them. Systematic reviews in particular can be much more powerful when they can help determine what worked but also what did not work and why.
- **Make contributing your evidence a regular part of your program routine.** Given the overloaded schedules of most conservation teams, it's important to make sharing your data and results a part of your regular program routine. For example, upload your data on a monthly or quarterly basis to the appropriate repository or send your data when you send your reports to your funders. This sharing will be greatly facilitated if you store and manage your data in compatible formats with the global repositories.
- **Encourage others to contribute their info.** If you are the manager of a program or organization, you can encourage and even incentivize the projects and programs that you are responsible for to make sure they share their experiences with the appropriate public repositories. And if you are a funder, you can go one step further and encourage or even insist that if projects and programs are using your funds, they have to contribute relevant results to appropriate public databases of experience. You can also provide the resources to facilitate this.

For example, in the world of genomic research, the leading institutions, funding agencies, and scientific journals have all come together and established a policy that if research is managed or funded by them or appears in one of their journals, the researchers *must* deposit all relevant genetic sequence data in a standard format in one of three approved and interlinked repositories around the world. It doesn't seem unreasonable that conservation projects that are funded through public support or by foundations should have to do something similar.

Developing Collaborative Learning Programs

In addition to serving as a basic unit for implementing conservation strategies, programs can play an important role in actively promoting learning. This can be done through different mechanisms for connecting people and projects in a learning network within a program or across programs. Marcia Brown and Nick Salafsky (2004) researched collaborative learning in a number of different fields and identified three approaches to promoting learning networks that could be applied to programs:

> ▸ **Approach I: Information exchange networks.** 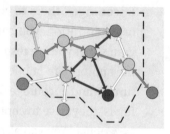 In these networks, learning is guided primarily by participants' specific requests for information, although the network may also have some high-level learning questions. The network thus has a loosely defined boundary shown by the dashed border that can shift depending on who is in the network and their current information needs. The members of the network are represented by the shaded circles inside the dotted line. Differences in shading show that the participants have different roles (e.g., managers, field practitioners) and areas of expertise. They exchange different types of information, as represented by different shaded arrows. Some people serve as central nodes of information, and others benefit from their knowledge and their connections. Information is shared not only within the network but also with some people outside the network. Their membership process is usually open, and they can be any size. They usually require very little commitment from their members, and they rely primarily on informal incentives for participation. In terms of coordination and communication, they typically have a paid coordinator and a "fishing net" communication structure. Some well-known examples of this type of network in conservation are the Environmental Grantmakers Association, Conservation Finance Alliance, and Ecosystem-Based Management Tools Network.

▶ **Approach II: Best practices networks.** In these networks, participants define specific learning questions and collaborate to document, validate and disseminate best practices around these questions. The network thus has a more tightly defined boundary. They tend to have a formal membership approval process, and therefore they are not as large as the information exchange networks. They also 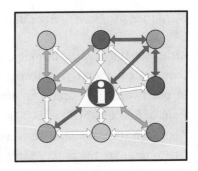 require a formal or informal commitment from participants, but they tend to rely on informal incentives for sharing information. They have paid coordinators and a bicycle wheel or spider web hub-and-spoke communication structure, with varying levels of participation in decision making. The coordinators help the members define learning questions, gather information from participants, process it, and return the processed information (best practices, lessons learned) to the participants. They usually rely on face-to-face communication but also create shared central information bases and websites. Some examples of this type of network in conservation are working groups set up by the CMP and the Conservation Coaches Network (CCNet).

▶ **Approach III: Collaborative research networks.** In these networks, learning is centered around a formal learning framework designed to answer specific research questions. Members are thus carefully selected as "replicates" that use one or more strategies that are the focus of the learning network. 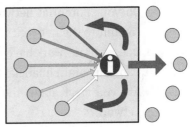 They tend to be small or medium in size. The process for joining the network can be entirely closed (by invitation only) or regulated by an approval process. They require a formal commitment and often offer formal incentives for sharing information. They have a paid coordinator and usually have a hub-and-spoke communication structure with a strong center core. The core defines the learning questions and learning framework, collects data and information from all participants, and analyzes them to draw conclusions. It then documents the results and shares them with the network participants and with outside parties interested in the topic. Participation in decision making varies. Some prototype examples of this type of network in conservation are the Biodiversity Conservation Network and the Locally Managed Marine Area Network.

Guidance for Developing Collaborative Learning Programs

Although the idea of bringing your program's members together in a network to promote collaborative learning sounds great in theory, it can be very challenging in practice. In the spirit of sharing failures, Richard and Nick launched Foundations of Success (FOS) in 2000 with the idea of using learning networks—particularly Approach III: collaborative research networks—as the main strategy that we would use to improve the practice of conservation. Although we had ambitions of creating dozens of these networks around different strategies, two decades later we have not been able to sustain or replicate the success of our initial prototypes. Based on this experience and the work outlined in Brown and Salafsky (2004), we can offer the following advice:

- **Start with the basics.** Perhaps the most important finding from our research and experience is that there are certain conditions that any learning network, regardless of its type, will have to meet. Specifically, before forming a learning network, consider the following initial questions:

  - Do you have a fairly specific subject or domain for your learning network?
  - Do your potential network members have the interest, desire, and time to commit to the network?
  - Does your network have the ability to hire a paid coordinator?
  - Can you obtain financial resources for network activities?
  - Are you clear about the questions you want to answer with your learning network?

  If you answer "no" to any of these questions, then you should probably reconsider trying to form a learning network. In particular, you need to pay attention to the people in the center of the network. As Malcom Gladwell (2000) says, networks depend on the principle that in any situation, roughly 80 percent of the work will be done by 20 percent of the participants.

- **Think hard about the right approach.** After considering the above questions, if you are still interested in going forward with a learning network, the decision of which type of approach to use involves balancing your needs and your available resources. As a starting point, consider the question:

- What types of learning are the members of your network interested in? If your members are interested in sharing experiences around a variety of topics, then using an Approach I information exchange network might make most sense. However, if your members are interested in discussing specific best practices or pursuing research questions, then an Approach II or Approach III network may make more sense. If you are interested in an Approach II or III network, then think about the following questions:

  - Do you have specific learning questions? Could you develop a learning framework?
  - Will membership be open or subject to approval or by invitation only? What might be the conditions for inclusion?
  - Will your members be willing to make a formal commitment to the learning process?
  - Can you provide formal incentives for sharing information?
  - Who will be on the coordination team?
  - Will your members support a centralized communication structure?
  - Is this a virtual network, or will the group meet together?

Depending on your answers, you will probably find that your situation is more comparable to one or the other of the two approaches. However, you may also find that you really don't have the resources to make an Approach II or III network function. In these cases, you may be better off starting with an Approach I network. It may also be appropriate in many cases to start with an Approach II network and let it evolve into a more intensive Approach III network over time. Although setting up learning programs can be challenging, we need to develop this critical set of tools for collaborative learning. In particular, this work may be informed by newly emerging work on how networks can be used to promote behavior change (Centola, 2021).

Building the Discipline of Conservation

This book is based on our own high-level strategy pathway (Figure 6.3). As shown at the far right-hand side of the diagram, this pathway makes a fundamental assumption that (1) successful conservation at scale in complex systems requires effective conservation programs. Furthermore, it also assumes that (2) programs that effectively use evidence and that (3) adopt and (4) have the analytical resources needed to use good analytical practices (per the *Conservation Standards*) will be more effective. There is also an assumed feedback loop (5) in that if conservation programs can demonstrate that they are effective, they will be able to attract greater levels of resource investment from society. And conversely, if programs cannot demonstrate effectiveness, available resources flowing to them—and the conservation sector as a whole—will decrease. Finally, although analytical resources and thinking are necessary for effective programs, they are not sufficient. There is also (6) "everything else needed" for the conservation community to achieve its ambitious goals, including sufficient human and financial resources, supportive leaders and stakeholders, functional organizations, enabling policies, and appropriate enabling conditions that contribute to program success but are beyond the scope of this book.

Given the magnitude and urgency of global conservation needs, we collectively don't have the time or the resources for each program or even each organization to (7) build on its own the evidence base needed for effective conservation, as described earlier in this chapter. We also collectively need to figure out how to (8) enhance the analytical capacity that programs need to use evidence as part of their good practices. And as is the case with getting any set of practices adopted, we jointly need to (9) actively promote these analytical practices by raising awareness, building abilities, providing incentives, and developing mandates. Or in other words, we need to harness collective impact to build the discipline of conservation. Key high-level strategy pathways include:

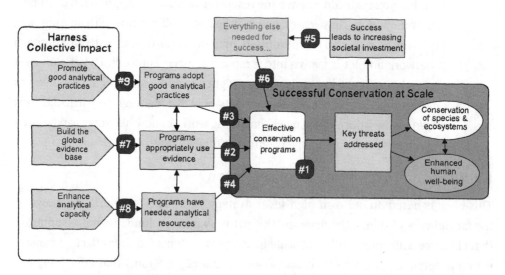

Figure 6.3. Overarching pathway for collectively building the discipline of conservation.

▸ **Build the global evidence base.** We collectively need to develop the global evidence base for conservation so that evidence can be generated and accessed when needed. As discussed in more detail in the first section of this chapter and Figure 6.2, this requires:

- *Developing a common analytical framework.* A shared conceptual framework for capturing and sharing evidence about conservation work
- *Creating and curating evidence libraries.* Four different types of repositories that can be used to capture and share evidence at all stages of the evidence production process.

▸ **Enhance analytical capacity.** In addition to building the global evidence base for conservation, we collectively need to build the surrounding systems and infrastructure to give practitioners the analytical resources they need to use this evidence. In particular, this requires:

- *Building compatible information technology systems.* Building the global evidence base will be greatly facilitated if we can develop common information technology systems that support this work. These include systems for planning and managing projects and programs, managing and using spatial data, agile work planning, data analysis and reporting, and building evidence libraries. The key is not to try to build one overarching system but rather to develop a common data framework and the connecting application interface pipelines that will allow information to seamlessly flow as appropriate throughout the conservation information ecosystem. For example, Miradi Software provides support for *Conservation Standards* analytical approaches and provides interfaces with many other key technology systems.
- *Developing a cadre of professional research practitioners.* Even more important than systems are the people who build and use them. In medicine, in addition to the frontline practitioners who treat patients (e.g., doctors, nurses, pharmacists) and the researchers who extend the science (e.g., laboratory researchers, drug developers), in between these two groups is a vast cadre of research practitioners whose entire careers focus on studying the effectiveness of clinical practice. These include clinical researchers, evidence synthesizers, and agency regulators. Likewise in education, in the space between teachers or administrators and academic researchers, there are many professionals involved in

evaluating and synthesizing evidence about the effectiveness of different curricula and approaches. In conservation, by contrast, these bridging and synthesizing roles are mostly either absent, sparsely covered on the margins of conservation organizations, or filled by volunteers and a few contract evaluators. There is thus a great need to develop the people who have the skills to fill these roles and the positions to support them both within existing conservation organizations as well as new ones focused on this type of work.

▶ **Promote good practices.** The biggest barriers to getting people to adopt desired practices are usually not technical but rather social, political, and institutional. To this end, we can collectively use the classic behavior change levers:

- *Increasing awareness and creating norms (i.e., "show me" or "sway me").* We need to make people aware of the need to adopt these practices and make the case that they will indeed lead to more effective conservation programs. Although there have been growing efforts to develop the stories, studies, and other evidence to support this hypothesis, there is still a great deal more to be done along these lines. Going further, we need to create social norms that make these practices business as usual.
- *Enhancing abilities (i.e., "help me").* We also need to provide guidance, coaching, and training to build capacity to use these practices. This includes building on the efforts of the CMP and the Collaboration for Environmental Evidence (CEE) to provide standards, guidance, and tools; the CCNet to develop skilled coaches around the world; and the Teaching Adaptive Management Network to provide training in these practices to students around the world who will become the next generation of conservation practitioners.
- *Providing incentives (i.e., "tempt me").* We need to provide meaningful incentives to individuals and organizations to adopt good analytical practices. We need to build this type of work into people's job descriptions. We need to provide support to and rewards for people, projects, programs, and organizations that do this type of work well. And we need to stop enabling those who don't do it well and cannot produce evidence that their work is achieving the desired or promised results. If you were an investor looking to fund a business venture, you almost certainly would not put up substantial funds unless the team had a solid business strategy and implementation and business information plan. Why should your conservation investment be any different?
- *Creating defaults and implementing mandates (i.e., "nudge me" or "make me").*

Finally, we need to build these practices into existing business processes and systems so they become default ways of working. We could also consider making these practices standard operating procedure. Organizations can require that their programs be based on good practices and conduct audits and assessments to ensure compliance. Governments can make and implement policies that require evidence-informed decision making. Foundations and other donors can preferentially or even exclusively fund programs that follow these practices. And society can bake impact assessment into the analysis of charities and other organizations done by groups such as Candid or Charity Navigator. Although on first consideration the concept of mandating good practices may seem extreme, given the growing and ever more urgent need for real and measurable conservation success (instead of just, in the words of Gordon Moore, "losing more slowly") coupled with the overall scarcity of resources, it seems reasonable to ask, "How can we not do what it takes to be as effective as possible?"

▶ **Harness collective impact.** Finally, in order to efficiently undertake the three pathways described above, we also need to organize and coordinate across the conservation sector. To this end, John Kania and Mark Kramer (2011) developed what they called a collective impact approach. As they wrote,

> Some social problems are technical in that the problem is well defined, the answer is known in advance, and one or a few organizations have the ability to implement the solution. Examples include funding college scholarships, building a hospital, or installing inventory controls in a food bank. Adaptive problems, by contrast, are complex, the answer is not known, and even if it were, no single entity has the resources or authority to bring about the necessary change. Reforming public education, restoring wetland environments, and improving community health are all adaptive problems. In these cases, reaching an effective solution requires learning by the stakeholders involved in the problem, who must then change their own behavior in order to create a solution.

Shifting from isolated impact to collective impact is not merely a matter of encouraging more collaboration or public–private partnerships. It requires a systemic approach to social impact that focuses on the relationships between organizations and the progress toward shared objectives. And it requires the creation of a new set of nonprofit management organizations that have the skills and resources to assemble and coordinate the specific elements necessary for collective action to succeed.

Kania and Kramer describe five conditions of successful collective impact initiatives. We consider each of these conditions with respect to the CMP and the CCNet, two of the leading conservation communities of practice.

- *Common agenda.* All participating organizations have a shared vision for social change that includes a common understanding of the problem and a joint approach to solving the problem through agreed-upon actions. At CMP's inception, founding member organizations ratified a charter that describes, in part, the vision and goals of the consortium. According to the CMP charter,

  > CMP was formed with a mission to advance the practice of conservation by developing, testing, and promoting principles and tools to assess and improve the effectiveness of conservation actions, and provide evidence of results achieved. By participating in CMP, member institutions seek to capitalize on their individual and collective experience to avoid duplication of effort, bypass tried but failed approaches, and quickly identify and adopt better practices.

- *Shared measurement system.* All participating organizations agree on the ways success will be measured and reported, with key indicators. Ultimately, like CMP, CCNet measures its success through its role in facilitating the global adoption of the *Conservation Standards*. However, its theory of change focuses on CCNet's role in developing the capacity of conservation coaches and their participation in global learning networks to improve conservation action. Thus CCNet gauges its success through a system that tracks the number and quality of certified coaches around the world, the number of the projects and programs CCNet coaches have helped facilitate, and lessons generated by the network.
- *Mutually reinforcing activities.* A diverse set of stakeholders, typically in multiple sectors, coordinate a set of differentiated activities through a mutually reinforcing plan of action. CMP and CCNet act as sister communities of practice, advancing their own set of fully complementary activities, all focused on improving the practice of conservation. Interestingly, the units of operation for CMP and CCNet are distinct and yet completely mutually reinforcing. CMP is composed of member organizations that are represented by one or two

individuals. CCNet derives its power and strength from the individual member coaches who make up the network. Frameworks, standards, definitions, and tools developed by the CMP members are field tested and applied by CCNet coaches around the world, and feedback from these coaches is incorporated back into CMP development activities, thus closing the loop of mutually reinforcing activities.

- *Continuous communication.* Frequent communications occur over a long period of time between key players within and between organizations, to build trust and encourage ongoing learning and adaptation. In this respect, both CMP and CCNet place great emphasis on active and dynamic communications within their respective communities of practice. But in addition, the networks go to great lengths to ensure communications and integration among their collective membership and constantly reach out to other like-minded individuals and organizations to extend their area of influence and impact.

- *Backbone organization.* Ongoing support is provided by an independent and dedicated staff that supports the overall work. The Nature Conservancy served as the backbone organization of CCNet when it was first established. Similarly, since its first meeting in 2002, CMP has relied on FOS as its backbone organization. In this role, FOS has served CMP by coordinating member activities, serving as de facto CEO, and acting as fiduciary agent, enabling the consortium to receive and disburse funds.

Measured against these criteria, the *Conservation Standards* community has made substantial progress over the past two decades in our ability to collectively support good conservation analytical practice. Our challenge is to build on this foundation and to continue to build the discipline of conservation.

Guidance for Building the Discipline of Conservation

As described above, building the discipline of conservation is an enormous undertaking that requires all kinds of contributions from all kinds of people and organizations. Therefore, it's hard to give specific advice to any one individual or group. But returning to the perspectives of the four managers we introduced at the start of this book, here are some examples of how you might be able to contribute to the discipline of conservation:

- *Community program manager.* If you are managing a local program, you can use the analytical approaches in this book with your program team. You will want to make sure that you consult with relevant external sources of evidence as you analyze your program situation and develop your program's strategies. In particular, ensure that you collect and record your monitoring data so that it can easily be rolled up and shared with your neighbors or broader programs that provide you with support or funding. As a local program manager, you are also in a great position to ensure that local and traditional knowledge is collected and incorporated into your program's evidence base. It also can be really helpful to capture quotes, narratives, photos, audio clips, videos, and other snippets of information that can help you tell your story about your work. Also, don't be shy about writing up your experiences and results and sharing them via blog posts, websites, podcasts, academic publications, or whatever channel seems appropriate. Real-world case examples can be incredibly helpful to your peers and other folks who are doing similar work. They also can provide attention and ultimately enhanced resources for your program.

Ideally, you are also well positioned to contribute to networks of people who are working on similar issues. If there is no obvious learning network to join, then consider starting your own. You can also push your program team and your program partners to improve your collective capacity to implement relevant good analytical practices.

- *NGO regional program manager.* If you are managing a regional program, you are in a great position to promote and implement the analytical approaches in this book across the projects in your program and with your overall program team. You can encourage the development of common strategy pathways and use your program to collectively test key learning questions that might emerge across them. But don't just work with your program in isolation. Reach out to other programs in your organization and beyond to find other people working on similar issues.

As a regional program manager, you are also in an ideal spot to create a learning culture within your program. You can develop true peer review mechanisms in which you have representatives of different project teams serve as auditors and reviewers of each other's work. You can also organize cross-project learning efforts, perhaps as part of regular pause and reflect sessions. And you can encourage the people on your team to develop their skills and even to become conservation coaches. Where possible, you should reach out to your organization's science teams and engage with them to compile evidence to test critical claims and to frame and answer key monitoring and learning questions that require extra resources and thinking. Don't be shy about writing up and sharing your results in relevant evidence libraries and journals.

- **Government agency monitoring expert.** If you are overseeing a government program that is setting fishery policies for your region, you are well situated to use the analytical approaches in this book to work with stakeholders to help frame and answer key questions. You can make sure that the decisions your agency makes incorporate all relevant evidence from different scientific, informal, and traditional sources. And where there are conflicting views and opinions, try to use your strategy pathways to work out where the sides differ and where they overlap, based on their assumptions about the underlying system.

  To the degree that your agency and situation allow, you can also play a key role in sharing your work and your findings with the broader world. Many governments have explicit policies about the use of evidence that you can build on and use.

- **Foundation program officer.** Finally, if you are managing a funding program, like any other program manager, you can implement the analytical approaches in this book with your program team as you design and implement your program strategy. But you also have an ideal opportunity to influence the adoption of good analytical practices in your grantee organizations by providing them with the awareness, abilities, incentives, and even mandate to do this kind of work. And of course, you can provide the resources necessary to undertake these practices.

  You are also in an ideal position to incentivize or even require that your grantees share their results in appropriate fashion. In particular, you make sure that you create a climate and incentives for your grantees to share their successes and to share and learn from their failures.

Finally, across all these roles, perhaps the most important thing you and your team can do is improve your own skills and ability to achieve your purpose. As Robert Pirsig said in *Zen and the Art of Motorcycle Maintenance* (1974):

The real cycle you're working in is a cycle called yourself. The machine that appears to be "out there" and the person that appears to be "in here" are not two separate things. They grow toward Quality or fall away from Quality together.

In the end, all each of us can do is try to become as effective in our work as possible.

Sources and Further Information

(See FOSonline.org/pathways for links and updated guidance material.)

Contributing to the Global Evidence Base

Key sources for this section include:

Annette Stewart, Nick Salafsky, and Richard Margoluis (2018), *Evidence Libraries: A Guide for Practitioners and Funders.* A review and analysis of evidence libraries in medicine, education, policing, conservation, and other fields.

Nick Salafsky et al. (2019), "Defining and Using Evidence in Conservation Practice" (*Conservation Science and Practice* 1: e27). Figure 6.3 in this book is derived from a more detailed version of the strategy pathway for generating, accessing, and using evidence in Figure 4 of this article.

Conservation Actions and Measures Library (CAML). A web-based library of generic pathways for single-action and compound conservation strategies.

Developing Collaborative Learning Programs

This material has drawn on the following sources:

Malcom Gladwell (2000), *The Tipping Point: How Little Things Can Make a Big Difference.* A classic book on how to create more effective networks.

Etienne Wenger, Richard McDermott, and William Snyder (2002), *Cultivating Communities of Practice: A Guide to Managing Knowledge.* A summary of the theory and examples of communities of practice, drawn primarily from the business world.

Marcia Brown and Nick Salafsky (2004), *Learning about Learning Networks: Results from a Cross-Disciplinary Study.* A review of learning networks that is the basis for this section.

Damon Centola (2021), *Change: How to Make Big Things Happen.* A book describing fascinating research on how networks can be used to promote behavior change.

Building the Discipline of Conservation

The overall theory of change in this section is based on similar thinking outlined in sources including:

CMP (2017), *CMP Strategic Plan 2017–2022.* A situation assessment and theories of change for transforming conservation practice.

FOS (2020), *FOS Strategic Plan.* A situation assessment and theories of change for improving the practice of conservation.

There is an extensive literature about the concept of collective impact based on an original article:

John Kania and Mark Kramer (2011), *Collective Impact.* (*Stanford Social Innovation Review*).

Key Learning Questions

1. How do we incentivize and enable practitioners and organizations to contribute their data and knowledge to appropriate evidence libraries?
2. How can we incentivize and enable groups to form learning networks to develop our knowledge about key actions?
3. How do we build and support the cadre of research practitioners to bridge the gap between science and research?
4. How can we better show, help, tempt, or make all relevant members of the conservation sector use good analytical practices?
5. How can we improve the collective impact of CMP, CCNet, CEE, and other communities of practice?

Some Final Words

We hope this book will serve as a catalyst for developing the effective large-scale programs that are desperately needed to address the complex conservation, environmental, and human well-being challenges we are collectively facing. We have tried to provide a guide to the most useful analytical frameworks and tools to help you and your team improve the ongoing design and management of your programs.

As we said in the preface, no book by itself will automatically turn you and your team into expert conservation practitioners; good conservation is as much an art as a science. And like any art, it requires years of hands-on practice to achieve mastery and to know when to follow the rules—and when to break and reinvent the rules. But it is our hope that this book can help you realize what knowledge and analytical skills you need, what you currently lack, and where you can go to find additional training and support and, most importantly, give you confidence in taking the next steps on your journey.

Large-scale programs in complex systems can be daunting endeavors that involve swimming upstream against a strong current with enormous barriers to overcome. But like the fish in our final illustration, if you can use the analytical approaches presented in this book to break up these challenges into more manageable tasks, then you can surmount these barriers and continue on your pathways to success.

Glossary

The following entries define the technical terms introduced in the book. These definitions are based in part on those in the *Open Standards for the Practice of Conservation 4.0* and our original book *Measures of Success*. We have also built on some definitions from the systems thinking literature and from Wikipedia. In some cases, these technical terms have narrower definitions in the context of program design and management than their wider common meanings.

In a few instances, we have adapted existing *Conservation Standards 4.0* terms or introduced some new terms as necessary to represent new concepts or provide greater clarity where existing terms are imprecise or have multiple and conflicting meanings. We have provided some notes to explain these changes.

We are not proposing new terms lightly. We recognize that people are both attached to and passionate about their language. And at the end of the day, the choice of a term for a concept is arbitrary. As Shakespeare eloquently put it, "A rose by any other name would smell as sweet." Nonetheless, having a common and precise language matters if we are going to continue to build conservation as a discipline. As Wittgenstein said, "The limits of my language mean the limits of my world. . . . What we cannot speak about we must pass over in silence."

The criteria we used in choosing a given term are to:

- Maintain established *Conservation Standards* conventions
- Fit standard use of terms in other related disciplines
- Be easily understood by practitioners coming new to the *Conservation Standards*,
- Make sense in English
- Reduce foreign language translation issues (although note that foreign language translations do not have to use the closest cognate if they prefer another term)

No one set of terms will optimize all these criteria; the art of this work thus lies in deciding which criteria take precedence.

Accurate. One of the criteria for a good *method:* The data collection method has little or no margin of error.

Achievable. One of the *SMART* criteria for a *goal* or *objective*: Practical and appropriate within the context of the program including the political, social, and financial context.

Action (or *intervention*). A set of activities with a common focus that work together to achieve specific goals and objectives by targeting key intervention points, optimizing opportunities, and limiting constraints. A good action meets the criteria of being *linked, focused, feasible,* and *appropriate.* Compare to a *strategy* (which includes one or more actions and their associated results) and an *activity* (which is a subcomponent of an action). Represented by a yellow hexagon in Miradi Software.

> **Note:** The *Conservation Standards 4.0* defines an action as "A general term used to refer to the work of project and program conservation teams. This includes strategies, activities, and tasks." We are deliberately redefining action to be more specific, essentially equivalent to a *strategy* per the *Conservation Standards 4.0*. This allows us to then redefine *strategy* at a higher level as a combination of both *actions* and *results*, which is much more consistent with how the rest of the world (e.g., the development, evaluation, business, and military communities) uses this term.

Activity. A set of specific tasks that need to be completed as part of implementing an *action*. Compare to *action* and *monitoring activity*.

Adaptive management. The incorporation of deliberate learning into professional practice to reduce uncertainty in decision making. Specifically, it is the integration of design, management, and monitoring to enable practitioners to systematically and efficiently test key assumptions, evaluate the results, adjust management decisions, and generate learning. Adaptive management is particularly useful when practitioners need to take action but don't have the evidence to act with certainty. *Basic adaptive management* is typically less resource intensive but also less precise, whereas more *rigorous adaptive management* is more resource intensive and precise.

After action review. Synonym for *pause and reflect.*

Agile planning. An approach to work planning originally from software development that focuses on small, incremental, rapid, and user-focused advances within a rough overall framework for implementing a given strategy. Agile planning is most useful in uncertain and complex situations in which it is not possible to fully spec out the desired solution in advance. Agile planning thus advocates iterative development cycles, continual improvement, and flexible responses to change. Compare to *waterfall planning.*

Analytical need (or *information need*). Something that a program team or program partners and stakeholders must know about a program. Often expressed more precisely in the form of a *monitoring question* or *collaborative learning question* and ultimately a *hypothesis*.

Appreciative inquiry. An approach to program planning that focuses on what a program team or group of stakeholders does well. Instead of 'problem solving,' appreciative inquiry is geared toward discovering the untapped positive potential of a system.

Appropriate. One of the criteria for a good *method:* Acceptable to and fitting within cultural, social, and biological norms.

Assumption. A general term used to describe what a program team believes to be true, such as an assumed causal relationship between two or more factors in a situation assessment or a strategy pathway. We are using *assumptions* as a nontechnical, catch-all term to describe both *claims* and *hypotheses*.

Attribution. The degree to which a given program, project, or strategy can claim sole or primary responsibility for a given outcome. Compare to *contribution*.

Audience. The specific people who will receive and use the information generated by a given analytical effort.

Balancing feedback loop. In systems thinking, a feedback process that works to keep the system in a certain state, such as a thermostat that activates a heating or cooling system to keep a house at the desired temperature. Compare to *reinforcing feedback loop*.

Basic adaptive management. See *adaptive management*.

Best practices network. See *learning network*.

Biophysical factor. An ecological or geophysical element within a system. Most often, part of a situation assessment showing the mechanism of how a *direct threat* affects a *target factor*. For example, inappropriate logging practices (a threat) cause loss of stream shading (a biophysical factor), which raises stream water temperature (another biophysical factor), which then affects salmon populations (a target factor). Represented by an olive green rectangle in Miradi Software diagrams.

Biophysical result. A factor in a strategy pathway showing the desired state of a biophysical factor. Represented by a bluish-green rectangle in Miradi Software diagrams. Compare to *intermediate result* and *threat reduction result*.

Black swan event. In systems thinking, a rare and usually unpredictable event that is beyond what is normally expected of a situation and that has the potential to majorly disrupt or change the system, such as a large oil spill in a coastal ecosystem coming from an oil tanker gone off its normal route.

Bright spots. Success stories that are typically discovered within a system rather than designed by a program team, such as a traditional farming technique that provides sustainability benefits.

Burden of proof. In the context of making decisions under uncertainty, the level of evidence a decision maker needs to meet to justify making a change from the status quo, such as taking a proposed risky action that will have consequences for different actors in the system. The degree of burden of proof in a given situation depends on the relative consequences of taking action where no action is warranted (*Type I error*) or not taking action where action is warranted (*Type II error*) as well as the reversibility of the situation.

Causality (or *causation* or *cause and effect*). A relationship between two or more factors in a system in which change in one factor (a cause) contributes to a dependent change in one or more other factors (an effect). Compare to *correlation*.

Censusing. In a monitoring plan, measuring all *units* within a *population*. Compare to *sampling*.

Claim. A proposition about a system that is supported by existing evidence. Claims are thus the basic unit of analysis for evidence synthesis. For example, claims in a situation assessment may be related to the status of target species or the cause of a threat. Claims in a strategy pathway may be about the effectiveness of an action or the conditions under which a given action might be effective. Compare to *hypothesis* or *assumption*.

> **Note:** Although many people use the term *claim* synonymously with *hypothesis*, we are deliberately reserving *claim* to refer to a proposition that is assessed with existing evidence. We are using *hypothesis* to refer to a proposition that needs to be tested as part of a future *monitoring question* or *learning question*. And we are using *assumptions* as a generic term to refer to all propositions including claims and hypotheses.

Coach. A person who provides support and training to project and program teams. Compare to *facilitator*.

Collaborative learning plan. A description of how a program will answer *collaborative learning questions*. Usually developed in conjunction with other collaborators.

Collaborative learning question. An *analytical need* that can be addressed through cross-program analyses. Typically converted into one or more *hypotheses* that can then be assessed. Compare to *monitoring question*.

> **Note:** There has been a great deal of confusion over the years between the "lowercase l learning questions" that every team ideally answers as they go through the project or program cycle and the "Capital L Learning Questions" that need to be addressed at a cross-program or even discipline level. We are explicitly using *collaborative learning questions* to refer to the latter and *monitoring questions* to refer to the former.

Collaborative research network. See *learning network*.

Collective impact. An approach to collaboration across a group of organizations that involves five conditions: a common agenda, shared measurement system, mutually reinforcing activities, continuous communication, and a backbone organization.

Complex system. A system composed of many dynamically interacting factors. Complex systems are intrinsically difficult to model because of the dependencies, competitions, relationships, or other types of interactions between their parts and their external environment.

Compound strategy pathway. A *theory of change* that has two or more actions that work together as part of an overall strategy. Compare to *single-action strategy pathway*.

Confounding factor. An element of the system that could affect relationships between given factors of interest in a core pathway.

Conservation target factor. Synonym for *ecological target factor*.

Consistent. One of the criteria for a good *indicator*: Not changing over time so that it always measures the same thing.

Constructed indicator. See *indicator*.

Contract. An agreement between two or more parties in which a funder provides money and other resources to an implementer who is then responsible for providing specified services or *deliverables*. Compare to *grant*.

Contractor. The organization or individual responsible for implementing a *contract*.

Contributing factor (or *driver*; historically also *indirect threat* or *opportunity*). A factor in a situation assessment that leads to a *direct threat* or *biophysical factor*. As opposed to the previously used terms *indirect threat* and *opportunity*, *contributing factor* is deliberately neutral because many factors (e.g., ecotourism) can be both part of a problem and part of a solution. Represented by an orange rectangle in situation diagrams in Miradi Software. See also *enabling condition* and *exogenous factor*.

Contribution. The degree to which a given program, project, or strategy is partially (as opposed to solely) responsible for a given outcome. Compare to *attribution*.

Cooperating partner. See *implementing partner*.

Core team. Individuals and organizations directly involved in designing and managing a program. The core team also typically includes one or more *coaches* or *facilitators* who can provide process support and advice.

Correlation. A relationship between two or more factors in a system in which change in one factor is associated with change in one or more other factors, but dependence has not been established. Compare to *causality*.

Cost-effective. One of the criteria for a good *method*: Does not cost too much in relation to the data it produces and the resources the project has.

Current status. The most recent measurement for an indicator or rating value for a factor that represents the present condition of the factor. Compare to *desired future status*.

Current threat. See *direct threat*.

Data. In evidence-informed conservation, a set of raw observations about a situation of interest collected through monitoring and research efforts. The bottom layer of the *data*, *information*, *knowledge*, and *wisdom* evidence pyramid. Sources of data include details about the conservation targets, threats, stakeholders, actions, and other basic data for evidence-based practice from program records, monitoring data, or key informants. They also include global data sets of target status, threats, and conservation actions.

Decision makers. The people who are collectively responsible for setting policies for and managing an organization, program, project, or other entity.

Declining payments. A form of payment in a multiyear *grant* in which a higher proportion of the grant is paid out at the beginning of the grant, and subsequent payment amounts decline until the end of the grant.

Deliverable. Specific goods, services, or *outputs* that must be produced by the implementer as part of a contract. Can also less formally refer to the *results* produced by the implementer of a grant that feed into an overall funding program strategy.

Dependency. In work planning, a relationship between two or more *activities* or tasks such that the initiation or completion of one relies on the initiation or completion of the other.

Desired future status (or *target value*). The targeted measurement for an indicator or rating value for a factor that a program team intends to achieve by a specific future date. Often the *target value* for a goal or an objective. Compare to *current status* and *milestone*.

Detail complexity. In systems thinking, refers to a system with a large number of factors or parts. Compare to *dynamic complexity*.

Developmental evaluation. See *evaluation*.

Direct threat (or *pressure*). A human action that immediately degrades one or more conservation target factors (e.g., illegal logging or unsustainable fishing). Direct threat factors can also be natural phenomena altered by human activities (e.g., increase in extreme storm events due to climate change). *Current threats* are actively negatively affecting target factors, *future threats* are likely to affect target factors at some point in the future, and *historical threats* negatively affected target factors in the past, but are no longer active. Represented by a pink rectangle in Miradi Software diagrams.

Direction of effect (or *sign*). An assessment of whether a given evidence source or overall evidence base supports or argues against the case for a given claim. *Supporting* (or *positive*) *evidence* builds the case for a claim. *Refuting* (or *negative*) *evidence* reduces the case for a claim. Compare to *strength of effect*.

Driver. A synonym for *contributing factor*.

Dynamic complexity. In systems thinking, a system with factors that interact with one another in a complex and often nonlinear fashion. Compare to *detail complexity*.

Ecological target factor (or *conservation target factor*). An element in a situation assessment that represents part or all of the ultimate biodiversity outcomes that a program is focused on. Typically species, ecosystems, or ecological processes. Compare to *human well-being target factor*.

Enabling condition. A *contributing factor* in a situation assessment or strategy pathway that is either necessary for or greatly facilitates implementation of a strategy. Often, an *exogenous factor* that is beyond the control of the program team, such as a legal framework or the level of corruption within a country.

Entrepreneurial program. An initiative that seeks to attract additional and often increasing sources of revenue to fund its work. Compare to *steady-state program*.

Evaluation. A formal assessment of the effects of a program, typically conducted by a third party. Evaluations can be subdivided into *developmental*, *formative*, or *summative evaluations* depending on whether they occur before, during, or after the strategies or programs being evaluated. Evaluations can also be *independent* (or *external*) or *participatory* depending on the degree to which the implementers are involved in the evaluation. Finally, evaluations can be divided into *process audits* versus *impact evaluations* depending on whether they focus on the actions taken or the results. Compare to *monitoring*.

> **Note:** Many people use *evaluation* more generically to describe the process of analyzing and making sense of data, particularly as it relates to the effectiveness of an intervention. In this book, however, we distinguish continuous internal analysis of monitoring data (i.e., evaluative thinking) from external evaluation, which is often done infrequently by a third party. We therefore restrict use of the term *evaluation* to the latter case.

Evidence. The relevant *data, information, knowledge*, and *wisdom* used to assess one or more *claims* related to a question of interest.

Evidence base. The body of all evidence (i.e., data, studies, syntheses, and theory) used to assess a particular set of *claims*.

Evidence-based conservation. Synonym for *evidence-informed conservation*.

Evidence-based practice. Synonym for *evidence-informed practice.*

Evidence-informed conservation (or *evidence-based conservation*). *Evidence-informed practice* as applied within the discipline of conservation.

Evidence-informed practice (or *evidence-based practice*). The explicit use and generation of relevant *data, information, knowledge,* and *wisdom* in all steps of any outcome-oriented discipline. Specifically, practitioners make decisions and take actions informed by systematic analyses of both their own and the world's previous experiences. Practitioners also document their results and contribute their findings back to the global evidence base.

Exogenous factor. A *contributing factor* in a situation assessment or strategy pathway that is beyond the control of the program team, such as the global price of gold or the level of corruption in a country. See *enabling condition.*

External evaluation. See *evaluation.*

External validity. Synonym for *relevance.*

Facilitator. An individual or organization who helps organize and lead workshops and other group meetings. Compare to *coach.*

Factor. A generic term for an element of a *situation assessment* or *strategy pathway diagram* such as a *direct threat* or *intermediate result.*

Feasible. One of the criteria for a good *method:* Can be implemented by people on the program team.

Feedback loop. In systems thinking, a set of cause-and-effect relationships that forms a circuit so that there is a reciprocal flow of influence. Every factor in a feedback loop is thus simultaneously both a cause and an effect. *Reinforcing feedback loops* cause increasingly rapid change in the system, whereas *balancing feedback loops* stabilize the system.

Focal interest. Synonym for *target factor.*

Focus. The center of attention for a program's work. Defining a program's focus includes clarifying the program's *purpose,* selecting *target factors* and bounding the program's *scope,* and assembling the right *program team* and *program partners.*

Formative evaluation. See *evaluation.*

Funder. An organization, agency, or individual that provides financial support to other entities that implement strategies, projects, or programs. Compare to *implementer.*

Future threat. See *direct threat.*

Generic claim. A proposition about a generic situation that is often a composite of many specific case situations, such as "Rats are a primary cause of seabird nest predation on islands around the world" or "Outreach campaigns will change target audience attitudes and behaviors." Compare to *specific claim.*

Generic evidence. *Data, knowledge, information,* or *wisdom* in an *evidence base* from the rest of the world outside the specific system or program of interest that is *relevant* to a given *specific claim.* Compare to *proximate evidence* and *specific evidence.*

Generic strategy pathway. A general theory of change describing how one or more types of actions leads to desired outcomes in different conditions. Generic strategy pathways are derived by comparing experience and evidence from multiple specific strategy pathways. They ideally capture the accumulated knowledge and even wisdom about conservation strategies and thus can serve as templates to develop new specific pathways. Compare to *specific strategy pathway*.

Goal. A formal statement detailing the desired ultimate outcome of a *strategy pathway*. Often equivalent to the *desired future status* of a *target factor*. A good goal meets the criteria of being *specific, measurable, achievable, results-oriented*, and *time-limited* (SMART). Compare to *objective*.

Grant. An agreement in which money or other resources are given by a *funder* to an *implementer* to achieve certain outcomes. Unlike a *loan*, the implementer does not have to pay back the money. And unlike a *contract*, grant funds are usually not used to directly purchase a specific service or deliverable from the implementer.

Grantee. The organization or individual that is the recipient of a *grant*.

Group. In a monitoring plan, a specific subset of the overall *population* that is the subject of monitoring efforts.

Historical threat. See *direct threat*.

Human well-being target factor. An element in a situation assessment that represents part or all of the ultimate human welfare outcomes that a program is focused on, such as food security, livelihoods, protection from severe weather events, or cultural traditions. In conservation programs, human well-being targets are typically linked to the program's ecological targets, although some groups do not divide ecological and human well-being targets into separate categories. A program's human well-being targets should collectively represent the array of human well-being needs dependent on the ecological targets. Compare to *ecological target factor*.

Hypothesis. A proposition about a system that requires additional evidence to assess. Hypotheses are thus the basic unit of analysis for program monitoring, research, and collaborative learning. For example, hypotheses in a *situation assessment* may be related to the status of target species or the cause of a threat. Hypotheses in a *strategy pathway* may be about the effectiveness of an action or the conditions under which a given action might be effective. Compare to *claim* or *assumption*.

> **Note:** Although many people use the term *hypothesis* synonymously with *claim*, we are deliberately reserving *hypothesis* to refer to a proposition that needs to be tested as part of a future *monitoring question* or *learning question*. We are using *claim* to refer to a proposition assessed with existing evidence. And we are using *assumptions* as a generic term to refer to all propositions including claims and hypotheses.

Impact evaluation. See *evaluation*.

Impact trajectory. A high-level model of a program's expected effects relative to the status quo in which the program is not implemented. Liz Ruedy's six models of impact trajectories are transformative, proactive, opportunistic, stabilizing, preventative, and palliative.

Implementer. An organization or team responsible for designing, managing, and executing a strategy, project, or program. Compare to *funder*.

Implementing partner. An individual or organization involved in helping to implement a project or program. Generally people who can be assigned activities and tasks used to implement program strategies. Specific types of implementing partners include *program staff* who work for the core organizations involved in the program, *funders* who provide financial and other support through grants and contracts, *grantees* and *contractors* who use financial and other support to implement activities, and *cooperating partners* who participate in program implementation without direct compensation.

Independent evaluation. See *evaluation*.

Indicator (or *metric*). A measure related to a specific analytical need, such as the status of a target, change in a threat, progress toward an objective, or association between variables. A good indicator meets the criteria of being *measurable, precise, consistent, sensitive*, and *understandable*. When used to assess progress toward goals or objectives, indicators are sometimes called *key performance indicators (KPIs)* in the business world.

Indicators can be subdivided into *quantitative indicators*, which include both continuous and discrete variables, and *qualitative indicators*, which include both ordinal and nominal variables. Indicators can also be subdivided into *natural indicators*, which are direct and usually quantitative measures of a variable of interest; *proxy indicators*, which are indirect and usually quantitative measures of a variable of interest; and *constructed indicators*, which are assessments of a variable along a rating scale or through some type of index.

Indigenous knowledge. Typically, evidence that has been sourced from the cultural traditions of indigenous people. See also *traditional knowledge*.

Indirect threat. See *contributing factor*.

Information. In evidence-informed conservation, the product of *data* that have been analyzed to help assess a claim or a hypothesis. The second layer of the *data, information, knowledge*, and *wisdom* evidence pyramid. Sources of information include documentation of specific adaptive management or research efforts that describe the question, situation, analytical method, results, and conclusions of specific cases. These sources can range from peer-reviewed scientific publications of randomized controlled trials to gray literature case studies or informal field notes.

Information exchange network. See *learning network*.

Information need. Synonym for *analytical need*.

Information system. The software, databases, and other components used to collect, analyze, and share a program's *evidence*.

Initiative. Synonym for *program*.

Intermediate outcome. See *outcome*.

Intermediate result. A factor within a *strategy pathway* between an *action* and a *target outcome*. Represented by a blue rectangle in Miradi Software diagrams. Compare to *threat reduction result* and *biophysical result*.

Internal validity. Synonym for *reliability*.

Intervention. Synonym for *action*.

Investment approach. A high-level description of a funding program's strategy for selecting its investment options. Investment approaches can be put on a spectrum from more *responsive philanthropy* to more *strategic philanthropy*.

Key attribute. In the *viability analysis* framework, an aspect of a *target factor* that, if present, helps define a healthy target and, if missing or altered, would lead to the outright loss or extreme degradation of that target over time.

Key performance indicator (KPI). See *indicator*.

Knowledge. In evidence-informed conservation, *information* that has been put into context. The third layer of the *data, information, knowledge,* and *wisdom* evidence pyramid. Sources of knowledge range from formal systematic reviews and evidence maps to subject-wide evidence syntheses to more informal summaries of available evidence. Sources of knowledge also include decision support systems that summarize evidence and make it available to practitioners when making decisions. These sources can range from simple decision trees, to more sophisticated searchable online information technologies and decision support software, to traditional knowledge systems used by indigenous peoples.

Learning network. A group of individuals or projects engaged in collaborative learning. Networks can be subdivided into *information exchange networks*, *best practices networks*, and *collaborative research networks*.

Learning question. See *collaborative learning question*.

Loan. An agreement in which money or other resources are given by a *funder* to an *implementer* to achieve certain outcomes. Unlike a *grant,* the implementer has to pay back the money.

Magnitude. Synonym for *strength of effect*.

Measurable. One of the *SMART* criteria for a *goal* or *objective*: Definable in relation to some standard quantitative or qualitative scale (numbers, percentage, fractions, or all/nothing states).

Measurable. One criterion for a good *indicator*: Able to be recorded and analyzed with quantitative or qualitative data.

Method. In a monitoring plan, a specific technique used to collect data to measure an *indicator*. A good method should meet the criteria of being *accurate, reliable, cost-effective, feasible*, and *appropriate*.

Metric. Synonym for *indicator*.

Milestone. An interim target value for an indicator of a factor, goal, or objective that a program team intends to achieve by a specified date while moving toward the ultimate *desired future status*. A milestone is structured like the ultimate desired future status for a goal or objective but almost always represents a lesser amount of achievement in a shorter period of time. Compare to *desired future status*.

Mission statement. A written description of an organization's purpose, strategies, and values. Compare to *purpose*.

Model. A simplified representation of reality, often presented in the form of a diagram. A model is used to synthesize different perspectives, collect relevant evidence, compare alternative courses of action, and create a framework for ongoing learning.

Monitoring. The periodic collection and analysis of data to test specific *hypotheses* that answer specific *monitoring questions* about a program's *situation assessment* and *strategies*.

Monitoring activity. A set of specific tasks that need to be completed as part of implementing a monitoring plan. Compare to *activity*.

Monitoring plan. A description of how a program will collect monitoring data. Components of a monitoring plan include *monitoring questions*, *factors* and *indicators*, monitoring design and methods, *monitoring activities*, and a monitoring data information management plan.

Monitoring question. An *analytical need* that can be addressed by a program's monitoring efforts. Typically converted into one or more *hypotheses* that can then be assessed. Compare to *collaborative learning question*.

> **Note:** There has been a great deal of confusion over the years between the "lowercase l learning questions" that every team ideally answers as they go through the project or program cycle and the "Capital L Learning Questions" that need to be addressed at a cross-program or even discipline level. We are explicitly using *collaborative learning questions* to refer to the latter and *monitoring questions* to refer to the former.

Natural indicator. See *indicator*.

Negative evidence. Synonym for *refuting evidence*.

Neighboring evidence. Synonym for *proximate evidence*.

Nested factor. In systems thinking, elements in a model that are wholly contained within a higher-order factor. For example, species target factors may be nested in an ecosystem target factor.

Objective. A formal statement detailing a desired result in a strategy pathway, such as reducing a critical threat. A good objective meets the criteria of being *specific, measurable, achievable, results-oriented*, and *time-limited* (SMART). Compare to *goal*.

Operational plan. A description of how a program will implement its strategic plan. Components of an operational plan include a work plan and budget, an analysis of funding, human capacity and skills, and other nonfinancial resources required, a risk assessment and mitigation strategy, an estimate of program lifespan, and an exit strategy.

Opportunity. A *contributing factor* that represents a positive aspect of the system that could be built on to help achieve a program's goals. See *contributing factor*.

Organization. Typically used to refer primarily to nonprofit groups, but in this book also a generic term encompassing all types of entities including nonprofits or NGOs, consortia, government agencies, communities, tribes and other indigenous groups, foundations, and firms.

Outcome. What a program seeks to achieve with its investments of time and treasure. *Ultimate outcomes* are equivalent to a program *purpose*, whereas *target outcomes* are equivalent to the desired future status of a target factor (which is then converted into a SMART *goal* statement), and *intermediate outcomes* are equivalent to the desired future status of a result (which is then converted into a SMART *objective* statement). Compare to *result*.

Note: Some people use the term *outcome* to refer only to the ultimate endpoints of a strategy pathway. Other people expand the definition to include more intermediate results. As you can see above, our definition of *outcomes* allows for both, to represent the desired change in or status of people, institutions, or other system conditions.

Outcome-oriented philanthropy. Synonym for *strategic philanthropy*.

Pareto-optimal allocation. In economics, a situation in which total benefits have been maximized across all stakeholders. Thus no individual stakeholder can be made better off without making at least one other stakeholder worse off.

Participatory evaluation. See *evaluation*.

Pathway. A set of factors in a system that have an assumed causal relationship to one another. A pathway can be described in text, a table, an economic cash flow analysis, mathematical notations, or even a three-dimensional sculpture. In this book, however, pathways are generally represented as flow diagrams. See also *situation pathway* and *strategy pathway*.

Pause and reflect (or *after action review*). As part of *adaptive management*, an interval in which a program team analyzes actions and results to date and uses the information to adapt strategies as needed.

Pilot strategy (or *pilot project*). A small-scale, preliminary implementation of program actions carried out to evaluate feasibility, duration, cost, outcomes, and adverse events so that the strategy can be expanded to a greater scale.

Population. In a monitoring plan, the collection of all sampling *units* that could potentially be observed.

Portfolio. A suite of programmatic activities or investment options that, in combination, work toward a shared goal.

Positive deviance. An approach to program evaluation that focuses on finding what is working and determining why it is working, especially in a context that is not conducive to success. Related to the concept of *bright spots*.

Positive evidence. Synonym for *supporting evidence*.

Practitioners. People who design, manage, and monitor strategies, projects, and programs. Includes people involved in funding programs.

Precise. One of the criteria for a good *indicator*: Defined the same way by all people.

Pressure. Synonym for *direct threat*.

Process audit. See *evaluation*.

Program (or *initiative*). A set of related projects or strategies designed to achieve a specific purpose. A program can be thought of as both a larger-scale project in its own right and a functional unit to think about managing, funding, or learning from a group of related component projects. The concept of program can also be subdivided into implementation programs and funding programs, although many programs have elements of both of these roles. Compare to *project*.

Note: *Programs* and *projects* are relative rather than absolute terms. A "parent" program is at a higher-order scale than its lower-order "child" projects and thus contains work at multiple scales—a roll-up of project-level actions plus other actions being taken at the program-level scale.

Program advisors. Individuals and organizations who provide advice and oversight for a program. Advisors can include organizational leaders and board members. They can also include key stakeholders such as community elders, citizens' groups, watchdog organizations, or researchers.

Program partners. The wider group of individuals and organizations involved in designing and implementing a program.

Program plan. A living set of documents and associated evidence base that contains a program's *purpose, focus (scope, targets,* and *team), situation assessment, strategic plan, operational plan, evidence base,* and *monitoring* and *collaborative learning plans.*

> **Note:** The *Conservation Standards 4.0* defines a *strategic plan* as the sum of all documentation for a project including "descriptions of a project's scope, vision, and targets; an analysis of project situation, an action plan, a monitoring plan, and an operational plan." We are deliberately proposing to define *strategic plan* to be more like an *action plan* in the above *CS 4.0* definition and then introducing the term *program plan* to represent the broader concept.

Program staff. See *implementing partner.*

Program strategy pathway. One or more *actions* being undertaken by a program team to achieve specific program-level results. A program strategy pathway can include both "rolled-up" project-level strategy pathways and its own independent actions. Compare to *project strategy pathway.*

Program team. The group of practitioners who are responsible for designing, implementing, and managing a program as well as oversight of the program's component projects. Compare to *project team.*

Project. A set of *actions* being taken by a defined team of people to achieve agreed-upon outcomes, often at a specific geographic site, or within a thematic scope. Although technically projects can be at any scale, in practice they tend to be smaller site-based endeavors. In addition, they are often developed and managed as groups of related projects within a *program.* From the perspective of a funding program, a project is often equivalent to the work being done under a grant. Compare to *program.*

Project strategy pathway. One or more *actions* being undertaken by a project (or grant) team to achieve specific project-level results. A project strategy pathway is a building block of a project; put another way, a project is composed of one or more project strategy pathways. Compare to *program strategy pathway.*

Project team. The group of practitioners who are responsible for designing, implementing, and managing a project. Compare to *program team.*

Proximate evidence (or *neighboring evidence*). *Data, knowledge, information,* or *wisdom* in an *evidence base* that may not be from the specific system or program of interest but is from a spatially or conceptually close situation that makes it potentially more *relevant* to a given *specific claim* than evidence from the other side of the country or the world. Compare to *generic evidence* and *specific evidence.*

Proxy indicator. See *indicator*.

Purpose (or *ultimate outcome*). A high-level statement of what a program would like to accomplish with its time and treasure. Compare to *mission statement*.

Qualitative indicator. See *indicator*.

Quality. Synonym for *reliability*.

Quantitative indicator. See *indicator*.

Question. See *collaborative learning question* and *monitoring question*.

Refuting evidence (or *negative evidence*). *Data, knowledge, information*, or *wisdom* in an *evidence base* that helps reduce the case for a claim. Compare to *supporting evidence*.

Reinforcing feedback loop. In systems thinking, a feedback process that drives the system in one direction, often at increasing rates. When the reinforcing loop moves toward an undesirable direction, it can be called a vicious cycle. For example, soot from shipping causes ice to absorb heat, thus causing more melting, thus increasing the shipping season, and therefore causing an additional increase in soot. When the reinforcing loop moves toward a desirable direction, it can be called a virtuous cycle. For example, as stakeholders gain trust in a program, they are more willing to participate, which further builds trust. Compare to *balancing feedback loop*.

Relevance (or *external validity*). An assessment of the degree to which an evidence source or overall evidence base applies to a given claim (very high, high, medium, low). More relevant evidence addresses the claim in question and matches key enabling conditions of the situation of interest. Less relevant evidence either does not directly address the claim in question or does not match key enabling conditions. Compare to *reliability*.

Reliable. One of the criteria for a good *method:* Results are consistently repeatable; each time that the method is used, it produces the same result.

Reliability (or *quality* or *internal validity*). An assessment of the quality of an evidence source or overall evidence base for a given claim (very high, high, medium, low). More reliable evidence comes from a higher-quality source or evidence base and thus has higher internal validity (e.g., a systematic review, a controlled study, or a reliable source of traditional knowledge). Less reliable evidence comes from a lower-quality source or evidence base and thus has lower internal validity (e.g., a single case study or an anecdote). Compare to *relevance*.

Report element. A component of a communication product such as a chart, table, dashboard gauge, photo, or story.

Research. Systematic investigation to evaluate one or more *hypotheses*, usually beyond routine strategy implementation and associated *monitoring* and *adaptive management*. Compare to *monitoring*.

> **Note:** Many people use *research* more generically to describe the process of collecting, analyzing, and making sense of data to evaluate a hypothesis. In this book, however, we distinguish between the internal collection and analysis of monitoring data while taking action ("small r research" that is part of ongoing adaptive management) from more formal "Capital R Research" that is typically done outside the course of routine strategy

implementation and monitoring and is aimed primarily at expanding general knowledge. We therefore restrict use of the term *research* to the latter case.

Research practitioner. A person who focuses on studying the effectiveness of clinical practice. Research practitioners include clinical researchers, evidence synthesizers, and agency regulators.

Responsive philanthropy. A funding *investment approach* that involves supporting individuals or organizations that are doing good work without being too involved in determining specific strategy pathways or outcomes. Compare to *strategic philanthropy*.

Result. Narrowly, a factor within a *strategy pathway* between an *action* and a *target outcome*. Represented by a rectangle in Miradi Software. Results can be subdivided into *intermediate results*, *threat reduction results*, and *biophysical results*. An *objective* is a formal statement providing *SMART* details of a result. More broadly, the term *result* can also be used to describe any output or outcome of a program's actions. Compare to *outcome*.

> **Note:** Some people use the term *results* to encompass everything that stems from an action, including outputs, intermediate outcomes, and ultimate outcomes. Other people restrict the term results to be a subset of outcomes, focused in particular on the more intermediate outcomes. As you can see above, our definition of *results* allows for both.

Results chain. Synonym for *strategy pathway diagram*.

Results-oriented. One of the *SMART* criteria for a *goal* or *objective*: Represents necessary changes in target condition, threat reduction, or other key expected results.

Rigorous adaptive management. See *adaptive management*.

Sampling. In a monitoring plan, measurement of a subset of *units* within a *population*. Compare to *censusing*.

Sampling frame. In a monitoring plan, a description of the set of all *units* that a project team can sample.

Scale. The level at which a program is working and having an impact. Dimensions for considering scale include spatial and ecological (a run of salmon in a specific stream vs. the entire population of salmon in an ocean), temporal (over a week or over decades), and social, political, and institutional (part of a project being implemented by a local NGO in a municipality or by a consortium of agencies and private foundations across international boundaries).

Scope. The broad spatial, thematic, and temporal *focus* of a project or program.

Sensitive. One of the criteria for a good *indicator*: Changes proportionately in response to the actual condition being measured.

Sensitivity analysis. An assessment of how a model responds to changes in key parameters.

Sign. Synonym for *direction of effect*.

Single-action strategy pathway. A *theory of change* that has only one action leading to the desired results. Compare to *compound strategy pathway*.

Situation assessment (or *situation analysis*). An analysis of a program's context that includes defining the program's *scope* and *target factors* and the various biophysical, social, economic, political, and institutional factors that affect them. This analysis includes investing the appropriate level of resources in collecting and synthesizing relevant evidence to support key claims about factors in the system. *Situation assessment* also refers to the documentation of the results of this analysis.

Situation model (or *situation diagram*). A visual depiction of the findings of a *situation assessment*. A situation model represents relationships between key factors identified in a situation assessment believed to affect or lead to one or more target factors. It is also used to organize existing evidence for key claims about the system, identify key intervention points, and determine future monitoring and collaborative learning questions.

Situation pathway. A set of factors in a situation model that have an assumed causal relationship to one another. Most situation models can be subdivided into multiple situation pathways for different analytical purposes. Compare to *strategy pathway*.

SMART. An acronym used to describe a *goal* or *objective* that meets the criteria of being *specific*, *measurable*, *achievable*, *results-oriented*, and *time-limited*.

Spatial scope. See *scope*.

Specific. One of the *SMART* criteria for a *goal* or *objective*: Clearly defined so that all people have the same understanding of what the terms in the goal or objective mean.

Specific claim. A proposition about a particular real-world case or situation, such as "Rats are the primary cause of seabird nest predation on the islands within our program scope" or "An outreach campaign to our community members can persuade them to install rat barriers on their boats." Compare to *generic claim*.

Specific evidence. *Data, knowledge, information,* or *wisdom* in an *evidence base* from within the specific system or program of interest that is presumably more *relevant* to a given *specific claim* than evidence from the other side of the country or world. Compare to *generic evidence* and *proximate evidence*.

Specific strategy pathway. A *theory of change* describing how one or more *actions* leads to desired *outcomes* in a particular real-world case or situation. *Specific strategy pathways* are sources of information that can be used to derive *generic strategy pathways*. Compare to *generic strategy pathway*.

Stakeholder. Any individual, group, or institution that has a vested interest in or can influence the system that a program is working or that potentially will be affected by program activities and has something to gain or lose if conditions change or stay the same. Stakeholders are all those who need to be considered in achieving program goals and whose participation and support are crucial to its success. These can include people who need to be engaged or informed through two-way or one-way communication.

Steady-state programs. An initiative that operates under or allocates a generally fixed set of resources. Compare to *entrepreneurial program*.

Strategic philanthropy (or *outcome-oriented philanthropy*). A funding *investment approach* that involves supporting specific actions in service of specified outcomes as defined by a clear strategy pathway. Compare to *responsive philanthropy*.

Strategic plan. A living document that contains a program's strategy and scaling pathways. Compare to *program plan*.

Note: The *Conservation Standards 4.0* defines a *strategic plan* as the sum of all documentation for a project including "descriptions of a project's scope, vision, and targets; an analysis of project situation, an action plan, a monitoring plan, and an operational plan." We are deliberately proposing to define *strategic plan* to be more like an *action plan* in the above *CS 4.0* definition because it seems confusing to have an *action plan* describe *strategy pathways*.

Strategy. See *strategy pathway*.

Strategy pathway (or *strategy*). A model of a *theory of change* showing how one or more actions lead to (or, in more scientific terms, "are assumed to cause") desired outcomes. Strategy pathways can be further broken down into *single-action* versus *compound*, *specific* versus *generic*, and *project* versus *program strategy pathways*. Represented by a block arrow in Miradi Software diagrams.

Note: The *Conservation Standards 4.0* defines a *strategy* as "a set of activities with a common focus that work together to achieve specific goals and objectives by targeting key intervention points, optimizing opportunities, and limiting constraints." This narrow use of the term *strategy* to denote an *action* goes back to our original book *Measures of Success* and The Nature Conservancy's 5-S Planning System in the 1990s, which (as the name suggests) deliberately chose to use only terms starting with the letter S. Unfortunately, this definition of *strategy* is at odds with most of the rest of the world (e.g., the development, evaluation, business, and military communities), who use the term to refer to both actions and their anticipated results and outcomes. To this end, we are deliberately redefining *strategy* at a higher level as a combination of both *actions* and *results*. By formally calling it a *strategy pathway*, we hope to minimize any confusion between the current narrower *Conservation Standards 4.0* use of the term and our broader use of the term.

Strategy pathway diagram (or *results chain*). A graphical representation of a *strategy pathway*.

Strength of effect (or *magnitude*). An assessment of the degree of support that a given evidence source or overall evidence base provides for or against the case for a given claim (strongly supports, weakly supports, mixed, weakly refutes, strongly refutes). Strong evidence convincingly supports or refutes a claim. Weak evidence only somewhat supports or refutes a claim. Compare to *direction of effect*.

Summative evaluation. See *evaluation*.

Supporting evidence (or *positive evidence*). *Data*, *knowledge*, *information*, or *wisdom* in an *evidence base* that helps build the case for a *claim*. Compare to *refuting evidence*.

System. A group of interacting or interrelated factors that form a unified whole. A system is described by its *focus*, boundaries, and structure and expressed in its functioning. Systems become more complex as the number of factors increase (*detail complexity*) and the way in which factors increase expand (*dynamic complexity*).

Systems analysis (or *systems thinking*). A set of synergistic analytical skills used to identify and understand systems, predict their behaviors, and devise modifications to them in order to produce desired effects.

Target factor (or *focal interest*). An element in a situation assessment that represents part or all of the ultimate outcomes that a program is focused on. In conservation programs, these entities typically include both *ecological targets*, including species, ecosystems, and ecological processes, and *human well-being targets*, which include aspects of human communities such as food security, livelihoods, protection from severe weather events, and cultural traditions (although some groups do not divide ecological and human well-being targets into separate categories). As programs expand into other disciplines, it may also be useful to consider target factors that represent other purposes such as human health, education, water and sanitation, environmental justice, social and racial equity, and human rights. Represented by an oval in Miradi Software diagrams.

> **Note:** The term *target* has been the source of endless confusion and discussion. The *Conservation Standards* community adopted this term as a shorthand for what was originally called a *focal conservation target*: a species, ecosystem, or ecological process that represented the biodiversity values of the system. Unfortunately, this use of the term is at odds with the rest of the world, which uses *target* primarily to represent the *desired future status* for a *SMART goal* or *objective* for any kind of factor. This includes the targets established by the Convention on Biological Diversity and the UN's Millennium Development Goals. We and the Conservation Measures Partnership have spent many hours trying to develop better terms to distinguish between these two concepts. It's proven to be surprisingly difficult to find good substitutes that fulfil all our terminology criteria. To this end, we have adopted *target factor* and *target value* to try to distinguish between these two meanings.

Target outcome. See *outcome*.

Target value. See *desired future status*. See also the note under *target factor*.

Temporal scope. See *scope*.

Thematic scope. See *scope*.

Theory of change. A series of causally linked assumptions about how a team thinks its actions will help it achieve *intermediate results* leading to *target outcomes*. A theory of change is often displayed in a *strategy pathway diagram*, although it also can be expressed in text, mathematical notation, or other forms. A theory of change approach is both the process and the product of laying out these assumptions.

Threat. See *direct threat*.

Threat reduction result. A factor in a strategy pathway showing the desired state of a threat factor. Represented by a reddish-purple rectangle in Miradi Software diagrams. Compare to *intermediate result* and *biophysical result*.

Time-limited. One of the *SMART* criteria for a *goal* or *objective*: Achievable within a specific period of time.

Traditional knowledge. Typically, evidence that has been sourced from the cultural traditions of regional, local, or indigenous stakeholders. See also *indigenous knowledge*.

Type I error. Taking action where no action is warranted, such as a judge convicting an innocent person of a crime, a firefighter responding to an alarm call when there is no fire, or a mayor ordering a hurricane evacuation when the hurricane misses the city. Compare to *Type II error*.

Type II error. Not taking action where action is warranted, such as a judge letting a guilty person go free, a firefighter not responding to an alarm call when there actually is a fire, or a mayor not ordering an evacuation when a hurricane ends up hitting the city. Compare to *Type I error*.

Ultimate outcome. See *outcome* and *purpose*.

Understandable. One of the criteria for a good *indicator*: Both the indicator and its underlying concepts can be clearly communicated and understood by different people.

Unit. In a monitoring plan, a single item or individual that can be observed.

Verification monitoring. Typically, less-intensive data collection and analysis efforts to ensure that activities have been completed or results have been achieved as expected.

Viability analysis. A framework for assessing the *current status* and *desired future status* of *target factors*.

Waterfall planning. An approach to work planning originally from software development that focuses on laying out in precise sequence all the tasks that need to be accomplished for a given strategy. Agile planning is most useful in situations in which it is possible to fully spec out the desired solution in advance. Compare to *agile planning*.

Wisdom. In evidence-informed conservation, *knowledge* that has been encapsulated into accepted principles and theory for a given discipline. The top layer of the *data, information, knowledge,* and *wisdom* evidence pyramid. Sources of wisdom range from rules of thumb to generic theories of change to codified guidance and principles.

Wisdom of the crowd. In social science, the concept that under the right circumstances, groups of people are often collectively far smarter than the smartest people in them.

Keys to Diagrams Used in This Book

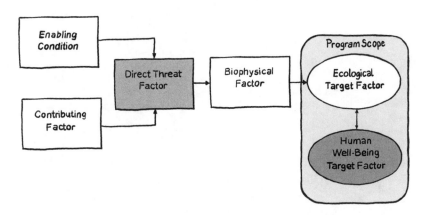

Situation Models

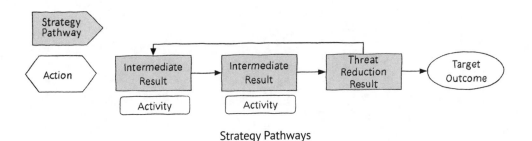

Strategy Pathways

About the Authors

Nick Salafsky is the executive director of Foundations of Success (FOS), the product manager of Miradi Adaptive Management Software, and one of the initial founders of the Conservation Measures Partnership. In these roles, he has over the past two decades worked with hundreds of conservation projects and programs around the world on strategic planning, adaptive management, and cross-program learning. Before starting FOS with Richard, Nick was a program officer with the John D. and Catherine T. MacArthur Foundation and the Biodiversity Support Program. Nick also worked as a researcher studying enterprise-based approaches to conservation across Asia and the Pacific, agroforestry land use systems and tropical forest ecology in West Kalimantan, Indonesia, and freshwater tidal wetlands in New York's Hudson River Valley. Nick's background is at the interface of ecology and economics. He has a BA in biological anthropology from Harvard University and an MA in resource economics and an interdisciplinary PhD in environmental studies from Duke University.

Richard Margoluis is the chief adaptive management and evaluation officer at the Gordon and Betty Moore Foundation, where he and his team support grant making in environmental conservation, basic science, patient care, and the San Francisco Bay area. Before joining the Moore Foundation, Richard worked with Nick as codirector of Foundations of Success and was one of the initial founders of the Conservation Measures Partnership. An epidemiologist by training, Richard has spent most of his professional life living and working in Latin America and Africa, applying the principles of epidemiology to conservation and development programs. He holds a BA in Latin American Studies from Northwestern University and an MPH in planning and evaluation and a PhD in epidemiology from Tulane University.

Foundations of Success (FOS) is a mission-driven organization and global collective dedicated to accelerating and amplifying the impact of the conservation community. FOS provides practitioners with the skills and tools needed to be more effective and efficient in their efforts to foster thriving ecosystems, conserve natural resources, and advance human well-being. FOS staff members are collectively coauthors of this book (in rough order of their service time with FOS): Caroline Stem, Marcia Brown, Janice Davis, Guillermo Placci, Vinaya Swaminathan, Ilke Tilders, Arlyne Johnson, Judy Boshoven, Armando Valdés, Nico Boenisch, Valeria Martinez, Amanda Jorgenson, Ashleigh Baker, Adrienne Marvin, Vladimir Milushev, Daniela Aschenbrenner, Annette Olsson, Paola Mejía Cortez, Kari Stiles, Varsha Suresh, and Jaclyn Lucas.

Index

uncertainty
  agile planning and, 153
  becoming less and less wrong, 63–64
  evidence investment and, 16–17
  investment portfolios and, 138
  strategy pathways and, 93–94
  in systems analysis, 61
  work planning and, 135, 136
"understandable" criterion, 195, 289
unintended consequences, 206, 223
units, 195–96, 198, 289

validity, internal and external, 178–79, 284

values, 24–26, 35
variance, 53
verification monitoring, 184, 199, 202, 289
viability analysis, 216–18, 236, 289
vision, 24, 25

Wade, Jon, 48
waterfall planning, 133, 134–35, 289
wisdom, 252, 289
wisdom of the crowd, 41–42, 289
Wittgenstein, Ludwig, 271
work planning, 131–36, 166, 197–98